GAP YEAR
How An Empty Nest Led Me To Grow Wings

A Travel Memoir by Catherine Maxwell

ISBN: 979-8-9875320-0-3

Acknowledgments

This book never could have been completed without the help of so many people! First of all, thank you to everyone I met on this amazing trip. It is you who have filled the pages with colorful images and conversations. Thank you for becoming characters in my story, and in my life.

Heartfelt gratitude goes out to all the writers who patiently helped me tweak this narrative into something resembling a coherent story. Special thanks to the Chopping Block Crew of Boulder and the Willamette Writers Group of the Pacific Northwest.

A big thank you to my editor, Elizabeth Cameron, who gave me so many insights about how to shape the arc of the story.

A big shout-out to my writer friends who helped encourage and guide me in the self-publishing journey: Alesa Teague, Pete KJ, Peter Garland and Brave Knight Media, and Deb Cerio.

And of course, thank you to my family for standing by me through the ups and downs of writing life and real life. I love you all!

You get a strange feeling when you're about to leave a place, like you'll not only miss the people you love, but you'll miss the person you are at this time and this place, because you'll never be this way ever again." – Azar Nafisi

⚭

"Travel isn't always pretty. It isn't always comfortable. Sometimes it hurts, it even breaks your heart. But that's okay. The journey changes you; it should change you. It leaves marks on your memory, on your consciousness, on your heart, and on your body. You take something with you. Hopefully, you leave something good behind."
     – Anthony Bourdain

The First Day of the Rest of My Life

I sit restlessly in the Miami airport, MIA. How appropriate. Missing In Action. Uncharacteristically early, I jiggle my legs as I watch the people walk by. My flight is not for hours. And although it's not really a vacation, it's not not a vacation either, so I decide to head to the bar.

The bartender bustles about as I plop myself onto a barstool and tuck my zebra tote under the bar. I try to catch his eyes, which I notice are bright blue. I extract my wallet as he approaches, flipping it open casually. He smirks and shakes his head, waving off my optimistic age-check.

"May I have a margarita, please?"

As he goes off to mix the drink I sigh. My legs are still jiggling; I hope the tequila will work to calm me.

I am panicking. There is a persistent voice like a fly that buzzes around my head, and if I swat at it, it buzzes off but never truly goes away. "You're an idiot," the little fly-voice says. "Quitting a job in this economy?" it chastises. "Is that really a smart thing to do?" I swat at it again, but doubt swells in my mind.

The barman returns with my margarita, a full fish-bowl of the potent drink. I take a tentative sip from the overflowing rim while I pull the goblet toward me, but it sloshes nonetheless, splashing my still-open wallet and a photo of my daughters. With the hem of my shirt, I wipe it away, whispering, "Sorry, Emz! Sorry V!"

Oh God, is this a sign? I'm leaving them alone while I traipse off to Spain, is it a mistake?

But in making this trip, I know I am being a good role model for my two grown girls. I am showing them that a woman can set off on her own and have adventures! They don't need me the way they once did, and my new chapter needs to begin.

I once said, during a discussion in a grad school psych class, that I was in my third life. "Maybe you have nine lives," the professor wisecracked. If so, I'm more of a scraggly alley cat than a well-groomed Persian, but I sometimes think he might have been right. Maybe we all do, as we move through the various incarnations of ourselves, as we change and grow. In this incarnation, I will explore and I will write. I am dedicating a year of my life to this trip; throwing my heart across the ocean to Spain and following it blindly. Broke as a joke, I'm volunteering to earn my keep along the way. Phase two will be a journey through South America, from Patagonia traveling north, ending with yoga training in Costa Rica. On this adventure, I hope to learn Spanish, to drink *vino tinto* and meet other travelers, maybe to even make love with a dark-skinned man on a remote beach as he whispers endearments that I don't understand and don't even care to. And throughout it all, I will write. That is my pledge to myself, to process the experience through my blog and somehow learn lessons I have yet to identify.

The airport is ripe for people-watching. I observe a steady stream of travelers pass by. At the closest gate I notice a pair of backpackers sitting on the floor, sharing a computer near the large pillar that boasts one of the few electrical outlets. Their tall backpacks rest beside them – dense and portable. I envy their ability to travel lightly. Before my departure I packed and repacked my ginormous red rolling duffle at least half a dozen times, taking things out, and then putting them back in. My sister helped me.

"What about another pair of jeans?" I asked.

She shook her head and pulled out a pair of suede-half chaps. "What's this for?" I pulled them out of her hands and put them back in the bag.

"Some of the places I'm volunteering have horses." She looked at me skeptically. "Really! I need them." I tucked them in snug against my leather riding boots that would double as hiking boots. As if I hiked. But you never know. I had flip-flops, Keens, and black sandals that I could wear with a dress. A few dresses in varying colors, because I certainly couldn't wear the same one twice if I went out. Shorts. Swimsuits. Many pairs of underwear, because I might not always get to the laundry. A few thongs, too, just in case. I can't rule out romance!

The bag is almost four feet tall when I hoist it upright on its wheels. I've been agonizing over having enough, having too much, worrying about having to pull the damned thing through airports and streets and flights of stairs. I prefer fretting about these details to worrying about the larger problems. How will I find my way? How will I fare as a woman traveling solo? People are envious. People call me brave. People are wrong.

A couple about my age pull out the barstools next to me. "Ya'all mind if we sit here?" the lady asks me. Smiling at the accent, I shake my head and scoot my bag out of the way. They order beers, then the lady turns back to me. "Tom and I are going to the Bahamas. We're celebrating twenty-five years together! Where are you headed?"

"To Spain, then eventually South America. I'm volunteering at different places for room and board, making my way around."

"By yourself?" The woman turns to her husband to see if he had caught that fact, then back to me. "I could never do that!"

I shrug, trying to look like the carefree vagabond that I so do not feel like yet. "I'll make friends," I assure her, although I am not at all sure myself.

Tom leans over. "You're gonna do just great!" he says, bobbing his head in affirmation. "Don't you let Louise bring you down. We don't travel much, I bet you're an expert." He squeezes his wife's hand affectionately

I smile ruefully. If only he knew! "Congratulations on your twenty-five years. I can tell you, as a divorced woman, I am in awe of you."

Louise looks sympathetic. "How long have you been divorced, hon?"

"Seven years." For a split second I imagine a man beside me, taking care of all the details of the trip, carrying my bag, arranging hotels. I am momentarily bereft in contrast to the way Louise must feel, secure with her husband by her side. Then again, maybe he's useless and she runs the show. As I now run my own show. I gulp down the rest of my drink and say goodbye, headed back to the gate to wait for my departure.

A family of three walks by, the man and woman separated by a sullen, pouting, preteen daughter who looks like she would rather be anywhere else in the world. She meets my eye and glares, hard. *Stop staring at me, creeper!* I can almost hear her thoughts. I shudder as I drift back to a time five years ago...

"I'm not strong enough to do this!" My voice was a ragged whisper, begging something, someone, to rescue me. I curled into a ball, trembling. Where could I turn for help?

I cradled my head in my hands. I had sent my daughter to her room after she had called me names I never thought I'd hear from the lips of one I loved so much, had created from my body and brought into the world only thirteen years earlier. She angrily slammed the door (which was loose on the hinges by now), threw some things around the room, and kicked a hole in the wall. The crumbling drywall sobered us both up and she apologized tearfully. Afterward, all was quiet in her room, but my insides were in an uproar. Tears streamed down my cheeks. "I can't do this," I whispered again. I sobbed on my bed, at a loss for an answer. How can you refuse to parent your own child? I couldn't. Yet she had a hundred big fights in her every day, and I had barely one on a good day. I could not keep up, and I could not control this high-spirited kid.

My daughter had earned a three-day suspension from school for coming to class high. She was disrespectful to teachers, failing several classes, not only hanging out with the wrong crowd but becoming its ringleader. And I was her mom: a single mom, a teacher myself in a district a forty-minute drive south, powerless to be there after school, powerless to enforce restrictions, powerless to do anything but beat my head against the wall. If I called my ex-husband, he went on about how I was at fault for being too lenient. I needed help. There was none.

I had been divorced for two years; I had to get through at least four more years of single parenting. I had never anticipated parenting alone. In retrospect, there had been warning signs about my husband. He was impulsive, jealous, and mercurial. I had married him anyway and quickly had two daughters, twenty months apart.

I must have loved him in the beginning, but that love dissolved as years tumbled by. He was an alcoholic who became gradually more abusive. As he delved into Internet porn, I went to college to get my teaching certificate. The space between us widened. Still, I stuck it out. So he liked pornography, was that so bad? Maybe he drank too much and his employment was unstable. Maybe he wasn't always the best dad, but the girls could get out when they were eighteen. I had said vows. I was stuck. Eventually, though, the list of reasons to leave him grew too long, culminating in his infidelity, and I broke free after fifteen years of marriage.

A year after that, I'd met Brad. Like a bird set free from her cage, I sang and flew. I fell madly and deeply in love. Loving him lifted me up, but I still had the difficult job of single-parenting two daughters who were going through their own journey, coping with the divorce and their teenage hormones all at the same time. Some days I didn't think I would make it through until they were both eighteen.

That was when I made The Calendar.

My oldest daughter Emily seemed to be on the right track, but Veronica was a handful. So I took a piece of paper and a pen, and I drew big boxes, dissecting each into twelve months. The rest of 2007. 2008. 2009. 2010. Finally, 2011. The year my youngest daughter would turn eighteen. There were forty-six months until then. And what, I asked myself, would be the reward I was working for, to not give up, to not quit or run away; to shepherd, however poorly, both daughters into adulthood? I wanted to travel. I could go to Spain. If Brad and I lasted until then, he could come with me and we could explore it together. All I had to do was make it through the next four years. The reward of this trip would carry me through.

I tucked the calendar between my mattress and box spring.

Once in a while, I'd take it out, more frequently in the beginning, and then as Veronica grew older and she and I agreed on some guidelines, less often. I crossed out the months like a bride awaiting her wedding day.

⟞⟞⟞⟞⟞⟞

Originally, I was to make this journey with the proceeds from selling my house. I listed the house for sale and waited. After two months, I had to make a decision; I had less than a month before I left the country. I decided to rent it out instead and moved all my remaining worldly goods into my parents' Colorado house. My parents have always been there for me, and this time was no exception; of course I could store my boxes and my aging dog there with them. But I was beginning to realize it was going to be time for me to return the favor; after this trip I would settle in Colorado where I could keep a closer eye on them.

Renting out my house in Washington would generate a little bit of income for me to travel on, roughly three hundred dollars a month after I paid monthly bills. Was I crazy? Even the cheapest hostel in Spain was thirty or forty euros per night. Even if I slept in parks I still had to eat. I needed to figure out something.

But what?

Inspired by Elizabeth Gilbert's renowned *Eat, Pray, Love* and a book by Joyce Major with the endearing title *Smiling at the World* about volunteering while traveling, I hit the Internet to do some research. Maybe Elizabeth and Joyce could motivate me, but they damned sure were not going to lend me any money. How could I manage to travel without spending the equivalent of two years' worth of my teacher's salary?

I typed in "volunteer" and stumbled upon what would become

7

my lifesaver, a website called Help Exchange. I signed up, created a volunteer listing, and began to search for hosts. The usual informal agreement is that the helper works about four to five hours per day, five days a week, in exchange for room and board. Jobs vary from construction to animal- or child-care, cleaning, or gardening. I scoured the site, sifted through over eight hundred hosts in Spain, and began firing off inquiries. I devised a tentative travel plan, arranging hosts throughout Spain.

But now as I sit here at the airport, panic sets in. I have only ever stayed in three or four-star hotels, and alone in a hotel is one thing. But volunteering to stay in strangers' houses and work for them? I could be enslaved, molested while sleeping, even murdered! How do I know who these people are?

"Have faith," a quiet voice advises. But I'm not sure I know how. I'm not religious, so who am I supposed to have faith in? A form of God I am not sure I believe in? My instincts? No, not those, they are short-circuited right now, screaming at me. The prospect of a year negotiating my way around Spain and South America as a tourist is a fun thought. But the reality of traveling on a shoestring budget and depending on strangers is scary. And after the year is up, what then?

I have started a blog, which helped me navigate through the pain of my breakup with Brad, and I would like to take it further. I want to blog about life, and adventure, and love, and whatever else interests me, finding that common thread that unites readers with an author. But I am terribly inconsistent. I have always written: romances, screenplays, novels, essays, poems. I published a story in a children's magazine when I was twelve. It has been pretty quiet since then.

Now, I will finally have time to write, because for the next year I will be free. I will be hauling around my stuff and relying on the good nature of random hosts to feed me and give me a comfortable place to lay my head. It sounds like an enjoyable freewheeling, gypsy life, but I am scared shitless.

My friends and family struggle to understand my reasons for the trip. Maybe that should be the first installment of my travel blog. I pull out my laptop and begin.

Blog Post: Who the Hell do You Think You Are?

This plan – to travel and reclaim my identity – has been forming for years. My divorce was necessary but brutal. Raising two daughters while working full time was just one step removed from impossible. The whole time I felt like I was drowning, gasping for air, praying to make the right choices for them and for myself.

My life raft was Brad – a man I loved all the more desperately the more I realized my love was unrequited. We were two lost souls escaping long marriages, and we clung to each other, but for reasons so disparate that they divided us in the end. I craved stability and someone to burrow into when things were tough. He craved romance and sex. I was his wild girl, building up his ego and appealing to the person he had buried under his CEO suit and tie. But in the end, he wanted the silk purse, not the sow's ear. I wasn't enough.

Now I am unmoored. My grown daughters have their own apartments, lives, and friends. My town in northwest Washington has too many ghosts, too many memories of the last fifteen years. The ice rink where I would watch my husband play hockey. The dance studio where my little girls dreamed of ballet and I bought the annual satin and sequin leotards for their spring recitals, year after year until they outgrew the dream. And then five years of Brad, draped throughout this place like fallen streamers from a party. Restaurants where we ate. Bars where we danced and laughed. His gym, my yoga studio. We would leave sexy notes on each other's cars. I can't bear to look at any of it any more. It's a town of busted visions.

Going back to Colorado, though, feels like defeat. This is where I grew up. I'm going backwards. It feels like running home with my tail between my legs. Forty-nine years old and living with my parents. I can feel my twenty-one-year-old self, with her New York party life and dreams as big as the city, gawking in horror at what she became. This is merely a place to get my footing, a safe harbor where my parents can pat my back, murmuring, "There, there." It's a place to stash furniture and boxes, and launch myself blindly into a new world with no boundaries, built of hope and tears and luck.

Healing comes differently for each of us. I am doing my best with the tools I have been given. Travel, I hope, will be the balm my wounded soul needs to turn my life around and onto a shiny new track. But first I need to gather my thoughts, examine my existence. In our culture we are encouraged to achieve. We are humans doing, not humans being.

I want to find out what I am if not a mother, teacher, wife, or lover.

For the next year I simply want to be a human being.

I close the laptop and close my eyes. I have left something out of the narrative. Brad and I have been talking on the phone again after a year of silence, talking about seeing each other when I am back for the holidays. The confusion of re-opening communication with him is just making me more anxious: am I making any of the right choices? Why is life so complicated?

I am not the only one with doubts about the trip. My mother has been alternating between sweet, affirming parental encouragement and the very embodiment of the voice of doom. Yesterday I had a hiccup-sobbing fit, panicked about the trip I am taking with no money, but unable to back down and say I will…do what? Live with my parents in Colorado and wait for my life to start up again?

"Well, you already have arranged Spain, but maybe you shouldn't go to South America, or do the spring yoga training in Costa Rica. You will need to get a real teaching job and make some money," my mom suggested. My dad, as always, stayed quietly in the background.

Take a short hiatus and then get a job? Well, maybe that's practical. But haven't I just taught for ten years, and done eight years of day care before that? I am tired of teaching right now. I need a break. Why can't I just claim it and not feel guilty? People do this all the time. *Yeah, young people!* Not nearly-fifty-year-old mothers. Not professionals with college degrees and mortgages. You take a gap year between high school and college. Does a woman in her late forties need a gap year?

Yes, as a matter of fact, I do. I am doing this. I am doing this!

It's not about being wild or irresponsible. It's about discovering my authentic self, helping others, widening my perspective on life. It's about changing something, learning another culture and language. It's about celebrating my freedom and my endurance, acknowledging the disappointments that life has brought and moving on. It's about finally being a writer. What do I have to lose? I'm forty-eight years old. I am homeless, unemployed, and single.

And I am doing this.

My flight gets into San Sebastian tomorrow, Sunday. From there I have instructions for how to get to my host family's house. I will be staying with a couple with two cats and no kids while I take a week-long Spanish course to brush up on my negligible command of that language.

I hope I will be able to sleep on the long flight to Madrid. I toyed with the idea of buying one of those bean-bag-filled neck pillows, but then I am stuck with hauling a bean-bag pillow all over Spain, and that just does not fit with the free-wheeling gypsy image I hope to attain. Of course, neither does my oversized shoulder tote that is proving so heavy with "necessities" that when I throw it over my shoulder I list to one side like a sapling in a strong breeze, praying the straps will hold up this whole trip.

I am a bit less sophisticated of a traveler than I had hoped I would be.

But I will soldier on. Mysteries wait to unfold like the sheets my mother put on the guest bed for me not even three weeks ago. I have stashed forty-nine boxes in my parents' crawl-space. I sold all my furniture save the faux wrought-iron bedframe that squeaks incessantly when the bed moves, and the bittersweet memory of Brad and I breaking it in would not allow me to leave it behind.

I first encountered Spain four years ago, the summer of 2007, on a trip with Brad. In our two weeks, we explored Barcelona, Sevilla, and Andalucia, where we'd rented a car and visited the white villages. We took this trip two years into our relationship, when he had just received a job offer in a city four hours away. I knew he would take it; it was a step up in his career. But we hadn't yet talked about whether we would try to stay together if he moved. Our time in Spain was fraught with high emotion, for it was possible it was going to be our last hurrah. In the end, we stayed together for three more years of long-distance, but the relationship eventually imploded when I tried to press for a bigger commitment.

Revisiting Spain is a touchstone for me, a baby step into solo travel. Starting with a place that I am somewhat familiar with is reassuring, but I also know that I will be haunted by the memory of the trip with Brad.

A few months ago, I had dinner with Brad after a year of his refusing to speak to me. He was probably wise; it took me the full year to heal. His first words were "I have one rule – no talking about anyone we've been dating." I agreed. After a margarita, though, he broke his own rule and told me about the woman he had met on the Internet and dated for six months.

"Do you want to know why I broke up with her?"

"Sure." *You can't hurt me anymore.*

"I wasn't in love with her." He looked at me meaningfully.

Had he expected me to feel flattered? All I felt was pissed off. "Brad! You don't want to be in love!" I twisted one of my blond curls tightly around my finger instead of giving into the urge to strangle him. How could he have forgotten? We had magic, and somehow it wasn't enough. But I shrugged it off. I didn't want to care anymore, and I didn't want to bring anger in – too little, too late.

On our way out, he walked me to my car and I kissed him. I don't even know why. I was so used to kissing those lips; I had kissed them a million times in the previous five years. It felt good, natural, and wonderful. I am still not completely healed from the breakup, and maybe I never will be. But I want to move on, reluctantly, finally. People don't change and I needed more from him than he could comfortably give. I once accused him of having the emotional depth of a houseplant. Our differences in communication and emotional connectivity caused too much grief to make this a permanent arrangement. I had to resolve this before I could go on, but the pain was more than I had anticipated. I was hoping the trip would be what I needed to finally break free of the hold he had on me.

Now he has told me he is still in love with me. He says he realized this after our kiss. Damn that kiss! I am confused and a little angry. I feel like he wasted the chance when I presented it, when it was possible. Yet I couldn't resist jumping back into communication when he gave me the chance. Perhaps the time and distance will give me real perspective on whether I can somehow have him in my life again when this trip is over. And here it is at last; this journey, this adventure, this foray into the unknown. For the next four months, this will be my life. If I can successfully travel through Spain and Morocco, I will take another big step after returning to the US for the holidays to see my family. I plan to travel through South America starting in January, finishing up with a two-hundred-hour yoga training in Costa Rica in April.

On the plane, sleep eludes me and I only nap sporadically. A youth group is aboard the plane, loud and flamboyant in all their teenage glory. It's hard to tell how old they are, maybe fifteen? Just a bit younger than my own girls. I smile fondly, secure in the feeling that I have left my kids behind in good shape. Emily was starting school and working part time, having broken up with the leech boyfriend who made her pay all the bills while he didn't look for a job. As for Veronica, after going away to live with my brother for her senior year of high school, she had returned as a mature and capable young adult. I helped her find an apartment and a roommate. She was due to start a new job within the week. She and I have fixed our relationship in the last year or so; the tough years were water under the bridge, as wise people (whom I didn't dare believe) told me they would be.

I close my eyes and settle into the airplane seat, tightening my earplugs when the teenagers continue talking loudly through the night. I am relieved when the flight attendant shushes them.

When we land in Madrid, I rush to the other terminal only to find that my flight to San Sebastian is almost three hours delayed, and they don't have a plane for us. In the past I would have been frantic, but I am in no hurry. Worry can no longer be part of my vocabulary; I am traveling alone and shit happens! I settle in and take my first photo: a sign in Spanish and English advertising the airport lounge. The translation makes me giggle: "Feel yourself! For just twenty-five euros." Wow, I think, it must be a very private lounge! I walk around the airport. I can already feel my Spanish improving as I decipher conversations and read signs.

Finally, there is an airplane for our group to board. I fall into slumber immediately upon leaning against the window. It is a short flight. When I awaken, we are approaching San Sebastian, making our descent. San Sebastian has a horseshoe shaped beach called La Concha, "the shell." From above, the golden sand is sprinkled with sunbathers on towels like bits of brightly colored confetti. Likewise, boats speckle the harbor, neat white squares against a blanket of blue. As we descend farther, I spot a lone seagull crossing under the plane.

I feel ready. I'm doing this on my own. I'm not vulnerable, but capable. Strong. Tired, but who wouldn't be after twenty plus hours of travel? Bring on the adventure!

As we disembark, the sea air caresses me. I inhale deeply. *Yes.*

The last challenge of my day is finding the bus stop, getting the bus and telling the driver in my fast-improving Spanish where I want to go. I am wiped out from the long day, but feel confident. I am doing this! I totally rock! We stop at a traffic circle and the bus driver tells me to exit.

I stumble from the bus, disoriented but obedient. I wander about this pretty seaside village, pulling my heavy overloaded duffle, taking in the rustic benches facing the sparkling sea, scattered restaurants along a boardwalk. It's a lovely town! Smaller than I had pictured San Sebastian, it feels quaint. But I need to get to my host family. I'm beat. Where the hell am I, anyway? I ask a waiter as I pass a café, and discover that I was dropped off at not just the wrong street, but also the wrong town. I'm in a place called Hondaarribia. Charming, indeed, but not my destination. I haul my heavy bag around the streets, trying to find another bus to get to San Sebastian, getting frustrated.

"Don't be a baby!" I scold myself as tears threaten. "This is just the first day, and these things are going to happen over and over again!" I acknowledge, trying to be kind to myself, that I am tired and jet lagged and hungry and lost. Who wouldn't cry?

I end up at a bus stop where I crumble into a folding seat. I am exhausted, fighting tears. I meet the eyes of a short but handsome man with kind crinkly eyes and long straight hair. Although he speaks no English, he takes me under his wing and we speak in Spanish as we ride the bus. My brain hurting from all the mental translation efforts, we get off the bus in San Sebastian and he takes on the job of hauling my bag around and asking people where my street is. I feel relieved, cared for. Someone else is taking over and I don't mind. My new friend drags my big red bag down narrow streets, stopping to ask in staccato Spanish if anyone knows the street. Finally, a lady points us to the square that faces the apartment building.

Calle Navarra is in a small plaza with a children's park, an

Irish pub, and a wine store. The building where my hosts live is three stories tall and modern. It has a double glass door flanked by bronze mosaic glass squares.

I ring the bell and my hostess, Laura, buzzes me in the front door. Thanks goodness there is an elevator, for I cannot imagine carting my heavy bag up flights of stairs after twenty-two hours of travel. My companion, gallant to the end, rides up with me.

At the apartment, I turn to thank him and he dives onto me with a kiss - not the standard Spanish cheek-to-cheek kiss, but a full-on lip-lock. I startle, then melt into him. At this point, the door opens and I push him off. I haltingly say hello to Laura, a thin elegant woman with dark hair, a long nose, and a knowing twinkle in her brown eyes. What a great first impression, I think, here is our student houseguest, making out on the doorstep! I hope I don't have to attempt to explain this in Spanish!

I greet my host family and sheepishly retire to my room to change and to contemplate my reaction to being kissed. My main emotion is that of surprise. Not only that he kissed me, but at how my body reacted. I am embarrassed. No one has touched me in so long. But a strong physical response to a kiss is not only normal, it's a good omen. My sexuality has not yet atrophied. I smile to myself and let it go. My Spanish classes start tomorrow!

San Sebastian – Spanish And French Kisses

Classes go well. I can speak a lot of Spanish and make myself understood but my grammar is horrible. I think of it as baby talk Spanish. It's humbling. I remember when I was teaching ESL as part of my university classes. A Japanese student said to me in broken English: "In my country, I am very smart and I know a lot. Here, because I cannot speak good English, I feel more stupid." That is exactly what it is like for me. I definitely feel more stupid here, trying to communicate in my feeble second language. As evidence, I have the bus fiasco.

Vicente is my host papa. He is the same age as me, but I feel just like a little girl – lost and scared. So papa it is! He walked me to school today, since I got lost and was late on my first day. Each day I spend time with Vicente and Laura at the end of the day, sitting on their pristine white couch, conversing in Spanish while they coax me through difficulties with the language. When I am uptight and worried, my hosts encourage me to relax. I am learning much already about the Spanish attitude: no pasa nada, no worries! I decide that this is the ideal time to write another blog about my experiences.

Blog Post: No Tengo Prisa

There is a saying in Spanish, to be in a hurry, "tengo prisa." In America, everyone seems to be in a hurry. People rush from one place to the other. I do too. My motto has always been "walk and talk". I multi-task. I cannot sit and have a leisurely conversation, except for with my therapist. Even then, I fidget.

Buddhists speak of being in the moment, of mindfulness. With mindfulness, one is aware of everything at that moment. At Plum Village in France (the teaching center of famed Buddhist monk Thich Nhat Hanh), if the phone rings, one arises slowly, mindfully walking towards it, wishing blessings upon the caller.

This was told to my mother by a friend who had visited there. Meanwhile, we wondered, is the person on the other end of the phone fuming, knowing that someone is slowly and mindfully approaching to answer, but taking their own sweet damned time?

What's your hurry?

Typically, we cram a full day in around a job that lasts at least 8 hours. Add the commute and it's nine or ten hours. Then there are children to feed, houses to clean, errands to run, dogs to walk. Not to mention some of the pleasures of life: for me, riding a horse, taking a yoga class, writing for a few hours. Then, in the happiest of times, there is also having deep conversations with a partner, making love. How in the world do we ever fit all of these things into a day? I cannot see any way to do it well in a normal life. We want to have it all, so we hurry. Tengo prisa.

But now, as I travel freely (not always contentedly), no tengo prisa. It is a hard adjustment. I feel rushed, as if the ghost of my former life is urging me on, hurry up and get there! Where? Does it matter? Next, next, next. There is little mindfulness in this approach.

Yesterday, as I was lost again on the way back from my Spanish class, here in beautiful San Sebastian (it would be the second of four times in that particular day), I caught myself being anxious. I stopped and thought about it. What, indeed, was my hurry? I had nowhere to be. I had no one to report to. No timetable. My back and shoulders hurt from carrying my tote, heavy with my computer, some books, and a bottle of wine. I was tired. I was hot. So I rested in the shade, and leisurely examined the map. I got "home" eventually. On the way, instead of feeling hurried and anxious, I thought of myself as deliciously lost. What a wonderful way to examine a new place. Delicious lost-ness.

I think I'll try that approach for a while. Perhaps Thich Nhat Hanh would approve.

It is my second evening here, and I sit at a café by the beach, having splurged on a pinxto (a tapas-like snack) and red wine. A car drives by and Rihanna's voice drifts out: "Just gonna stand there and hear me cry…" *Love the Way You Lie* was my song last summer, when my heart was still in pieces from breaking up with Brad. I feel a sharp twang of pain.

The wine is rich and mellow. The pinxto is made of cheese that looks like Brie and tastes like goat cheese, piled on a piece of crusty bread topped with roasted red pepper and mushrooms.

The tastes mingle in my mouth deliciously. Surfers stroll by, their waists wrapped in damp towels. I gesture for the bill and decide to check out the beach.

The breeze is cool and fresh, salt-infused. I'm glad to be wearing jeans and a sweatshirt, for even though it is August, it is cool by the ocean. Surfers in black wetsuits dot the water like seals. A kid body-surfs, plunging into waves, his feet sticking straight up, the very picture of boyish exuberance. I smile, missing not only my own youthfulness, but the kindergarten kids I typically surround myself with every fall. And yet, I don't want to be anywhere other than here. Right here, right now.

⸎

Even though I am a traveling, free-wheeling gypsy, I still have some responsibilities, and I can't stay in my Zen Zone for more than a few sweet moments, as logistics rear their ugly head. I forgot how stressful travelling from one place to another can be, especially when you are trying to save money. Where is... anything? Was I better at this when I was younger? I honestly can't remember. And, like Blanche DuBois, I am always depending on the kindness of strangers. I sometimes find myself at the edge of tears, getting frustrated with myself.

One night while trying to find the welcome party for students in my school, I am wandering around lost once again, map in hand. A man approaches. He is short with an olive complexion, a tumbled mane of dark hair, and glasses.

"Can I help you find something?" he asks.

"I am trying to find this bar, to meet some friends. It's around here, somewhere." I poke my finger at the map, and then shrug helplessly at the maze of small streets and tucked-away shops around us.

Together, Victor (for that is his name) and I negotiate the narrow streets and talk, mostly in English. We finally encounter the pub, hidden in a small plaza that I had previously walked right past. We make a date for later.

At the party I have a great time with the other students once we all warm up to each other. I am one of the oldest people in the group, but I am determined to be social and not hide in the corner. After talking to some others for a bit, I develop a crush on a German architect, and we create a private joke that keeps us in stitches. He is far too young for me. Still, I can enjoy some mild flirtation, can't I? The sangria is sweet and refreshing, and I am hesitant to leave the party, but perhaps a private party will be better. I walk just a few meters to meet my date on the corner.

Victor and I walk to a nearby bar, where we sit and speak in both English and Spanish. He tells me he lives by the beach. There is sadness in his big lonely eyes. I decline the offer to see his house; instead, we take his car to the far beach, where we sit in the sand and talk until the wee hours. He is recently divorced with a seven-year-old son and still heartbroken over the split. We chat about love and marriage, and make a date to meet a few nights later. I kiss him goodbye. I think we can be friends.

A few nights later we have another date. The bar looks out over the busy cobblestone street. Tourists and locals stroll by in the warmth of the summer evening.

"I like this area," I tell him. "San Sebastian is beautiful."

"It's just a twenty- minute drive to France," Victor tells me. He is polite and a little reserved. Laura has said that the men from this area are timid. I get the urge to shake things up a bit.

I lean in mischievously and whisper to him, "We should drive to France!"

Victor looks surprised. "Why?"

"Because it's so close. I would love to say I went to France on this trip!"

He smiles indulgently and shrugs. "Very well. Let's go." I down my remaining wine and grin. Off we go to France!

Since the European Union has formed, there is an open border agreement between most of the countries. We drive into France the way one drives between Oregon and Washington: no border, no hassles. And unfortunately, no extra stamp in my passport. A road sign tells us we are now in France. The tiny port town of Saint Jean de Luz is deserted. Angels on the side of a building stare down as we get out of the car and walk to a small balcony of cement overlooking the water. The face of a smaller angel carved into a wall peers out at us from the shadows as we walk arm in arm. Victor points out the lights of San Sebastian on the other side of the bay, glowing like playful fireflies in the dark night. We kiss.

Something stirs inside of me. I feel so hungry for physical touch while waiting for a relationship that has some meaning. But this night in France as we walk on the beach and the clouds scud across a sliver of yellow moon, the blue lights from the casino glow, the breeze lifts the smells of the salty sea air, and the sand is soft as silk beneath my feet, I let go of my inhibitions. How can I not make love at the seaside with this sweet Castellano?

In the darkness of the night, we fumble at each other's clothing. Victor produces a condom from his pocket and we have a hasty tryst in the sand. Afterward we walk on the beach and he draws a heart in the sand, pierced by an arrow with our initials at each end. The night is cool and he draws me close to him. We walk into a deserted courtyard and he points out the architecture of the buildings, arched doorways and wooden vigas. It is late, and golden lights bathe the courtyard. It looks like a storybook picture of days gone by.

"You have a beautiful smile," Victor tells me.

I duck my head, a blush warming my cheeks. Whether or not I fully believe the compliment, I know how hard-won that smile is.

In my marriage, I learned the fake smile: the one that said everything's okay, even when it wasn't. And the longer the marriage went on, the more of it wasn't okay. I had my two beautiful daughters, a scant two years apart, and I had what might appear to be a good partnership.

My whole family did theater together; we balanced work and parenting, sharing the load as I went to school. I ran a day care in my home from the time Veronica was six months old, taking classes first at the community college, then the local university. And as I bettered myself by finishing my education, my husband deteriorated. He was a steady drinker who dabbled in drugs and was starting down the dark path of an Internet porn habit.

I stayed in that marriage far too long; fifteen years. They say that hindsight is 20/20, and I know now I should have left sooner than I did. But at the time I felt like I had made my bed and needed to lie in it. Right or wrong, I had chosen him.

The light had gone out of my eyes, faded from my smile in those days. My husband would often tell me when we looked at pictures, "You have a haunted look." Did he really have no idea that it was he who was haunting me?

It was only later, after I had met Brad, that I learned to relax and authentically smile again. I had been in love. The trip Brad and I took together to Spain was memorialized in dozens of photos where I rediscovered my smile –beaming and true.

How fitting that here I was, back in Spain, and my smile was still bright enough to be notable. I had lost Brad, but kept my inner radiance.

Victor and I get into the car for our drive back. "Do you want to see my house?" he asks.

"Okay." I watch the dark scenery as we drive back into town in a comfortable, tired silence. There is sand in my hair and in my shoes.

We arrive at his place. We kiss in the elevator. Making love in an elevator is on my bucket list, but I resist telling Victor this. In the apartment he asks if I need anything, a drink, perhaps? But what I really want is to have sex again. On the beach, it was a quickie. I am ready to spend more time. We get into bed, stripping off our clothes. But as we begin, his penis goes soft.

"I'm sorry…" he says in Spanish.

"No, no. Esta bien." I shush him and try to coax his penis back to life, but Victor begins to cry softly.

Uh-oh.

"I'm sorry," he tells me again. "I just can't do it here, in our bed. The bed I shared with my wife. At the beach I was okay, but I can't do it here. I'm sorry."

It's the Ex-Factor. There is no getting around that! "I understand," I tell him.

At first, I don't take it personally. But he goes on, "She is so tiny, and your body is so much bigger…" um, thanks, Pal. How about you stop right there?

"Okay," I tell him. I try not to show that I am irritated. I swing my leg back over his and reach for my clothes. "Maybe you should take me back now." I can't be upset with him; he is obviously torn up. But inwardly I roll my eyes. You picked me up on the street, buddy.

I kiss him goodbye when he walks me to the apartment. "Nos vemos." Until we meet again.

I knew, though, that I would not see Victor again. He was

still in love with his ex. How could I possibly pass judgment as I grapple with my own lingering feelings for Brad? I hope that I helped Victor forget her, if only for a few precious moments on the beach in France. I smile at the thought of sand sticking in his curly hair that would likely keep coming out for days – a tangible reminder of the Americana Selvaje – wild American woman.

Barcelona - Mosaics And Meals

Barcelona. It's a city I have been to before, with Brad, during two days of our Spain trip. I loved the distinctive architecture and vibrant street life. I have a few days to spare before I am due in Madrid; why not revisit one of my favorite places? Taking the bus will be cheap, thirty Euro, and save me the need for a hotel, as I can take a midnight bus that arrives in Barcelona at 7:30 AM.

So that is what I will do. My bag has been so awkward for me to deal with that I have to take that into consideration, so I try to book a hotel before I travel. The process is frustrating: availability that disappears when you try to book, prices that are based on two people for the room (so it is double the quote if you are alone), mixed dorms of eight or more inhabitants. I am too old for that. I could never sleep in a bunk bed dorm. I find a cheap private room with a shared bathroom in a hostel and I book it immediately, feeling fortunate to find it.

On the bus I sleep the whole time, and wake up next to a young woman. As she awakens and smiles at me, we introduce ourselves. Her name is Evelyn; she is Polish and travelling alone. She is a slim brunette with a friendly smile and I instantly like her. We decide to explore Barcelona together for the few days we are here, both grateful for the company.

I find and check into the hostel. It is a tiny room, with an unkempt shared bathroom down the hall, but with friendly staff and WiFi access. It is beyond cheap for Barcelona– less than thirty dollars a night – and walking distance to the Ramblas, a pedestrian street lined with trees where tourists and natives can experience vendors, entertainers, restaurants, and bars.

As I walk down the street to the subway I take in the sights of Barcelona. It's a city with a gypsy-hippie vibe, even though it is the second largest city in Spain. Artistic touches are everywhere in the architecture, especially in the famous "block of discord," comprised of famous modernist buildings. My favorite buildings are designed by Gaudi, an important influence in Barcelona architecture.

Evelyn and I meet and tour the famous Sagrada Familia cathedral, designed by Gaudi in the late 1800's, with its Gothic design of winding carved spires. We take the Metro to eat dinner off the Ramblas. We swap cameras and take pictures of each other. Just twenty-four years old, Evelyn is on vacation here after finishing medical school. Over dinner later she tells me she isn't sure she wants to be a doctor.

"It is a safe job; I will constantly be working. For me this is important. But I will have six more years of school to learn a specialty, and it is so much, all the time studying. Perhaps I don't have the passion for being a doctor." She shakes her head and looks to me for guidance.

I am twice her age; I should have some good advice, shouldn't I? But I am coming up empty-handed. What the hell do I know?

Instead, I tell her how I came to teaching late, after a rather wild life in New York, and that having children was what really changed me and made me choose a career. I tell her I enjoy teaching, but not in the passionate way she is talking about. I have always wanted to write, and I will write, but whether I make a living at it or not is another question. There will be time, I say, to change your path whenever you want to. But meanwhile, medicine is a noble profession with many directions, and maybe something will ignite her interest when she interns. She nods, and tells me she will continue towards a career in medicine, but she hopes to build confidence and find a specialty she loves.

Evelyn points to a distinct 6-inch scar that runs down her chest. Earlier, at the beach, a man we were talking with asked about it, and she said, "Someone broke my heart." Cute. But now she tells me that she had heart surgery at five, that she has battled a rare heart disease and never knows if it will return; it is for this reason she chose medicine.

"No one had time to talk to me about it, doctors are not paid to talk, merely to do their work, quickly, quickly, then on to the next. I would never want to treat a person like that."

I remember when my own daughter Emily was sick and hospitalized at the age of four, thinking how scary that was for our family, and how frightening it must be for a child who is barely capable of understanding the purpose of surgery.

"That's the best reason for going into medicine; you really want to help people," I tell Evelyn. "So that means you'll probably be really good at it." We go into the restaurant to pay and the owner asks how long we are both in town. He introduces himself as Leo, makes some recommendations, then asks me to dinner the next night. I take his number; why not?

I have to wait for the bathroom the next morning, and I longingly remember the nice hotel Brad and I stayed in on my first trip to Barcelona. We have spoken through Skype a few times on this journey, and reminisced awkwardly about that trip. How could I have ever guessed back then that on my next visit I'd be on my own, sharing grimy bathrooms with strangers? I have a deep pang of missing Brad as I walk out into this incredible city that I first discovered with him.

I shake it off, go meet Evelyn, and together we explore the beautiful Parc Guell. The park is another Gaudi masterpiece, full of beautiful mosaic art, twisted stone columns, winding paths, and large expanses of platforms with spectacular panoramic views of the city. Feeling reflective, I encourage Evelyn to explore while I sit in the central amphitheater, gazing at the colorful mosaic art on the ceiling high above and writing in my notebook.

Blog Post: Making Beauty from Something Broken

I have been drawn to mosaic art for some time now. The last time I was here in Barcelona it was with a man I thought was the love of my life. Now, a few years later, I have returned solo. I remember sitting on the famous Gaudi bench that winds around the top of Parc Guell giving spectacular views of the city, wrapped in my lover's arms. Now I am wrapped only in my own thoughts. I lean against a column in the center of the park, running my finger along a small porcelain beige triangle in the structure. How many people have found and lost love here in this city? I am among them.

But I am not broken.

Perhaps this mosaic shard was a plate, a planter, a candlestick holder. Now it's part of an amphitheater. It is just as beautiful and useful as it once was; maybe even more so. One is not defined by what tragedies have happened in one's life, but rather, by what we do to move forward.

I'm learning to be by myself, to enjoy the gift of a single day. A sunny day in Barcelona, or maybe in my backyard in the U.S. I am whole, complete, and happy. I am not what I once was – a wife, a young mother, a wild divorcee – and I am not yet what I might become. I stand on the precipice of something fresh and bright. I am a mosaic made of my life experiences.

The best is yet to be.

As I finish writing, Evelyn returns.

"This place is so beautiful," I sigh as she plops down on the ground next to me.

"Yes," she answers, "but it is spoiled a bit by so many people. I think it loses some of the beauty when it is so crowded. You cannot be peaceful, as it was intended, with so much crowds and so much noise."

We push our way through the throng on the stairs, past dozens of people jockeying for position to have their picture taken by the famous mosaic dragon fountain. Bursts of German, French, Spanish, and languages I cannot discern drift past as we hustle down to the main exit.

I say goodbye to Evelyn, giving her a long hug and wishing her luck. A sad smile lingers on my face as I watch her board the train; fleeting friendships are part and parcel of the journey I am on. It's odd to become so close, so fast, and then know that I will never see that person again (except perhaps on Facebook.)

In the evening, Leo and I go out to a restaurant he knows, a local seafood place, bustling with both Barcelonans and tourists.

He orders for us, and we sample mussels, shrimp, and a succulent regional fish.

Leo makes me feel safe and cared for. He is generous and kind, with greying curly hair and a commanding manner. After dinner we have a drink at his restaurant and part ways after some kissing and his multiple suggestions that we get a hotel room. I decline, too tired for romance.

On my last day in this beautiful vibrant city I spend the morning writing and sipping coffee, window shopping and watching the world go by. At midday I meet Leo again on the beach. We nap there a while, the sun caressing us into a dreamy state, listening to a lullaby from the cacophony of voices of the beach vendors.

"Mojito, mojito!" "Cerveza!" is the cry from several men with coolers, threading through the crowded sand.

"Masaje, masaje," call the Asian women.

Others shout, "Henna tattoo?"

I doze, letting the sounds swirl around me like an impromptu concert. I could record this and make it the backbeat to a song, I think. Leo's hand is warm, resting on my thigh.

After the beach, we go out for more food at a place called "Pato Borracho", the drunken duck. We order Spanish paella de mariscos, seafood, and sangria. I tell Leo if I stayed in Barcelona with him any longer I would become quite fat! When we part at the entrance to my hotel he implores me to return to Barcelona before I go home. I love Barcelona, and I enjoy Leo's company. We shall see.

Hauling my large bag around on the Metro and through city streets is a pain in the ass. When I arrive at ten PM, I discover that the bus ticket I thought I had reserved online did not come through; the eleven, eleven-thirty, and twelve midnight are all full. I get a ticket for the one AM bus, an aisle seat, as there are no window seats left. I hope I can sleep with no window to lean against. I am tired and hot, but I try to take the bus change in stride. After all, what better have I to do? I am a little grouchy now, though; in the waiting area, noises are bothering me. Every time the door to the women's bathroom bangs shut, which is often, I cringe. A girl sits back-to-back with me, leaning back, tickling my back with her wet hair. I sigh loudly and move. I hear a sound I vaguely recognize: click-click. A man nearby has his shoes off and is trimming his toenails. Click-click, bang goes the door, click-click, bang, bang.

This is going to be a long night.

Me on the Gaudi bench in Parc Guell, Barcelona

Gaudi house design, Block of Discord

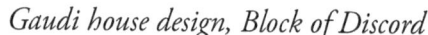

To Madrid, And Beyond – Perfecting My English

Travelling alone and broke is a bit like being accompanied by the seven dwarves' bastard cousins: Bitchy, Dirty, Achy, Lonely, Weary, Sweaty, and Loopy. There is no reassuring "I don't feel like walking, I'll just take a cab," or "This four-star hotel looks nice". It is a dog eat credit card world out there!

The bus to Madrid from Barcelona was the obvious choice for my budget: thirty Euros versus one hundred eighteen for the train, a night bus replaces a hotel night, saving another forty Euros or so. I have become, out of necessity, a bus traveler.

Exhausted, I finally find sleep, or it finds me. I am happy to discover upon arrival in Madrid that the bus station is directly connected to the Metro. I make my connection and brave three long flights of stairs – up, up, up. At last, a young man takes pity on me and helps me carry my duffel up the last flight. Panting with exertion, I drop off my monstrous bag at my hostel, less than half a block from the station, and quickly freshen up in the shared bathroom. The room isn't ready, but I can already tell that this hostel is much nicer than the one in Barcelona I just left.

Off to explore Madrid until the check-in time!

At the Plaza Mayor in Centre de Sol, a group of young children marches by, each with a bright lime green backpack. I meander down the pedestrian street to the next plaza. From the subway emerges a group wearing red t-shirts with the words Puerto Rico emblazoned on the back, each holding a small Puerto Rico flag as they walk along. A chubby man selling lottery tickets under an umbrella sings out "Viente Milliones de Euros, loteria...." I find it fitting that he is here in the Opera Square, with his strong melodic baritone.

On the Plaza de Oriente, in front of the magnificent palacio, a toothless Spanish man sings "Proud Mary." I doubt he really knows what words he is singing; they have a funny sound: "Lowwling on the Reeva!" I laugh and put some money in his cup.

My next volunteer job is called Pueblo Ingles – a conversation exchange where Spanish speakers practice their English with native speakers. Volunteers are given room and board in exchange for their work. It sounds like fun! I'm excited to meet a group of ready-made friends.

The next day is my last morning here in Madrid, so I walk around the city. August is the time of "Rebajas," or sales, in Spain. I try window shopping but it is only frustrating. I'm an American, a born consumer. I want to consume, damn it! I keep in mind two crucial things: that I am currently unemployed, and that my bag already weighs a ton! I wander on, glancing longingly into the stores, full of clothing and shoes that I dare not try on. I lust after a pair of furry boots, but this is not the season for them. It is way too hot.

At Opera Plaza I linger in a café over some coffee. It's less hectic than Plaza Mayor in the Puerta del Sol, but still great for people-watching. I am weary of cities, though, and tired of worrying about every Euro I spend. I'm ready to work hard in exchange for being taken care of.

It's Friday, the day the Pueblo Ingles group is to take the bus to La Alberca, where the language camp is to be held. I check out of the hotel and haul my bag (I have come to call it "Big Guy") through the Metro and, with the help of another kind stranger, find the street and the pick-up place for the bus.

On the bus, volunteers are asked to sit with a Spaniard, as "the English starts here!" Jez, the program leader warns. No one is allowed to speak Spanish from this point forward. The four-hour ride, out of the busy city and into the dry rolling hills peppered with low dusky green trees, passes pleasantly as I get to know my seatmate.

The English only thing is a mixed blessing for me. I desperately want to work on my Spanish, so a week of only speaking English cuts into my own language learning goal.

On the other hand, it is a sweet relief not to have to remember how to conjugate this Spanish verb, or whether this noun is masculine or feminine. Also, I don't have to think about how much the hotel costs, or wonder where my next meal is coming from, as this is all part of the program. I can unpack, relax, and enjoy the pool at free time. The site is distinctly Un-Spanish: the accommodations have an alpine feel, white panels with large dark wooden beams on the ceilings. The exteriors are stone on the bottom and dark wood on the top, with wrought iron stair railings, clay tile roofs, and window trim painted red, blue, or green. It is as if the designer of these houses changed courses at least three times in the building of them, but somehow the result is one of singular beauty and charm. Rough-barked trees sprinkle the gentle hills of the complex, and red brick paths wind between houses. There are benches and wicker seating areas throughout, so that when it is time for our one-on-one conversations, we have many choices of areas to sit and talk.

Everyone seems relaxed here, even the Spaniards, who are working incredibly hard. I can sympathize, having an intimate familiarity with the difficulty of learning a language well. They are all here to learn, to immerse, and to advance. Some have come on their own, but for many their week was paid for by their employers so that they can improve for work. A week, of course, is not enough. But the immersion and the play and friendship here is a good start. We all enjoy each other's company and are here as friends and helpers.

The schedule is deceivingly fluid, but when all is said and done it is a long work day. Breakfast at nine, one-to-one conversation for four one-hour slots afterward, lunch, then siesta (one and a half or two hours), then group activities, more one-to-ones, another group (entertainment time) and dinner. We converse at meals, of course, so this is a part of the work, informal as it may be. All told, it is at least an eleven-hour day. But it is pleasant work. It is delightful to meet all the Spanish speakers, and the English speakers (the "Anglos") as well.

As for me, I am having a great time. You never know when you will meet life-long friends, or someone who will somehow change your life. I am open to all experiences, but I am not planning to hook up with someone in this closed environment. I have been told this happens frequently. For me, it would be like high school, sleeping with a boy and then having to deal with seeing him "in the halls" as it were, and pretending that everything was normal. No thanks! Not that anyone has offered; many of the Spanish men are married anyway and others are very young.

Being on this trip and communicating with Brad seems surreal. When I envisioned this journey, I imagined he might accompany me, or would be part of my past. This limbo is unsettling; at the moment I am completely unavailable and I feel like that might be the appeal for him. Brad enjoyed the long-distance relationship we had for three of our five years while I agonized over every moment apart. I have a sneaking suspicion that he just won't ever let himself be authentically close to anyone. Perhaps I can just let this be his problem and not mine. But we have agreed- thus far, anyway – to meet when I am back in the area in December, to see what we feel like when we spend some time together. But do I really want to continue a relationship where true intimacy is avoided through excessive physical intimacy?

I call him one night through Skype, as arranged. We talk about what we are doing and avoid talking about our relationship, and for some reason, perhaps too much red wine at dinner, I begin to cry. Hearing his voice is so nice, so familiar, and unleashes a tide of emotions in me. "I don't know whether what I'm feeling is real or if it's all nostalgia!" I wail.

"Shush, don't cry," he says, but he does not offer more comfort than that, or a glimpse into his own emotions, if he has any. He is, as always, detached. I vow not to talk about these feelings with him anymore. Soon enough, I will know. Until then, there is nothing I can do. What scares me the most is that if the feelings are real, there may still be nothing I can do. It was hard to deal with his detachment when we were together. Now, after all the healing, why rip myself open again?

Here at the Pueblo Ingles program, we mostly talk of things that are familiar to us: family, jobs, where we live. Occasionally the conversation drifts into more personal ground: relationships and disappointment and joy. My first one-to-one is with a lovely young woman from Chile, and we walk up the hill while we talk. She tells me the story of how she met her boyfriend. They were friends and co-workers in Brazil for over a year, and when they finally discovered they both wanted more and their relationship was in the full bloom of beginning love, she was offered a job in Spain. Difficult as it was, she decided to take the job and move, keeping long-distance with her boyfriend until he could also find a job here.

"Wasn't that hard?" I ask. I remembered how I had been ready to give up all my dreams to live with Brad, just to not lose the love I thought we had built up over time, and I also remembered how the whole thing crumbled when I offered him that option.

She takes my hand. "Of course. But it was an advance in my career. He could say that we were done in a month, and then what? I would have given up my life to be with him and have neither thing." I thought about this. How strong she must be to be in love and to risk losing that to be true to herself! I didn't do that. I was willing to live in eastern Washington instead of travel Spain and South America, all for a love that was not even durable. I gave him the choice, and then I waited for him to decide my fate. A woman like my Chilean friend would never have done that; she was stronger than to compromise her path. That is the kind of strength I want to cultivate, and I hope this trip will help me to achieve it.

I tell her then about my recent contact with my ex. She surprises me with some advice: "You should see him and find out how you really feel. If you don't try, you will never know." I tuck this away to think about later.

But I know if I do go see Brad what that means – we will fall into bed and although that would be nice, it won't solve this issue of whether we should try again. I am scared. I always feared that sex was our only real connection. Isn't it okay for me to say that's not enough anymore?

Blog Post: Lament of a Weekend Sex Toy

Lately I have been puzzling over whether to get re-involved with my ex. We had a relationship that was physically intense, we had compatibility in many areas, and I cared about him deeply; for his family, his child, his friends. But I fear that for him the relationship really was just based on sex. Sex with a girl who never said no, even at six AM before coffee, never said, "I couldn't possibly; what if someone sees us?" I was his perfect weekend sex toy.

Well, I am more than a sum of my sexual parts and talents. I am sweet, funny, and generous. I have a big heart and I'm easy to talk to. I'm a good listener. I have strong empathy. I have faults, too. I am unfocused at times, over-emotional, and occasionally have really bad ideas that I am determined to put into effect at any cost. I almost always burn grilled cheese sandwiches. I blow my nose really loudly. I am a complete person. Not just a walking sex doll. And I deserve to respect myself and be with a man who can respect me for all those things.

I want to find a romantic partnership with a man who will always be there for me, as I will for him. Someone who would sit by my side a whole weekend while I visit my mother in the hospital and nursing home (I did that for him). Someone who would take two days off work and help me find a house in a new town, even if it tore him up that I was moving (I also did that.)

Why is it so hard to get past endings? Why do we overlook so many things until it is impossible to go on? Do we want to believe the best in someone, or just believe our own delusional fantasies? The fantasy in my heart that I had someone I could truly love and be with, that I would get a second chance to get it right (even though my head always knew it was wrong) – well, that fantasy died hard.

Is it worth going back into this union and re-examining it? I guess only time will tell.

I am making friends here, relaxing, doing some minimalist flirting. I am one of the oldest participants. I don't quite know how to accept getting older. I am afraid I cannot do it gracefully. I don't feel my age. I enjoy connecting with all the people here – young girls, young boys, and older men and women, too. One of the Spanish men is 32, an adorable rogue. Sixteen years difference between us, and when we talk I get butterflies. I just shake my head at myself. Harmless. A small fantasy. And in these moments, I don't feel too old. It could happen!

But a Canadian woman points out after dinner one night that my eyes look tired - is she concerned or just rude? - and I must face it, I'm closing in on 50. I bless the years I have been given; I know they are a gift. I have good health and good luck. I am fortunate, blessed, and… growing old.

If I were still married (and believe me, I am glad as hell I am not) – perhaps then I would not worry about aging. I would have a partner to age with, someone who would love me "no matter what." I would relax into the idea that I have earned these stretch mark by having his children.

Instead, here I am, saggy eyes and stretch marked belly, trying to figure out how to market this rusty old used car so that someone will want to drive it. Men are trained to look at the sweet young unmarred things. Hell, I look at them as well, lying by the pool, smoking at the bar (not knowing that both these things will damage their perfect skin even if having babies does not.)

We are allowed some leeway in our last conversation sessions, and a group of us end up passing around a rum bottle and playing Taboo. The Spaniards mostly decline the rum, so it's me and another American doing shots. After dinner when we return to the hotel, the rum comes back out, and one of the English guys brings out his guitar. Handsome Arturo, one of the Spaniards, borrows it to play some flamenco tunes for us. I talk the Englishman into playing Springsteen on his guitar so I can sing (not as well as I imagine) "I'm On Fire." I only sing when I am drunk, and I am sure the world is grateful for that! The night ends abruptly at four-thirty AM when the sprinklers come on and unceremoniously soak the whole group sitting on the patio. We shriek and disperse.

I am barely back to my own villa when the Englishman knocks on my door, claiming there is a spider in his room and he can't go back. He climbs into the spare bed. I declare aloud that am not sleeping with him! Later, though, he crawls into my bed. No surprise. Half asleep and still drunk, I fool around with him and hate myself for doing it.

The next day, I am hung-over and sleep deprived, and I cry when I say goodbye to the others. I avoid the English guy. I hug my new friends hard when I say goodbye. Waving sadly, I watch their bus as it reverses, edges forward, and finally accomplishes the tight turn-around to leave. Goodbye, fashionable Madrid girls. Goodbye sweet older man who secretly told me a few new Spanish phrases. It feels strange to know I will never see any of these people again. Pueblo Ingles was a unique experience. I blink back more tears and take a deep breath. My cab will be here soon and I will be on to a new adventure.

Ledesma, Sleepy Town

I am a few days into my first Help Exchange experience, and already feeling moody and fidgety. This does not bode well for the remaining months! I am sitting in a small café. A bullfight is on TV. I had thought, at one point, that I might be able to go see a bullfight, to enjoy the ambiance of this very Spanish tradition. But I know now I could never sit through it. The one on television has me in tears. I don't comprehend it. The only thing I like is the matador's outfit. The bull has a back covered in blood as he charges the cape, half a dozen picadors, or small spears, stuck in his hump. My heart goes out to the poor fellow. What kind of sport tortures an animal like this? The bull, laden with the broken small spears, bows his head and pushes his shoulder against one of the horses that are part of the support team, as if he were trying to ask for help of a fellow animal. What is the poor beast thinking?

My host Ron here in Ledesma would say that bulls don't think at all. Ron is an Englishman who enjoys arguing and debating almost any subject, and I must admit that the intellectual stimulation is fun. Also staying here are two British boys the same age as my oldest daughter. Tristan has dark blonde dreadlocks and is tall and strapping; Eifian is dark-haired and slight. The boys helped me haul my bag up the stairs of Ron's house and into the tiny bedroom where I will be sleeping. "How do you manage?" grunted Tristan as he struggled with my luggage.

I drum my fingers on the café table as I turn from the television. I think my idealism has tripped me up once again. My Barcelona friend, Leo, called me to scold me for not contacting him. He told me he is going to Turkey and I want to say, *take me too*! I am not sure what I'm craving now, but I feel so restless. I think of myself in a warm, Spanish-speaking family, helping with the children, the garden, or the animals. Walking to town and meeting people. Sitting under a flowering tree with my computer, writing brilliantly. In these fantasies I am thinner, with long flowing hair and a stellar wit. And I am never ever bored!

At another table here, there is a group of four girls who look to be about the age of my own youngest daughter, who is eighteen. They have hair piled up on top of their heads and black eyeliner circles their eyes, making them look like sexy raccoons. Teenagers are the same everywhere. I smile to myself, missing Veronica.

⁙⁙⁙

That night I dream of kissing Tristan and I wake up mortified. To get some energy out I decide to go visit a place I came across the day before: a series of three stone staircases and a platform, leading from a low street to a higher one, and covering about fifty yards from bottom to top. I got winded just walking up them, which annoyed me. I am getting out of shape. I normally go daily to the gym or a yoga class, sometimes both, and now I'm doing next to nothing. So, I "go to the gym" and run up and down the series of stairs ten times. I break a sweat and get my heart rate up. When I get back, so the boys are carrying in some wood, so I join them, happy for a job at last.

At dusk we all go for a walk and end up by the seldom-used bullring in town. A local man is outside, playing a drum that is fastened around his chubby waist and blowing a flute-like instrument, attached with a gadget that allows him to blow into it hands-free. The effect is surreal, haunting. The boys and Ron walk over to the garbage dump and rummage around while I watch the sun set behind the bullring and think about this odd evening; one I will probably never duplicate. Cows in a field moo mournfully while the music plays on and the sun lights the white walls of the bullring with a faint pink glow.

I decide, for lack of other options, to schedule another week at an English-language immersion site like Pueblo Ingles. I will return to Madrid on Saturday and in the meanwhile try to contact potential hosts on Help Ex. I need to spread my net a little wider. One of my most anticipated stays, at a yoga retreat, was cancelled. I don't know where I am going next, and the uncertainty of that sets panic in my heart.

I am in a state of Limbo. I have never been away from home this long, and I am between homes anyway right now, in a major transition. I feel disconnected from real life. But what is it that makes a life? I have been contemplating this question, and not sure I have come up with a definitive answer. I think it is a combination of things: some real, some imagined. Matters of the heart and material goods. For me, it boils down to being around the people I love, having interactions: making dinner, making love, going for walks with the dogs, planning a vacation. If I were not traveling alone, this would be a very different trip. Perhaps this adventure is not what I thought it would be – I thought I would learn how to be strong, how to conquer fears, how to be alone. Yet I dream of my body intertwined with another's. Daily I wish for a friend. The lesson I am learning is that, yes, I can be alone, but I still don't want to be!

I use Skype to keep in touch with both Brad and my daughters. With Brad, I only use the phone application, but with my daughters I video chat. We have to navigate the time difference, but I check in with them every few weeks.

"How are you?" I ask Veronica when she picks up my call. Her dog Zepher is beside her, wagging his tail.

"Good, Mom. How's Spain?" She takes a drink of something; I wonder if it's alcohol. I squash the urge to ask. She is independent now.

"It's wonderful." I tell her about Pueblo Ingles, and about the place I am staying now. I can feel her attention wane as I go on. "What about you?" I prompt.

"Not much. Work. Hanging out with friends."

We wind up the call with "I love you" and I sigh. I miss her, but I am here now.

In Ledesma, the sky is blue, the sun is shining on the plaza below, and it is a beautiful day, unfurling with not much to do, true, but also no expectations.

On one of our group walks, the boys climb around on big rocks down by the stream. They find a dead fish and wave it at us. I laugh at their youthful play. I have come to call them cachorros, the Spanish word for puppies. Ron and I walk together, surveying a beautiful valley with a trickle of a stream and boulders scattered all around. An old Roman bridge stretches over the larger stream, and Ron and I sit on rocks to watch the boys scramble around. Ron is curious about Americans – our lifestyle, our politics, our patriotism.

He turns to me with a familiar glint in his eye. I await his question. "Do you think that Disney has ruined America?"

I smile. Here is a subject I have contemplated many times. "I don't know about ruined, but it certainly gives us unrealistic expectations."

Ron nods. "If everyone in your country grows up on Disney movies and their imagery, it must be a huge disappointment when you see what life really is like."

"I like Disney, though." He responds by arching a cynical eyebrow. "I do!" I insist. "I want to believe in magic."

"You can't want to believe in something. Either you believe in it or you don't."

On the walk home, I consider this. I disagree with Ron's statement. I think you can want something to be true while still doubting that it is. Magic is difficult to find; that doesn't mean it doesn't exist. You can search something out while still questioning its existence, can't you? Isn't that how most people find God?

The following day I ask Ron if we can make a trip over to Portugal if I pay for gas, and he agrees. We all four pile into his small car and drive about 45 minutes to cross the border into Miranda du Douro, where we do a bit of wandering and shopping. We visit a church and some shops and have a beer at a bar at the edge of a river. A girl is throwing sticks for her Rottweiler. It's a wonderful day: sunny but not scorching.

On the way back, we stop for a visit with some of Ron's friends who live in a neighboring village, smaller than Ledesma. They are not home, so we wait. When they come, they are accompanied by five children – two of their own and three neighbors. The children run around pretending they are pirates. The littlest boy keeps hurting himself, running in tears to his mother, then recovering and picking up his sword once again. As I watch them, I feel a sharp and fleeting pang of missing my school kids.

Antoine, the papa, is a Frenchman married to Isabel, a Spanish lady. They are artists. He is a drum maker, and he hauls some out of his workshop for us to play. Ron brings out a loaf of bread he bought in Portugal and they bring out some sharp and smooth local cheese. Isabel makes tinto de verano, a wine and lemonade mix that is popular in Spain. We sip and play the drums.

Antoine offers Tristan a guitar to play and teaches him to pick the strings in flamenco style. We form an impromptu drum circle with a single guitar. As night descends, we fall into a groove of music and friendship. It is these kinds of experiences that I have been craving. Not fancy, not always planned out, but making connections with others, making music, real or theoretical. Experiencing small moments of joy with other humans.

On the drive home, I tilt my head up to see the multitude of twinkling stars in the onyx-black sky. They are glowing and dancing, and bright little pinpricks of smaller stars cast a fuzzy glow. It is like looking into a dark ocean full of phosphorescent creatures. I sigh a deep contented sigh. I want to keep this feeling deep in my heart so I can bring it out and hold it when I'm feeling disconnected.

⸎⸎⸎⸎

The next afternoon I decide that I simply must do a yoga practice! I take a beach towel down to the hard stone floor near the main entrance to the house. At some point Tristan walks out to have a cigarette. When he returns, he asks me to show him some yoga, so I do. Then we sit on the floor, legs crossed, talking. We talk about how yoga affects the body and the spirit as the light grows dim outside and the large dining room of the antique palace is cast into shadow.

"Do you think some people are naturally more in touch with their emotions?" he wonders.

I stretch my legs out, wiggling my toes. "I'm about the most open person you'll meet," I say. "But I was always that way. I don't know if yoga opened me up to others, but I think it made me more open to myself."

He nods, dreadlocks bobbing. He is cute – the boys don't like that word, but I can't help it. I am getting used to the lilting rhythm of the three English accents, but I miss trying out my Spanish. It's getting to be time to move on again, if developing a crush on a boy of twenty is any indication, and I need to find an assignment that keeps me busy. Ledesma is charming in a quiet way, but short on action.

On the last night, I go out with Tristan and Eifian, my cachorros. I convince them by reminding them that it is my last night there. I have grown to enjoy the company of these boys, the dinner-time debates with our host Ron, a high-spirited game of Trivial Pursuit, and the many quiet moments in our days together. I guard my secret crush on Tristan, corralled by the stern voice in my head that reminds me he is the same age as my oldest daughter.

We stay out far too late drinking and listening to live music, but I don't regret it. I will sleep on the bus tomorrow when I return to Madrid. Back at the house, the three of us sit outside, reluctant to say goodbye. I wonder what these young lads think of me -- a woman their mothers' age who drags them out to bars. I hug them both and we stumble off to our separate beds.

In the morning, after my two hours of sleep, Ron helps me take Big Guy to wait for the bus. We do the Spanish double-cheek kiss, and off I go.

My cachorros in Ledesma

Valdelavilla – More English Practice

After a quick stop in Madrid and a meet-and-greet with some of the participants in the Vaughn language immersion, I am off to another new place to help Spanish speakers practice English. We are going to a small hamlet called Valdelavilla, an hour outside the city. Cristina, a friendly and well-traveled lady from San Francisco, took me on an informal bus tour of Madrid last night. I hope to create some friendships here this week.

I am craving connection, but feeling lost right now. I stare out the window of the bus and think of my daughters, missing them with a sharpness that hurts my stomach. My girls live in the back of my mind like a golden cloud, never far from my thoughts, but removed from this life I am living.

We pass a field of sunflowers, their yellow heads bowed over. They look as forlorn as I feel; struggling with loneliness in this transition. I try to conjure up a good memory of my first trip to Spain with Brad, and find that my heart is numb. If I do have feelings for him, they will have to be re-born rather than a resurrection of the past. I need to move forward and reconfirm the reasons for this trip – to study Spanish and to write.

Arriving at Valedelavilla, I discover that I will have three house mates: two English women named Michelle and Liz, and Larry, a man from Washington state. On our first night together we ladies sit and talk about dating, and when Larry joins us, he is a good sport and shares some of his own experiences.

As the week goes on, I am faithfully doing a bit of yoga every day in the yard of our house, which has a wall around it so that I am slightly hidden from view and don't feel so dorky. One morning I come back upstairs to find Larry shaving with an electric razor in the hall mirror outside my bedroom; we say good morning to each other. *It's like being married,* I think. The thought makes me sadder than it should.

My marriage was not good. We met on equal terms: I, a high-school dropout, ex-stripper, aspiring writer, working waitressing jobs and trying to figure out what was next. He was also not college educated, and living on a houseboat in Key West Florida. We fell in love, got married, and had kids.

Having children was what changed the game for me. I could no longer settle for a inadequate existence; waiting tables at restaurants – and not the nice ones, where you make a lot of money, - and a husband who made laborer wages and always hated his boss. I took in children for day care and went back to school, slowly earning first my Associates, then a Bachelor's, then a Master's degree in education. Meanwhile, my husband went the opposite direction: drinking more, becoming angrier with life, verbally abusing our young headstrong daughter, and acquiring an addiction to trading internet porn.

I was no longer happy in my marriage, but I felt stuck. I had made promises, said vows. Wasn't that the act of sealing one's fate: making a commitment to stay with one person, even if they became a person you loathed? I thought it was. I spent time with my children, reading, and exploring. I went to the barn and rode my horse, taking my daughters with me when they wanted to go. My life was fine, except for my marriage. I grew to live with the fact that I had married a man who disappointed me over and over. My children were growing into amazing girls: smart, beautiful, interesting. I loved my horse and my friends at the barn. I loved getting my education. I hated being married.

Now I doubt I would ever marry again. Today I had a conversation with a man from Madrid named Nica. He spoke passionately against marriage.

"I think it's stupid!" he exclaimed. "Why sign a paper about feeling? If I love you, I love you. I don't need to sign a paper to say it!"

I agree with him, but when I get back to my cottage, I think more about it. I begin to write.

Blog Post: High Infidelity

I saw a news program recently about a new trend in Mexico: the short-term marriage. These marriages have a set term, perhaps two years, at which time they must be renewed or the marriage is over. Over without the necessity of a long expensive divorce process. Both parties must agree to renew the contract. I like this idea. It is still a commitment, but I think people might work harder if they thought they might be "fired" or replaced. Maybe every two years there would be another honeymoon phase as the couple try to secure their place in the other's affections.

And imagine no need for sneaky affairs! No one feels

stuck. If you meet someone that you think is a better fit for you, you don't have to wait forever. This can happen, we all know it! It is the reason people don't want to settle down and make a final choice; what if you just didn't wait long enough? What if the perfect person is just around the corner, and you're stuck with this one? I am sure this would not stop some people from infidelity, but I can see myself saying, "Darling, my marriage is due to be over in four months. Let's get together then!"

The biggest blow to my identity and my womanhood was my husband's infidelity. Although I no longer loved him, being cheated on brought me to my knees emotionally. It made me question everything about myself and our union. I shed that marriage like a furry dog leaving a pile of fluff on the grooming salon floor. I felt lighter, but also exposed. The specter of infidelity haunted me, haunts me still. I never again want to risk that kind of leveling doubt.

There are studies that conclude that biologically, men are not wired to be monogamous. But what if men aren't, and women are? That is a huge problem! How can a man and woman make an agreement that he fights with himself to keep?

Now, having had my children, made my way through school, bought a house, I don't feel like I need to be tied to one person for the same reasons as I would have if I were young. I am not struggling to have a career or raise a family. Why would I ever get married again?

I am finding the Valdelavilla group to be a little more serious and less merrymaking than the Pueblo Ingles crew. Many of the Spanish people have paid out of pocket to improve their English here. The group is older. The men are generous; someone is always buying drinks at the bar.

One night I am sitting with my female housemates, and I notice four of the Spanish guys on the other side of the room, sitting and watching people, but not talking. I think they are afraid to speak among themselves for fear they will start speaking in Spanish. So, with one and a half strong rum and Cokes in me, I head over to say hi to them: Nica, Angel, and two others. I don't know any of these men very well, and I scour my brain for a conversation topic. I bring up the subject of bullfighting. I have been curious about this issue since I entered Spain, especially since I saw the bullfight on TV in Ledesma.

I am happy to hear that none of these guys support bullfighting, due the cruelty of it. But we all enjoy the pageantry. I tell them that my daughter's name is one of the moves of the matador, a veronica. Then I whisk an imaginary cape past a charging bull.

"Ole!" they cry.

Angel stands and puts his fingers on his head as horns and charges me. I flip my cape to the side.

"No," says Nica. "That move is not the veronica. In the veronica, the bullfighter brings the cape up and over his head."

"Like this?" I flip my imaginary cape.

"No," Angel says. He takes off the sweatshirt tied around his waist and unfurls it over his head with a flourish. I grow finger-horns and charge. By now the rest of the small bar is watching the display.

"Let me try," I spin, whipping an imaginary satin cape above my head.

Nica laughs. "I think the bullfighters do not move their hips so much." I attempt it several more times, and someone buys me another drink. I never quite get the part about keeping my hips still.

Valdelavilla is an older hotel, way up in the mountains and isolated. The stone houses themselves are old; dangerous for people who have been drinking, with their low ceilings and steep staircases. Larry walks around our house like a hunchback, as he is six foot four.

Most nights someone pilfers an unfinished bottle of wine off the dinner table and we sneak it back to our house, which I have dubbed the Henhouse, for all the nights we stay up late talking. Usually, it is the three women at the beginning and Larry joins us later, after his own socializing is done. A single guy, I think he is trying to chat up the cute blonde from Chicago. I imagine him lurking outside our door, hearing us ladies still up talking around the kitchen table. He waits outside a while, hoping we will finish soon, knowing he must pass us to creep up the stairs to his bedroom. Finally, he gives up, sighing, and joins the Hen Party.

One night we are talking about children. We all have grown children; mine are the youngest. I have drunk a lot of wine, and I miss them.

"I think the worst thing imaginable, worse than anything in the world, would be to lose a child," I say.

Then Liz quietly tells us that one of her children got sick and died as a young adult, and I begin to sob. Even Larry is teary, sitting quietly at the end of the table wiping his eyes. I reach over and squeeze his hand through my tears.

"Go home to your children," Liz says to me. "Just go home."

But I can't. How can I explain to someone what I can't even fathom myself, that I have to see this through. The ups and downs, the disappointments of missed trains and missed opportunities, the quiet joy of a solitary sunset, and all the things I have yet to experience. My children don't need me the way they once did. And I realize that the only way I will now have a happy and fulfilling life is to understand exactly what that means for me; gathering up the resources that I have, and discounting the things I have no control over. I need a wider perspective. I am hoping and praying that a year of travel will give me that.

Finally, our week is over, and once again it is time to pack up Big Guy and head off to other places. This time I think I have made some friends that will last. A Spanish friend named Ana has said she might go to Morocco with me. Nica says I can stay with him in Madrid, and on the way back to Madrid on the bus we sit together and do an intercambio with him speaking English and me speaking Spanish and both making corrections for the other when necessary. I practically bounce with excitement; my pent-up Spanish tumbling out in a gush. When we get to Madrid, I say goodbye to all my friends and Cristina says I can stash my bag at her apartment until it is time to take the night bus to Sevilla.

We go to dinner at Montaditos y Cerveza, a popular and cheap chain restaurant. Over sandwiches she gives me advice and suggestions about what to see in Morocco. I tell her that Ana has promised to check her schedule and see if she is available to travel to Morocco with me. Cristina advises me not to be too hopeful.

"You meet great people, but if they invite you to visit them, do it right away or not at all. The Spanish are like this; they will invite you but most of them don't really mean it." She has done many programs and must know what she is talking about.

"Really? That's curious. I did email someone in Pamplona who invited me to stay, though, and I have not heard back."

She gestures pointedly. "You see?"

"But he seemed so sincere when he asked! He's a teacher; he invited me to see his classroom…"

She nods. "That's the Spanish. They are like that. They welcome you, but they move on. They forget quickly."

I guess I should not be surprised, but the knowledge makes me sad. I have extended many offers myself, sincerely meaning it every time. I love having visitors. I have even registered with the couch surfing network, for when I get back to the life where there is a couch to share.

The past week I have been told that my life is interesting, even exciting. "We live in the same towns our whole life," one woman told me in our one-to-one session. I drew a rudimentary map of the USA and pointed out the places I have lived: Colorado, San Francisco, New York, Key West, Washington state. She shook her head with admiration. "I am from a town three hours north of Madrid, and now I live in Madrid." She is a lawyer. "People think I am unusual, moving away from my family home. Spanish people don't normally do this."

Perhaps this is why there are very few Spanish hosts on the Help Exchange network. They don't seek unknown help; instead, they turn to family and friends. In fact, none of my hosts on this trip are Spanish; they are English or German, living in Spain. For this reason, I have not practiced nearly as much Spanish as I had anticipated. I planned to return home this spring with three things: an increased blog following, improved Spanish, and yoga certification. But instead, I am growing fat and lazy, struggling with ways to incorporate yoga into my day. And my Spanish is rarely used, thus not improved. I have been writing most days, though; a catalog of places I have been and people I've met.

Although what it all means I have yet to decipher.

The "veronica"

Me and Nica (eyeliner for Amy Winehouse night)

Algodonales, Swimming And Dreaming

In the evening, I make my way to the Madrid bus station, and I sleep on the bus all the way to Seville, stumbling drowsily into the small station there to wait. A bedraggled man with a bushy beard and filthy clothes – homeless? – enters the Seville bus station at 6:30 AM and begins digging through trash cans. He fishes out the paper I discarded moments ago with the Pueblo Ingles schedule and looks at it before putting it back. I approach him, ask him in Spanish if he is hungry, and offer some cookies I bought in Madrid. He answers in rapid-fire Spanish I barely understand, but what I do catch is that he does not like these types of cookies. Ah, a selective trash-digger. I watch as he systematically goes through each trash can in the station, and then leaves through the opposite door from which he came. I am vaguely insulted that he turned up his nose at my cookies.

People enter, slowly filling the bus station. The taquillas, or ticket windows, are not yet open. I have begun considering a new bag for the South America part of my trip. Big Guy is just too big.

He wouldn't fit in the lockers at the station if I wanted to store him and explore. He is difficult to get on and off buses and up and down Metro stairs. He has become like a burdensome person I really do not want to travel with but am forced to. Before my trip, I was feeling smug about being down to only one bag! Now I envy the backpackers, wishing I was enough of a minimalist to pull that off. I don't need this many T-shirts, and I have not brought any of the right pants! I packed too many yoga clothes, anticipating three weeks volunteering at a yoga center that was cancelled.

Finally, the bus arrives to take me to Algodonales, a white village, or pueblo blanco, in Andalucia. All around me on the bus are snippets of Spanish language, and I catch tiny bits of words: "azul," "veinteuno." Eavesdropping might be the true measure of mastering another language. Does Spanish have the equivalent of the word eavesdrop? Yesterday Nica told me my Spanish was good as we talked on the bus. Working with English learners and watching them battle their insecurities makes me realize that I also must fight my discomfort and just speak more Spanish.

From my seat on the bus after some sporadic napping, I recognize the white hilltop village Zahara, with white houses sprinkled like sugar cubes down the gently sloping green hills and a boxy brown castle standing watchfully at the top. Brad and I visited here four years ago. I'm proud of myself for recognizing it.

<hr />

The bed and breakfast where I will spend two weeks helping is situated in a delightful house, large, spacious and all done up in tile. My hostess Julie and her husband Martin renovated the house together when they moved to Spain. The idyllic setting of rolling hills, a sparkling pool and this charming B and B at the edge of the white village is deceptively tranquil, hiding a tragedy. Martin suffered a heart attack and fell off the roof while tackling a too-big project, leaving Julie a widow to run their dream alone. She lives here with their fourteen-year-old son, Warren. Although it has been almost four years, her eyes still shine with unshed tears when she tells the story.

Julie left the comfort of England and her friends to come here with Martin, who had run a successful B and B in Britain. They bought the house, which was stark and made of brick and wood. They plastered it over, knocked out walls, put in bathrooms, renovated the kitchen, and put in the outside decks and the pool. She showed me pictures of the original house. I could not believe the difference.

"You guys did an amazing amount of work!" I exclaimed.

She seemed genuinely pleased for the compliment. "In England, no one gave us any credit for that. They thought we were mad. And now, I sometimes forget everything we went through together, because he's not here anymore."

"But you two made your dream happen," I reminded her. I gestured around, and together we looked out the window at the happy families sitting and enjoying toast and coffee on the poolside deck.

"Yeah. I guess we did." The echo of sadness in her voice haunts me.

The question I am asking myself on this trip seems to be echoing within every encounter. What are the things that make life worthwhile? Is it worth having a beautiful home and business, horses in the field, a shimmering pool just outside your back door in a land of bright sunshine and cheap wine, if the person you most want to share that life with is gone?

My last host Ron lived in what could be a magnificent setting, an ancient palace. His days are filled with cooking elaborate meals in a grimy kitchen for company he finds on the internet through Help Ex. I see the value in this: new friends tromping through the door every week from different lands, with different stories to tell. He is a wonderful host, coaxing higher-level thinking from the most confused dreamy brains, such as mine. Still, it makes me sad. Where are his authentic connections? Where is the love in his life?

Am I still just a victim, after all these years, after a wild decade in New York, after divorce, after love gone wrong – a victim of the Cinderella stories of my childhood? Are these stories so firmly engrained that I cannot see the value in a life without the perfect prince (or at least a passable one?) I wish I could go somewhere to have my brain rewired and wake up with the truth of relationships implanted in my new cerebral cortex: that they mostly suck, and when they don't, they are snatched away prematurely. But I do not want to be this cynical! I am searching for a happy relationship in this world, or at least in Spain, to hold up as a model and shining example. It is like searching for Bigfoot.

Julie and her son both call me "Cath," which makes me feel like an old family friend or perhaps a beloved aunt, rather than a person here working for room and board. Julie is kind, but a task-master; wanting things done just so. She gave me a serious lesson on how to hang the laundry. I will be doing lots of gardening and horse care, and Julie allows me plenty of time for relaxation.

Her golden bay horse, Abu, snorts gently in his corral, glimmers of his shiny coat visible through the bamboo and fruit trees. I am drying off in the strong sun after a leisurely swim. A blue mosaic dolphin sparkles at the bottom of the water, trying to beckon me in for another splash. I close my eyes, siesta-ing in the languid afternoon.

I arrived here yesterday and have not left the property. Tomorrow Julie has to make a day trip and she will give me a free day to do some touring. The map and the bus schedule will determine where I go.

Last night I talked to Brad for almost an hour via Skype. This time it was easier to stay neutral. I told him about my difficulty finding someone to practice Spanish with, and about the dropped "s" regional accent (for example, adios becomes adio.) We spoke of my travel plans and the trip to Italy with his daughter he is embarking on in a day.

He said he was still struggling with the death of his mother and that it comes and goes. He broke down crying in a Taco Time restaurant. His brother says they are now orphans.

"That's why I'm moving back to Colorado," I reminded him as if it needed to be restated. "To be with my parents as they get older."

Unspoken, what hung in the cyberspace between us is the fact that we live in different states now, an airplane ride rather than a drive apart. We struggled through a harsh breakup a year ago, when I wanted to move in with him and he balked. If he thought that was too scary, why in the world did he open the door to reconciliation? Did he just miss the intensity of our weekend trysts, or did he really want me, and all my quirks, back in his life? And I am not sure how I feel anymore, either. Maybe we're both just living in the past because we fear the future.

At the B and B, I help Julie get the rooms ready for guests. The horses get fed and watered. I pet the elderly terrier, Libby, stroking her as if she is made of spun glass because at the lightest touch she falls over, she is so old and wobbly.

Julie has me working in the garden, the grounds, and the barn. Each day after my work shift I lay by the pool in the sun then do some yoga, turning my face up to the golden rays. In Washington I rarely saw the sun. Here I am constantly embraced by its glow. I swim. I siesta. I read Facebook posts by my teacher friends back in Washington, feeling nostalgic but not jealous as they ready themselves for their new students.

And yet, although I am on this extended vacation, this gap year, I long for the structure of a job. What would I choose if I could have any life imaginable? *A partner, a lover....* My mind whispers to me. The voice in my head insists that this is necessary. Okay, I placate, but besides that? The framework of a day: yoga practice, or perhaps teaching yoga to others. On some days, volunteer work. Writing each day. Cooking delicious healthy meals. Connecting with other people: family and friends. Having a writer's group, a yoga class, riding lessons. And who, I wonder, will accompany me in this next phase of life?

Brad is in Italy with his daughter right now. I wonder how they like Venice. I have not visited Italy since 1987, and I adored Venice. Brad and I used to talk about going there together. I think about all the things we didn't talk about. I would try, because I loved that "dreaming together" phase of being a couple: what kind of house we would live in together, the vegetables we would plant in the garden, and the dinner parties we'd throw. I am a fantasizer; my dreams feed me. I always had a nagging trepidation about Brad's inability to even commit to putting eggplant in an imaginary garden. What could that mean? When we walked the aisles of a Target and I saw some pretty bath towels, I asked him if he wanted that color scheme when we someday would design a bathroom together. He was as puzzled as if I'd asked him something in Chinese.

These are the signs we ignore, the things we see later, slap our foreheads and go, "Duh!" It was there all along, his reluctance to commit to anything. Some men's actions speak if they don't have to say the words. They can do togetherness as long as they don't have to label it as commitment. Like the lonesome cowboy, they do not want to feel fenced in, even if they love their corral. The moment they feel confined, they flee.

Wouldn't it be better, I wonder, to have someone who didn't have to be persuaded, someone who outright adores me and is proud to say it? Why is it so difficult to discover love? Couples should just naturally fall together if we all want the same thing. Why is it so damned hard to find?

On my next day off, Julie suggests I check out a nearby white village called Setenil de las Bodegas. I find the right bus and get there in an hour and a half. Setenil is a striking town, built into sheer rock caves. I gaze around in wonder. The buildings are literally part of the gigantic marbled rock cliffs that hang over the streets and serve as their roofs. Between the rock facades, streets climb, then descend, and are so narrow that it's best to step into a doorway when a car passes.

I wander up a winding street and find a hermita, a small church. The church is filled, like many are, with life-sized mannequins of Jesus, his large eyes full of complacent suffering as he carries a large cross on his shoulder. Just once, I think, I'd like to see Jesus turn around and deck someone! Stand up for yourself, man! To Hell with this long-suffering act. But of course, he never does.

Blog Post: Jesus and the Agnostic Girl

I find Jesus profoundly beautiful, even though I was raised without religion. I don't know what I believe in, but I cannot deny his power. He is such a big symbol in the world that he is difficult to ignore, much like a gorgeous fallen rock star who has made it into pop culture permanently. Jesus and Elvis have been compared before, I suppose.

And although I am not on a conscious search for God, I am drawn to the churches as I travel through Spain. I go into as many of them as I can. Their exteriors vary: large, small, and everything in between. They are stone or painted white, yellow, or brown. Some have beautiful ornate windows and stained glass that takes my breath away. When I am done marveling at the beauty, I always look for my amigo Jesus. He is somewhere inside, often many of him. Sometimes he looks like a mannequin with real hair. In some churches he is dressed in elegant robes, in others he wears a ragged loincloth. But whenever I see him, my heart sings. I look into his big puppy dog eyes and there I find love and compassion.

In these churches, I always look for the electronic box where you can insert a coin to light a candle. These boxes have replaced the old-fashioned set up of actual matches and candles. My prayer is generic. I'm not making a wish and I'm not asking for anything. I simply pray to be open. I drop the coin and inside the glass box, my candle flickers twice, then burns brightly.

They say not all who wander are lost. I think that's true for me. I am wandering, and I may not know what lies at the end of my road, but I am putting one foot in front of the other and walking forward the best way I know how, trying to be available for life lessons.

If Jesus wants to come along, that's fine with me.

I follow signs to Cuevas del Sol, or Sun Caves, a street along the river, scattered with restaurants under the rocky overhang of caves. Outdoor tables are shaded by a rocky ledge. Green clumps of vine hang over the edge like ponytails. Across a bridge are the Cuevas de Sombra, shadow Caves, where several shops are receded into the caves like their counterparts across the river. They are not open to the light, but shadowed by cave rock on one side and white houses on the other; the shops sell wine and Iberian ham in the cool interiors. I drink a frosty mug of beer as I reflect on my companions on this trip so far: my wonderful San Sebastian "parents," Evelyn and Leo in Barcelona, los Cachorros, Ron, Nica and Cristina, and now Julie and Warren. All have had something to teach me.

Have I grown on this trip, one and a half months in, and two to go? I'm not homesick often, possibly because there is no home of my own to go to, but I miss my daughters every day. I think fondly of friends I left behind. I think about my parents. I wonder how last year's kindergarten kids are doing in first grade. But mostly I plunge blithely into this journey, which has surely fallen short of some of my expectations while surpassing others. I fall into it like a weary guest falls onto a lumpy chair: grateful for whatever is offered after a long and strenuous trip.

◆◆◆◆◆

My time in Algodonales has done me some good. I have another week to go then I will plan a few days of sightseeing before heading down to Tarifa. After seven days in one place, I begin to feel ready to move on. When I first get in and unpack, I am profoundly content. But I have never really settled in. Moving from place to place seems to be the rhythm that carries me forward.

In the morning, I strip the two horse stalls of all their bedding. It is tiring and dusty work, but I thoroughly enjoy it. Give me something horsey to do and I am happy. A Help X host contacted me this week to work at their barn near Mijas (a town that holds more romantic Brad memories) and I have arranged to come for a week. They have thirteen horses; that should keep me busy. Tomorrow Julie and I are going riding. I am really looking forward to being on a horse, and it has been several months since I have ridden, so I hope I don't make a big fool of myself!

The next day we drive to the barn where she used to keep her horse and meet up with another lady who rides there. We drive through Grazelema, where the long stretch of lake is the exact color of turquoise. At the top of the town of Grazalema is a restaurant and, below that, a public pool. I remember being at the restaurant balcony with Brad, watching Spanish teens splash about on the hot July day. We held hands and thought of our own daughters, murmuring how lucky we were to have snuck away together, but secretly missing our kids.

The thought of Brad prompts the memory of our last brief discussion when he returned from Italy. He said he thought of me on the trip, and I try not to read anything into that. How easy it is to fall back into the traps of old! I have spent over a year covering up the trap door entrance, piling rocks on it, covering them with my blood and my tears, dragging huge boulders I once thought impossible to lift, barring that door from ever, ever being opened again. "There!" I finally said to myself, with an army of people nodding behind me: friends, my mother, my therapist, even my dog. I dusted off my hands and smiled radiantly at the group. "All done!" They clapped and breathed a collective sigh of relief.

But now, it is as if some of those strong rocks are crumbling, and the trap door is still there after all that work. I do not want to go near it. But if I don't, I'll never know. It is maddening!

So instead, I concentrate on the here and now. I saddle up the trainer's broad white gelding with the short ugly head. We ride out, three of us on white horses, through the Spanish countryside. The day is warm. The surefooted horses navigate rocks and spikey brush on the path. We duck under a few low-hanging branches. When the road opens, Julie's friend Jo encourages me to take my horse, Colino, for a canter. He complies easily. Jo told me earlier that this horse does piaffe (a very compact, athletic trot-in-place) and canter changes (in which the horse changes the leading leg mid-stride.) A mere touch of the reins slows him to the walk with a few steps. So unlike the hyper Thoroughbreds I have ridden!

On the way back to the barn, the horses perk up, as horses often do. Jo points out a worn circle of dirt ahead. "That's a schooling area," she tells me. "If you want to go do some things with Colino, go ahead."

I urge him forward, and we break into a rolling canter. He is so easy to sit, like a super-charged couch. I canter around the ring, feeling invincible. I am a star! I am the world's greatest rider! I will win the blue ribbon! I am...

"You're on the wrong canter lead!" Julie calls out. I look down. *Damn!* He's so balanced, I didn't even realize. I make a few false starts to get the correct lead. Finally we get it, and I do a few small circles at canter – not pirouettes, exactly, but small enough to make me feel special. I do a little lateral work at the trot, and Julie and Jo move forward back to the trail. I shrug, pat Colino, who I now think of as my handsome boy, and join them. I am elated. Tears collect in the corners of my eyes.

◄◄◄◄◄◄

I take my last swim in the pool in the late afternoon. A young couple from England is staying with Julie; they arrived a few days ago. We chat as I dry in the fading sun. The girl is a HelpX worker who was with Julie a year ago, and she has brought her boyfriend, a quiet Irish man. She is on holiday and will begin working on her Ph.D. when she returns. I am impressed by this, a girl of twenty-five knowing precisely what she wants to do and pursuing an advanced degree.

I think of my own daughters, who I Skype called yesterday. Emily is just starting University in a few days to earn her teaching certificate. Veronica has agreed to talk to me about school when I am back, and maybe start taking some classes at the community college. I am thrilled that they are both pursuing their educations! Maybe college isn't for everyone, but having a teaching degree enabled me to leave my dead marriage and be able to raise my children solo, and that has made all the difference in my life.

Sevilla: Past Longings Meet Present Insanity

I arrive in Sevilla at noon. It is a beautiful city, the largest in Andalucia. The Moorish influence is apparent in the tall towers that reign above courtyards strewn with gushing fountains. Whitewashed buildings are trimmed in saffron yellow, giving the city a glowing, sunny feel. Oranges that grow on trees lining most streets echo the sunny colors. Ornate bridges over the river Guadalquivir connect the east and west parts of the city, separating different Barrios, or neighborhoods. The clip-clop of horses' hooves echo in the streets as tourists ride the ubiquitous carriages to sight-see.

It is a warm, familiar place, another city I saw with Brad. The rushed anxiety I harbored earlier has melted away. At the bus station, I ask the friendly old man at the information desk about the train to Malaga tomorrow. I am told that it leaves from a station across town. No pasa nada. I ask him for a map and he helps me find the hostel. "Es cercatita!" (very close) he exclaims. He circles the street on the map. There is a line forming behind us, which would concern me if I were in his shoes, but it seems not to bother him. He takes his time to be sure I know where I am going.

"Usted es muy amable," I thank him, being sure to use the respectful, formal words. He seems touched to be thanked so profusely.

On the street, the horse-drawn carriages roll by. One carries a bride and groom. She is immaculately coiffed, holding a huge bouquet of red roses. I wave to her; she waves back. As I walk by Murillo Park, lovers are everywhere: strolling hand-in-hand, sitting on the benches. A woman in white jeans is straddling the lap of an ugly man, giggling. I avert my eyes as I pass.

The information man was correct, the hostel is very close and I find it with minimal problem. Unfortunately, there is no elevator, only a narrow winding set of stairs, and my room is on the third floor! But the desk clerk amiably helps with my heavy bag. They are just finishing cleaning the room, which appears small and plain, but adequate. And there is Wi-Fi. I'll share a bathroom again, but I have learned not to mind this much. Perhaps I will take a quick shower and a nap before setting out to explore. The hostel is in a small plaza, quiet and hidden. It is just a block from the busy Barrio de Santa Cruz.

In walking from the bus station to the hostel, I realize that Brad and I missed parts of Sevilla when we were here; we roamed closer to our own hotel then and skipped this area altogether. I daydream of meeting someone today who will invite me out to see flamenco in a hip bar in Barrio Triana this evening. Anything is possible! I put on makeup and a flirty short skirt, just in case. I look pretty, I decide, gazing in the mirror.

It is hot and humid in Sevilla. When Brad and I were here, we spent a torrid few days and nights, sampling local cuisine, going to a flamenco bar, and making love in our hotel. He snapped a picture of me, lying back on some pillows, my hand covering my breast, smiling like Mona Lisa into his camera, my blue eyes alight with adoration. But I need to stop dwelling in the past. I can reclaim this special city with new memories. This is my time now!

I pass the Alcazar - a famous heritage sight - and the Cathedral, both of which I hope to see tomorrow. I stroll. I have packed my computer, my camera, and some condoms, laughing at myself when I threw these in.

As I walk farther down this shopping street, Tetuan, a sign intrigues me: "Travesuras de la niña mala – sexy store." Tricks of the bad girl. It is on a side street and I find it easily with its hot pink store front. Inside the tiny store are corsets and g-strings, and in the back, sex toys. A glow in the dark green vibrator, waterproof, and bent to hit that special spot, is only fourteen euros. About twenty bucks. It is a perfect travel size. "What the hell," I think to myself. I buy it, and batteries too, feeling indeed like a niña very mala!

Walking on, I notice a handsome man with dark waves of hair wearing a white long-sleeved button-down shirt. He is sitting alone at a table outside. I linger by a store window, pretending to check out brightly colored flamenco dresses, hoping he will look up. He doesn't. Oh, well. I'm not bold enough to say anything. I've lost my touch, and I've lost my nerve. I feel fat, old, and sweaty. My new vibrator and I walk on by.

However, a half hour later and a few blocks down, as I take some time to write, the same man enters the bar where I am sitting outside at a table. I've ordered nachos and a beer. Why the hell didn't I get something a little more elegant? The man of my dreams is inside, and here come my nachos. I feel so American! Maybe he will recognize me, pause at my table to ask where I'm from, brown eyes twinkling with flirtation. Just in case, I won't eat the onions!

My antennae are up. Is he bar-hopping? Does he work here? Is he dating that waitress, perhaps? My back is to the door but my head is on a swivel. Possibly, sitting here in a cleavage-showing white top and flowing skirt, typing on my little pink computer, I look like an intelligent and approachable niña mala. But there he goes, walking right by. Damn. Guess I'll eat these onions after all.

Young people, elegantly dressed, stroll by. I pay my bill and get up to wander a bit, wondering where the mysterious dressed-up people are all going, and wishing I too had somewhere to go. I meander along the Paseo de Cristobol Colon. Palm trees sway, silhouetted in the dusky indigo light. Under the bridge of Isabel, a bride and groom are posing for pictures. An overwhelming sadness and longing creeps up on me. Fucking weddings! I will never get married again. I blew it; I squandered my one chance. I'll never have that perfect loving partner. I am certain I will die alone. We all get old. Even you, little bride and groom. Enjoy it while you can.

I am depressed now, feeling lonely and irrelevant. I have had no romance and no excitement other than the new vibrator, which I have decided to name Shrek due to its lime green color. I guess it will also be my lover tonight. Shit. I'm going back to my little hostel room. Brad and I have arranged to Skype, but it is no consolation for my dismal loneliness. I wanted adventure, not more self-torture. That I can do at home. Why am I even on this trip?

I go into a small shop to buy a bottle of cheap red wine. Making my way to my hotel, I nod at the drivers of the horse carriages going by. One waves and yells at me, and pulls over across the street. When the light changes, I cross. We talk in Spanish, tell each other our names. I promptly forget his, but his horse's name is Romero. I explain that I don't have the money for a carriage ride, which is normally fifty euro, almost seventy-five dollars. He asks if I want a picture on the horse.

"On?"

He explains that he can hoist me up and onto Romero's back, which he does, although I am none too light or graceful.

I thank him and he asks again if I would like to go for a ride, perhaps around the park. "I can't," I tell him, explaining again that I am broke.

"Not for money, just for love." I wonder whether I should walk away, but he seems sincere, and I think it will be okay, whatever I decide. He is average looking with a scruff of beard and friendly brown eyes. Not dangerous. This could be my evening's adventure; wasn't I looking for romance tonight? I hop up into the carriage beside this unnamed man.

He takes me through the park, telling me in Spanish about the sculptures. The statue dedicated to the poet Becquer is striking beneath a weeping willow tree. My driver tells me that the three women depicted in the statue represent Past, Present, and Future. Romero's hooves clip-clop on the path as we move through the darkened park. We get out by the statue of Maria Luisa, whom the park is named for. As we walk towards her, he kisses me and grabs my ass. I resist and then cave. It feels awkward. I taste the cigarette he just smoked. A lady is sitting on a bench nearby with her large dog, and when he sees her, he releases me and we return to the carriage. Thwarted! I think with a smile.

He asks if I am married as we go further around the park. I tell him I'm divorced, and ask him the same.

"Separado, no divorciado." He has a three-month-old son. So young! "Es la vida," *That's life*. It sure is.

He takes me though the Plaza de Espana. I remember being

here with Brad in the daytime. Beautiful blue and white porcelain tiles make up the arched bridges in the plaza. It is lovely at night. Another damned bridal couple is walking through. I look at the blossoming of new love in front of me, I remember how in love I was the last time I was here, and I glance at this sincere and horny carriage driver, wanting to weep for the turns my life has taken.

We stop again, and he leads me to the back of some bushes. He tries to kiss me again. I don't want anything as intimate as a kiss right now. I remember the condom and think, *What the hell, this is what I was looking for. Wasn't it?* He apologizes before we begin, the horse is standing in the road; we need to be fast. He fumbles with the condom. We do it standing up and it is over quickly. I feel numb and ashamed. Shouldn't I be feeling thrilled, naughty and sexy?

My two-minute lover leads me back out of the park, arm around my shoulders as he chuckles. "Estamos locos, Cathy."

We're crazy. At least he remembers the name of his conquest, which is more than I can say for myself! In awkward silence, we clip-clop the short ride back to the plaza where we met. Before I get down from the carriage, he asks for my phone number. Amused, I give it to him, reminding him that I am out of here tomorrow. He asks if I come to Seville often. Is he kidding? It reminds me of the guy who says "I'll call you," after an awful date.

Home seems so far away.

On Sunday I am exhausted from staying up late and not sleeping well. Julie and Warren are supposed to meet me at the Alcazar, but I don't know when. I spend the morning wandering, tired, and vaguely hung over. Every horse-drawn carriage makes me cringe as I fear it might be my nameless friend. One driver leers at me, and I feel self-conscious, humiliated. Do they all know who I am now? No, impossible!

I sit and have coffee at a café, watching the tourists stroll by. On the rim of my coffee cup, it says "un café, una vida." One coffee, one life.

Finally, I enter the Alcazar and coincidentally run into Julie and Warren, along with the young British couple. We ramble through for a few hours, admiring the architecture and the splendor of the gardens, taking pictures, and then go have a late lunch. Afterwards we part ways, promising to keep in touch. This time I splurge on a cab to the train station. The driver grunts as he loads up Big Guy. I smile apologetically and over-tip when we get there.

≈≈≈≈≈

The train from Sevilla to Malaga passes through rolling hills and white villages. Brakes squeal as we pull into a station. The sign reads Osuna. A wave of nostalgia washes over me. Osuna was another town Brad and I visited on our trip. We chanced upon a charming little hotel built in an old monastery. It had only a few rooms, but a large outdoor patio restaurant. It is my most romantic memory of our time in Spain. We wandered around the small quaint town in the heat of the Spanish sun, finding a tapas bar to escape the midday heat. The barman served up the coldest beer I have ever tasted. Later that evening after Brad accidentally locked the key in the room, we sat giggling with our feet in the pool, ordering wine from a waiter while the harried desk clerk dug through a basket of spare keys. All around us, elegant Spaniards dined al fresco and we gazed up at the stars in the sky, holding hands while we splashed our toes.

Brad begged me not to visit Osuna this time, to leave that memory alone. I spoke with him for an hour last night, but it was an achingly unsatisfactory conversation. He told me more about his Italy trip, and I confessed to him that I felt myself slipping right back into where I was before with him, a place I have worked so hard to get away from. I was drinking red wine, disturbed by my encounter with the horse carriage driver, which I, of course, did not mention.

"Just don't fuck with me, okay?" I implored. More than half the bottle of wine was gone by this time.

"What do you mean?" he asked. I reminded him how he's generally clueless about his emotions, how far apart we live now, and that there isn't much we can look forward to, except more long distance, and much longer than we had before.

"Yeah, I know," he said. And nothing more. He didn't offer me anything in the way of understanding or comfort. Still just clueless, I wonder, or is he regretting that he confessed his supposed love to me? If I was looking for reassurance from him, I was barking up the wrong tree. I was barking up a cactus.

Sentenil de las Bodegas

Romero, the carriage horse

Alhaurin – The Healing Power Of Horses

The train passes through a deep, rocky valley with a river running at the bottom. As we move south, the landscape changes. White villages. Orchards of fruit trees so bright they hurt my eyes to look at, the light of the setting sun bathing their leaves in a shimmering golden green. Palm tree trunks covered in dry leaf-husks like hula skirts. Rolling mountains spread out along the landscape, cradling the occasional village. Horses pepper the fields here and there, grazing. I smile contentedly.

I have been thinking lately about the possibility of having a horse in my life again soon. I miss the connection that happens when human and horse work together to produce moments of physical clarity, functioning as one entity. Some of the most fulfilling moments I have had were those shared with horses. Of course, before I can settle in and find a horse to buy or borrow, the trip to South America and more volunteer work looms ahead. I know I must have gained some knowledge on this adventure, but I am not sure how to put it all together. I still feel foolish and naïve, a bumbling middle-aged lady. Although I hope for wisdom that will apply to my future, I don't know if I've truly earned any.

My next hosts are a couple who run, as they say in British English, a livery, or boarding stable. Roland, my host, picks me up at the train station. I immediately like this big, no-nonsense guy with the sparkling eyes. While Harvey, a brown bull terrier mix, bounces around the back seat of the dusty blue Explorer, Roland and I talk horses. In his youth he rode jumpers, and he tells me about his riding adventures. As we get closer to the farm, he points out various villages cradled in the mountains: Coin, Alcala de Valle, Cartema.

"When you move here, you get a view of the mountains, whether you want it or not!" he jokes.

Near the stable he shows me the tiny caravan where I will sleep and we unload my bag. Debbie, Roland's wife, comes out of the barn to greet us. So do three more dogs. We all go up to the house, where Debbie serves dinner on their outdoor terrace. It is like a living room, with a dining table, couches, a TV, and a pool table. I tell them I love to play pool, but I'm not very good. Roland proceeds to beat me at two games (and will continue to beat me all week.) I lament that I am playing worse than usual, but Debbie assures me that her husband is thrilled to have someone to play with, bad or not.

After dinner, I walk back to the caravan in the dark, tired and ready for bed. We will start with the horses at 8:30, and Debbie has promised me a trail ride in the campo, or countryside.

My week here proves to be nice, calm, and predictable: feed and bring in horses in the morning, ride, go to the pool to cool off, take a siesta, then clean stalls, put horses out and feed again. Then a nice dinner with wine on the terrace, and off to bed.

The house was built on the site of an old fruit stand. Roland, who is in construction, built it himself: the house, the pool, and the landscaped gardens. My favorite place to relax in the afternoon is the pool deck. From this vantage point, you can see the lower paddocks where beautiful chestnut and bay horses stand swishing their tails. The open terrace where we eat dinner each night leads out to the sparkling blue swimming pool. Their little Jack Russell terrier, Pip, will usually jump in and swim with anyone who takes a dip.

Bright pink Bougainvillea flowers surround the yard, interspersed with the somber green-grey of olive trees. Further down is the orange orchard, its trees hanging with what look like large round limes, the oranges that will be ripe around Christmas time. A walk down the gravel drive leads to the caravan where I sleep at night.

Upon first sight of the caravan, I was simultaneously impressed and disappointed. It is small, cute, and clean, but the operative word is small. There is a horseshoe shaped couch to lounge on, but this is soon taken up by Big Guy and his contents. The tiny kitchenette is just inside the door: it consists of a sink, a mini-fridge, and a three-burner stove. What looks like a closet is actually the bathroom, a toilet in a space so close that your knees touch the wall if you sit, and a shower that is not big enough to turn around in, let alone wash anything you need to move your arms to reach. But the bed is spacious, surrounded by curtained windows for plenty of air and light. The mattress is comfy. I find that I spend very little time here in the caravan – I simply change clothes, sometimes make toast and coffee, and sleep a heavy sleep, only occasionally interrupted by barking dogs in the neighborhood, or early-morning rooster crowing.

Debbie is a friendly blonde, a few years younger than me, with a sweet elfin face and humming-bird energy around the barn. She is gracious and always thoughtful. She tends to do things quick and efficiently – there are thirteen horses and she is used to doing it all solo. I often meander a bit, scratching horsie necks and thinking up blog posts while I fill water buckets or muck stalls. We work well together, though, and I try to do things her way as much as possible, remembering how picky Julie was about having things just so, but Deb is more relaxed. She is happy to have help and invites me to the house to shower, use the pool, or just hang out.

I fall into a routine, pleased to have the structure. Although I am filthy by the end of each day, I am happy to be around these big creatures. There is a tall black horse named Murphy who lives in a lower outdoor paddock. I noticed him on my first day.

"He belongs to a friend of mine who's gone back to England," Deb tells me. "You're welcome to ride him." I gaze down the hill at him: almost seventeen hands high and solid black with just a tiny white star. He is calm and friendly in the paddock, and I imagine his personality is similar under saddle.

During the week, I ride Murphy several times, and, although he wears a blister in my right hand from pulling, we learn to get together and accomplish steering, finally. He accepts the bridle and is a willing partner. *If I were only a better rider!* I think, but we muddle through some simple things. We are both out of shape and sweat a lot when we work. He has a choppy trot for a big horse, and riding him takes a lot out of me, but feels good. By our last ride, I feel like we have made some progress.

Blog Post: The Power of Horses

In my travels through Spain I have had the great fortune of being able to ride horses from time to time. Winston

Churchill is quoted as saying, "There's something about the outside of a horse that's good for the inside of a man." This is true for me. I love everything about horses: their strength, their skittishness, the power and grace one feels when riding. Their big brown eyes, their manes and tails, even the way they smell when they sweat.

I have loved horses since I was a small child. My parents used to go to farm auctions to find a bargain antiques. If they turned around and could not find me, they went to where the horses were stabled. Once I crawled up over a wall and was sitting on top of a horse in his stall.

As an adult, I have owned several horses, and I have learned to ride several ways: first bareback, then Western, jumping, and finally, dressage. In dressage, the rider and horse fine-tune their communication so that, in the highest levels, it is as if the horse is dancing, fluid and strong, while the rider serenely sits on its back and guides the horse with invisible cues.

I love this the most - the dressage-ing of a horse. I hear the voices of all my past riding instructors in my head, reminding me of my position, the outside rein connection – all of the things that I need to keep in mind. I wish riding was something I had a lot of natural talent for, but it isn't. Every bit of progress I have made in this area is something I have worked hard to achieve. I'm a decent rider by now, but I have annoying bad habits that tend to creep up on me and it is a battle to remember all the things I am not supposed to be doing.

But despite my struggles, what I like the most is the connection, the communication with the horse, both riding and on the ground - in the paddock, grooming, feeding - all the things that go along with loving horses. And it strikes me as funny that these are the same things that I want in a human relationship. The day-to-day connection and harmony between two beautiful (but not perfect) beings. This connection is not easily given by horses or humans. It seems like you always have to work for it, with calm, patient understanding and persistence. You have to know when to push through a challenge and when to save it for another day. And the biggest element of all is trust. The rider has to trust the horse, and the horse must trust the rider. In human relationships we also must find trust. But I've been bucked off and trampled underfoot. My last attempt at trust put me in the metaphoric hospital. How do I find the courage to try again?

When I first got divorced and had to sell my horse, I used to exclaim, Mae West style, "I'll never have a horse or a husband of my own, ever again. If I need one, I'll just borrow someone else's." The horse is the easy part. A husband, well, I just don't believe in marriage anymore. In my experience, men don't feel obligated to be faithful to their wives, so who would want that? Not me! My husband had an affair. My ex-boyfriend Brad cheated on his wife, and also on me. The key lies in having a man you can trust. Even then, how does one ever really know?

Here in Alhaurin, I was propositioned for sex by a friend of Roland's who lives with his girlfriend. I turned him down. Brad, while claiming to still be in love with me, is chatting up some blonde on Twitter for the world (and me) to see. Trust is a scarce commodity, and doubly difficult with those who have proved to be untrustworthy. And of course, I am no saint. Although I was faithful in my marriage, I have cheated in relationships I was bored with, or on the way out of. None of us are perfect,

On Friday of my work week, Deb offers the day off, and I decide to go to Mijas. Mijas is another place I visited with Brad. Our final night in Spain was in Mijas, and I remember the town fondly. I have, unfortunately, been dreaming about Brad often and waking up mad at myself.

On the bumpy, winding road, the bus passes a collection of condos, buttercream yellow, each with an individual pool, like a splash of turquoise paint has been decoratively dropped behind each building. The condos border a lush green golf course with palm trees set on its edge. On the other side, more condos are being built. This, I think, is Andalucia: rife with Europeans from colder climates who have bought their dream home in Spain.

Once in Mijas, I walk into the main square of the Virgin of Pena. A man with a guitar is singing "Besame Mucho" along with a karaoke track. He is a horrid singer who keeps changing keys, but it still brings tears to my eyes. This is the song that was mine and Brad's.

"Besame, besame mucho, como si fuera esta noche la ultima vez,

Besame, besame mucho, que tengo miedo perderte, perderte despues…"

"kiss me, kiss me a lot, as if this night were the last time,

Kiss me, kiss me a lot, because I'm afraid I will lose you, lose you afterwards…"

It is an overcast, misty day, and because Mijas is set amongst rolling hills, fog is more typical here than in the lower lands. I sit in yet another café in yet another small square, sipping coffee. As I drink the rich beverage, I look around, thinking about my time in this country. Have I made any progress in my personal growth, having been in Spain two months? Who's to say? I know I feel calmer, "tranquila", able to shrug off small disasters. If I'm learning anything, it's what to pack – and not to pack – on my next long trip. Has Spain merely been a practice run for something yet to come?

The fog persists, heavy and damp. It suits my mood. In no other place have memories assaulted me as much as here in Mijas. I pass the hotel where Brad and I stayed; I have a picture of me standing on our balcony in a little black dress. There is the restaurant where we ate on our final night where Brad saw the bullfighter in his limo drive down the street after the bullfight. Angel was his name, and Brad did a marvelous impression of the poster for the bullfight. Here is the auditorium where we happened upon a children's dance recital, reminding us both of the days our daughters had taken dance at the same studio in Bellingham, but long before we met; when we were both married to other people, a lifetime before.

And here is the little store, Mijas Magic, where I tried on a ring with both of our birthstones. It fit perfectly, but he didn't get the hint, even though I exclaimed what a wonderful coincidence that the ring had our stones, and how nicely it fit. We left the store, me stormy and sullen, and him oblivious. Finally he asked what was wrong. When I explained, he said "Let's go back and get it!"

I said, "No. Too late. Now I want a diamond." I threw down the gauntlet. If he got the new job and moved, long distance would be excruciating for me, and I needed to know we had a future. I felt like a symbol of commitment would be appropriate. What did I know? I did get my diamond, but I found out that it hadn't meant commitment to him after all. Now, four years later, I am back in the same shop, with memories and unbidden feelings washing over me. I buy a ring with three metallic waves: brass, copper, and silver. Past, present, future. I am hovering on the verge of tears as I purchase it. What in the world is wrong with me today? I must need food.

I find a little restaurant and order tinto de verano and Spanish tortilla. A cat is wandering about – a sleek grey and black mackerel tabby missing part of its right ear. I call him over and with a little wiggle of my fingers, he is up in my lap, curled up and purring. He is so warm. I begin to cry. He sits in my lap as I write in my notebook, and when I pull the plate towards me, he stands up. Ah, he is hungry. I share several bites, and when the food is gone, so is he. Definitely a male cat, I think, gets what he wants and then leaves. He wanders toward another table to seduce another unsuspecting tourist.

Feeling a little more balanced, I attempt to analyze my feelings. I came here today not to relive the past but to revisit a place I liked. So why allow these memories to creep in? Then again, why not? Brad and I had a lovely time here. We mostly had wonderful times when we were together. Somehow I always knew it would end. And why now would I want to go back to someone who can not commit to his own feelings? A leopard doesn't change his spots, I remind myself, as the cat, who has returned to my lap, bites my wrist.

I know I am destined for something more: deeper, challenging, but not frustrating, with someone who can commit to what he really wants, and who knows that what he wants is me. Lack of commitment signals that someone is waiting for something better to come along. I never want to live that life again!

The plaza is beautiful, with three mosaic fountains spewing towers of water. Behind me on the tree-covered hill is a white church. There is a vista point edged with winding garden paths, and I remember that on a clear day you can look down and see the ocean and the Costa del Sol. But not today with the cloud cover. Perhaps my mood will lift with the fog.

After my lunch I encounter a church and put money in the box to light a candle. The church is aptly named Our Lady of Remedies. "Fix me," I silently entreat. My good friend Jesus, carrying his ever-present cross, looks down upon me with those long-suffering eyes. If he has a message for me, I still do not know what it is.

Wandering through the maze of streets winding up the hill among white houses, I am getting sleepy. Is my body just used to siestas now? It begins to sprinkle rain. I am bone tired and emotionally drained. I decide to go back to Alhaurin, where I will help with the evening feeding. Working, for me, is better than thinking.

⁕⁕⁕⁕⁕⁕

Saying goodbye at every turn has been one of the hardest parts of this journey. It is bittersweet: bidding adios to new friends, knowing that it is difficult to stay in touch. I always have a slight fear of the unknown as I move on. With each step of my adventure there are more new situations to navigate. And the endless packing, carting around Big Guy once again, at the mercy of unknown bus schedules. But I am more excited than scared about the next part of my journey. Tarifa, at the southernmost point of Spain, will be the gateway to a place I have always dreamed of – Morocco. Africa!

Bolonia, Where A Cow Encounter Changes My Life

The following Monday I get the bus, transfer, sleep a bit, and abruptly arrive in Tarifa. I stumble off the bus at the tiny station. I had pictured Tarifa bigger than this. Large condo buildings, abandoned half-finished, line the main street.

The bus station is a small one-room structure with no one behind the counter. I phone my host Ralph and apologize for my early arrival, and he tells me he will be almost an hour. It's okay, I can mosey around with Big Guy in tow.

I wander the mostly empty streets of Tarifa until my new host pulls up in a beat-up white truck. Ralph has a friend, a German girl, with him. (I later discover that she is one of his many girl-friends.) We all go to the grocery store and then begin the drive back to Ralph's place, which is outside the enclave of Bolonia, up in the hills. It is legendarily windy here on this coast, and the kite surfers are out in force all along the beach. The ocean sparkles as they gyrate along the waves, their colorful kites catching the breeze above. The kites in the air look like a rich array of jewels scattered against the blue sky.

A pale blonde sand dune stretches out above the beach and beyond that a rocky ridge. The landscape here is like nothing I've ever seen: a combination of things of the seashore and things of the mountains, all thrown together like someone cleaned up a landscape-building toy set quickly and did not bother to separate them into the proper boxes. We ascend the road above Bolonia, and the water of the ocean takes on a pewter cast in the fading light of day.

As we bump along the road in Ralph's truck, two black pigs cross the road and go into the ditch. He doesn't bother to slow. Behind us, two more large black pigs cross.

"I knew they were coming," he assures his girlfriend, who must have looked as worried as I felt.

Ralph explains that after we cross the cattle guard on the road, we are in "el campo", the countryside. Local farmers let their livestock roam and graze up here. Ralph himself has a small herd of five horses roaming around somewhere. He tells me they will probably stop and visit this week, as they often do.

Glancing back, I notice the color of the ocean has changed again, like a mood ring. This time it is deep blue, with the edges fading into a jade green. The road is bordered by fan palms, their spiky bush-leaves low and spread out. Ralph says that these plants produce a very sweet fruit. We drive past a dozen copper-red cows, lying contentedly on the ground, long horns curving up toward the sky.

Ralph's driveway is full of bumpy rocks and ruts that jar the truck as we pull in. We park outside a white-walled villa with a stone front and a green gate. The front is littered with discarded tools and building materials. A rusty cement mixer rests outside three sagging strands of barbed wire. Inside, a path of paver stones separates a low building on the right from the main house on the left, which sports a corrugated tin roof. The pathway is strewn with tools and broken machinery. Yellow and black power cords are intertwined like lazy tropical snakes basking in the sunshine. An old purple bike with a flat tire leans against the wall.

After depositing my bag inside, I cross the path that leads down the center of the dwelling and push open the door to a small walled-in terrace draped with fuchsia bougainvillea. Climbing onto the stone bench, I can see the ocean stretched out at the bottom of the rolling hills that embrace the small town of Bolonia, and beyond that, a whisper of muted land that is the north coast of Africa.

I walk over to the paddock, where there are two horses, small scruffy animals, and Ralph's burro stallion Romeo with his enormous ears and testicles, and loud, plaintive bray. There is a shiny calico cat and an elderly dog who looks like she could use a day at the doggy beauty parlor. Her coat is dingy and dull, and her nails are so long I'm surprised she can walk. Ralph appears to be a minimalist animal care person (although all the animals are at a good weight) which is a big change for me after the livery stable where Deb sprayed and dabbed ointments against flies and changed blankets and fly masks daily.

Ralph has given me a room of my own, which is an office, full of bookshelves and the computer desk. My bed is a sleeping loft above the desk. It consists of a mattress on a plywood platform and is hung with a mosquito net above. There is a reading light and two small fans. It is accessed by a metal ladder, which I will carefully scoot out on the brick floor when I begin my slow wary climb to bed. The bathroom is a wide-open space, half done with blue ceramic tiles (the other half are in boxes stacked against the wall), and a sheet hangs limply on a clothesline to give a smidgen of privacy.

The first day Ralph leaves me in the morning and I find my way around the kitchen where I make black coffee. There is no milk and I can't find the sugar. I meditate. I check Facebook. I write a bit. I do five minutes of yoga and then lose my focus. I go scratch the horses on their necks and talk to them. Finally, I put my boots on, scoot out through a barbwire fence, as Ralph locked the outer door when he left and I have no key, and go for a walk up the dusty road.

The hills up here remind me of the Rocky Mountains and I think of Colorado for a moment. More red cows are loose on the road, and although I would love to say hello, stroke their copper noses and look into fathomless brown eyes, they have sharp pointy horns, and I do not wish to risk encountering them. I pass one with a berth of only a few feet between us, and we regard each other calmly as she munches on a fan palm.

I pause for a moment. It has been a long time since I really looked at a cow. She is gorgeous. Looking into her eyes I see the animal equivalent of humanity. Some people might see hamburgers and steaks, but all I see is beauty. And it occurs to me that if I see beauty, if I see a soul in this cow just as surely as I do in my doggy friends, how is it possible for me to eat her without guilt? She continues to gaze at me. Something in me has shifted. She seems to know it.

Further up the road, I sit upon a flat rock and gaze at the mountains that ascend magnificently to my left. Four eagles ride the currents of the wind effortlessly as the clouds roll by like a fast-forward nature film. I inhale, breathing in the mountain air, letting the sun warm me. Eventually I trek back down the road to wait for Ralph's return.

I pass a few days here, readying for my trip to Morocco, making arrangements for a ferry ticket with an open return, checking the schedule for the night train to Marrakech. Finally the day comes. Ralph drops me off in Tarifa near the ferry and we say our goodbyes. I'm nervous but excited. One more continent to say I've set foot on: I'm off to Africa!

A cow like this changed my life

Kites over the sea, Tarifa

Marrakech – Color And Chaos

On the ferry to Tangier, the wind has kicked up and the boat rocks softly from side to side. I am a bit apprehensive about this part of the journey – being a blonde woman on my own in a country where I don't know the language. Fortunately, I was able to leave Big Guy behind at Ralph's. He gave me a dilapidated old leather bag that made me long for my sleek black spinner wheel carry-on back in Colorado. I wiped off the dust and part of an old wasp's nest and pull a condom packet from the side pocket. I was surprised and a little smug to find that all my clothes, shoes, and toiletries for the week fit into the bag. However, I know I'll want to shop in Marrakech. I've held off long enough, I've been financially responsible, and if I need one more excuse, Christmas is coming!

The water is choppy and steel-grey. The horizon all around is misty, as if the boat is inside a snow globe. I feel suspended between two parts of the journey, Spain and Africa. What adventures await me in Morocco?

Morocco is a place I have dreamed about ever since I read

Marguerite Henry's "King of the Wind", my favorite childhood book, about the founding fathers of the Thoroughbred racehorse, which descended from the Moroccan Godolphin Arabian. I picture blowing sand, chickens and camels in the street, turban-clad barefoot vendors with no teeth selling hand-woven rugs. In guidebooks you are warned about the throng of local guides who will descend upon you to get your money, take you to their cousin's shop to buy things, and generally run you around until they have squeezed you like a sponge of all your resources. I am therefore surprised to get off the ferry and step into a westernized, industrial port. A few taxis wait outside the customs area, but nothing more. No chickens, no camels, no aggressive turban-wearing vendors.

A man approaches me. "Are you the last one on the boat?" I tell him I am.

"Customs is up this way," the man says. He shows me his badge. "I am Allal. I work officially for the tourist bureau. Go through customs and I will see you on the other side."

I arrange with Allal to take a tour of Tangier as I wait for my night train to Marrakech. He takes me to carpet and jewelry stores where I resist sales pitches while admiring the wares. We have lunch by the sea--cold beer and many plates of food-- tiny salmon-like fish fried in a batter, garbanzo beans in sauce, a salad made of minced onion, cucumber, and tomato, succulent prawns with a wonderful flavor, as well as chicken tagine and lentils.

Over our meal I ask Allal about the tall towers that are part of every mosque.

"Those are the minarets," he points out. "They used to go to the top of the tower and call for prayer, but nowadays they have speakers." And sure enough, at the top of the tower, I see the speakers. It is Friday, the day of religion ("Like Sunday in the United States") and many shops are closed so that people can go to church to pray. I'd like to go into a mosque on this trip, but I don't say it out loud in case it sounds foolish. As much as I have visited Jesus in Spain, I would like to meet Allah, too. I think of the Om tattoo on my upper right arm. *We are all one.*

By five, I am tired, and I say goodbye to my guide. At the train station, I buy my ticket for the couchette so I will be able to sleep on the overnight train to Marrakech. I sit by a young woman in the waiting area and we introduce ourselves. She is also taking the nine-thirty train. Her name is Hasnaa. She is a radiology technician who lives and works in Tangiers, and her boyfriend lives in Marrakech and is in the military. She is going to visit him. We spend the next few hours talking and getting to know each other while throwing pieces of a muffin to a stray cat who lingers near our table. I tell her a little about Brad and she tells me about her relationship. "I don't know if I see myself with him for my whole life," she says.

I try to think of something wise to say, but I truly feel clueless about love and relationships. Having tormented myself about Brad in Sevilla and Mijas, sending him an email that begged for some kind of affirmation, and instead getting the usual detached bullshit that I remember so well from our whole relationship, I basically wrote him a "kiss off" email. No more Skype calls, no more dragging myself into what was and should still be dead and buried. His response was short and terse, "I don't want to distract or confuse you anymore." Good! I thought, while not answering it. I'm in Morocco now and you're in Yakima. Leave me the hell alone.

Hasnaa is looking at me intently, waiting for my wisdom. She's twenty-four, a few years older than my Emily.

I tell her, "If your heart speeds up when he walks in the room, maybe it's love."

She nods. She tells me that the long distance is hard and that she gets jealous. Her boyfriend has just called her and said his father showed up unexpectedly, so she can't stay with him. He wants to see her, but is leaving it up to her whether she wants to come. She thinks maybe it's an excuse, so he gets on his dad's phone to call her so she knows he's really there. I tell her that I was never jealous in my marriage, but my husband was meeting women from chat rooms and ultimately cheated. I tell her how Brad and I broke up after a year and he came back to me crying with a supposedly heartfelt confession of love when all the while he had plane tickets to meet another woman in Las Vegas.

She shakes her head in sympathy. "It's hard to trust," she says. "Sometimes I think it would be better to be with someone you don't love so much so it doesn't make you crazy to not trust them."

I see her logic. "Yeah, but you would miss the way that crazy love feels."

We both sigh.

"Stay with me in Marrakech," I say. I have a big hotel room and I'm all alone. Why not? She agrees.

On the train, I climb into the bunk bed to sleep. It is an erratic sleep, and for most of the night I dream about peeing. The bathroom is a horrible dirty mess, and I will have to climb down the ladder in the dark and put shoes on to do it. I can wait, but it's all I dream about.

Finally, I check my watch. It's six-thirty. I climb down the ladder, slip on my boots, and make my way, wobbling down the narrow aisle to the filthy bathroom. Afterwards, I stand in the aisle of the train car to watch the landscape drift by out the window.

I'm in Africa. It seems unbelievable.

The earth is dry outside, and there are trees I have only seen in movies. They are small with a narrow trunk and a great poof of greenery, like the afro of one of my fellow travelers on the train; a shock of hair on a scrawny person.

The train passes a man riding a donkey with side baskets loaded with straw. The ground is a reddish color. We must still be some distance from Marrakech. I walk back toward my sleeping compartment. A little man with white hair is standing at the window in the passage. He smiles at me. "Hello," he says.

"Hello," I say back.

We exchange the usual pleasantries: where are you from, is this your first time in Marrakech, where else have you travelled? This man from Malaysia is a seasoned traveler. His name is Isa, and he is also staying at a time share, one outside of town. He has worked in the travel industry and has seven weeks of time share per year. "I'm retired," he tells me, "But I'm not tired!" I laugh. He is charming. He invites me to visit him in Malaysia. I tell him I would love to.

"When you are a traveler, you open your heart and you open your home," he says. I nod. Isa says he and his friend may rent a four-by-four to go to the Sahara desert and would I like to join them? Yes, please! We exchange numbers.

I find Hasnaa and we get a taxi to the hotel. On the way there she begs the cab to pull over, and she opens the door and throws up.

"Are you okay?" I ask, digging in my pack for a tissue so she can wipe her mouth.

She nods and leans against the door until we get to the hotel. The room, of course, is not ready yet. We sit in the lobby and she calls her boyfriend. After a he had a fight with his father his dad left, so he is coming to join us. I know now that she will be staying with him. I'll be on my own again.

We go to breakfast and Hasnaa insists on having him take lots of pictures of us together, even though I feel old and frumpy in comparison to her dark beauty. I keep my shades on. Her boy-friend takes time to find the angles he wants. We laugh. He pays for our breakfast, I thank him, and we part ways.

Tired from the journey, I go to the quiet pool to splash around. It's refreshing enough to wake me up. I get dressed and find the grocery store, where the attendant leers at me as I stumble around looking for things. After unpacking my groceries, I take a nice siesta. If there is one thing I learned in Spain, it's the power of the siesta! Upon waking, I decide to get a bit to eat at the place we had breakfast, Le 6. I order a pizza and people-watch while eating half. The other half the waiter boxes up for me.

After dinner, I decide to stroll a bit, awkwardly carrying my pizza box. A young bald boy approaches me, speaking French. A beggar. "Non," I say, and cross the street. Before I finish my walk, several more beggars accost me, one grabbing my sleeve until I tell him firmly, "La! Stop! No!" and march away. I am shaken up by this violation of my personal space.

Reorganizing my thoughts, I walk on down the sidewalk. I receive several cat-calls, cars slowing down, boys on scooters yelling something I am glad I don't understand. I have taken care to wear my button-up blouse to cover my cleavage tonight. I can imagine what I'd be getting if I hadn't!

I decide to walk down the center of Avenue Mohammed VI, which is like a park. Small pink and white rosebushes, scattered like Easter jellybeans among the grass beyond a low brick wall, give off a sweet fragrance in the night air. Couples and families are sitting on the walls and walking the promenade. I smile at a toddler who is determinedly teetering down the walk, his father following with outspread arms. Two other children, older ones, walk past. I wave and smile. "Bye-bye," says the little girl.

A cat is roaming among the flowers. I open my pizza box,

pick off some ham, and feed him. Two boys on the brick wall are watching me. I remember a little French, "Le chat faime!" (The cat is hungry. Or did I say the cat is a lady?) They grin.

As I make my way back, the same bald child approaches me again. His round eyes are dark and imploring, and his head shines under the streetlight. Cancer? I wonder. "Madame," he pleads. And something that sounds like "Mange". *Mange*, that means "eat", I think.

"Pizza?" I ask, handing him the box.

"Merci!" He takes it and walks off. I stare after him, stunned by the fact that I am here as a tourist, and able to feed a child with just my discarded leftovers. And yet, even though I feel broke, I have so much more than some others, just by virtue of where I was born. It boggles my mind.

⸙⸙⸙

Sunday is my first full day in Marrakech. The hotel has arranged a welcome tour for free, so of course I will participate. As I sit and wait, I begin to talk to a nice English couple in their sixties who are celebrating their fortieth anniversary with this trip. Forty years. I can't imagine it.

Finally, the tour bus arrives with the passengers from the other hotel, including my new friend Isa and his traveling companion Johnny. We load into the bus. It is a hot day (40 degrees Celsius, I learn later) and the bus is not air conditioned. I sit next to a French couple who are probably the age of my parents. His hand rests sweetly on her knee as we ride along.

The tour takes us to see one of the water canals that were devised to supply Marrakech with water for agriculture. In this city where there is a drought every three years and it rarely rains, these canal systems keep the city in the middle of the desert lush and green, with palm and olive trees abundant in the landscape.

When we return, we are served orange juice on the terrace and the upcoming tours are explained. Isa leans toward me.

"I won't do any of their tours," he scoffs. "I am talking to a local guide about seeing the desert and traveling to some other cities. He's meeting me at the hotel. You want to meet him? You can come for a swim; the pool is beautiful." I agree and take the bus back to Isa's hotel.

The guide arrives to talk to Isa while I swim in the pool, which is indeed spectacular, with an island in the center complete with a palm tree.

The guide's is named Hussein. I discover that he also speaks Spanish, and he tells me with a grin that I can call him Jose. He takes us back to Marrakech in his nice air-conditioned Toyota SUV. He drives us by the finest hotels in the area- like the famous Mounmonet - and then into the main square.

And when I say into, I mean we drive right into the square, although it is closed to cars. Jose seems to know everybody in Marrakech, and he talks to one of the policemen for a moment, who then move the barricade so we can enter. The square is teeming with people – peddlers, tourists, performers, locals. We drive slowly and the sea of people parts as we pass. We find a small parking garage and proceed on foot to participate in the madness.

A man with an angry looking monkey on a chain thrusts him onto my shoulder. I squeal, but hand my camera to Isa. The monkey climbs on my head. His handler yells at him and jerks on the chain. Finally, he is off me, and I fumble in my purse for change. I hold out a few coins.

"This... this is nothing!" the man yells disgustedly.

"I'm sorry, I don't know the money here!" I tell him. I pull together a few more coins, put them into his outstretched hat and move along.

We circle the area, and walk through the restaurant line-up. Dozens of outdoor eating places are here, serving kabobs and tagine and shrimp, among other delectable treats. Waiters hold up menus and try to usher us in as we pass.

Finally, we return to the car, leave the square, and end up at a tucked-away barbeque restaurant where once again, everyone knows "Jose" and we are treated like royalty. The people at the next table eyeball us as we laugh and are served a special selection of goodies. Much of Marrakech is a dry city and we cannot order drinks, so I make do with water, although I would love a cold beer.

When the bill comes, it is only 180 Dhirum, about $23 for four people, and we had a lot of food. Isa generously pays for us all. They drop me back at my hotel.

I don't sleep well, tossing and turning through the night. In the morning I feel nauseous and dizzy. I have a tour of the Berber village scheduled. Isa and Johnny have gone into the desert with Jose. I really want to go on my tour, so I buck up, get dressed, and head out for the day.

Downstairs, the anniversary couple is also waiting for the tour. It turns out it is just the three of us and our guide, Ali, along with the driver. We drive up towards the foothills of the Atlas Mountains over a winding road. There is a pillow in the back seat and I clutch it to my stomach as we bump along.

We stop at a local shop. First we go up to the top of the hill to look at the views. The view of the mountains is spectacular; they stretch out below us like a rumpled quilt. Ali points out the highest mountain to me, and I want to take a picture but there is a telephone pole right in the way. I jokingly ask him to move it for me.

"I could lift you up," says Ali, and I shake my head, embarrassed. "You are built like a Moroccan woman, this is good," he assures me. "Moroccan men, we don't like the little skinny. We likes to sleep on meat." I laugh.

After a quick round of shopping, and much bargaining, I buy some bowls and a mirror. We get in the van and make our way up into the foothills, to the Berber flea market, where we walk past colorful stacks of vegetables and spices, pink plastic kids' toys, and stalls with dead chickens hanging from one leg. I see an elderly Berber gentleman with a beaming toothless smile playing a small, banjo shaped instrument strung with one thick string. Ali tells me the instrument is called a rebab.

We head down the food aisles, and my nausea comes spinning back, making me woozy. I soldier on. We come upon a snake charmer, a young handsome man in a red vest and hat. A black cobra sits patiently in front of him. He waves his hands and the snake gyrates with the rhythm. He breaks up a biscuit and waves it for the cobra, which follows his movements. He seems genuinely fond of the snake. I remember the rough, mean monkey handler of the night before, and am happy to give this man a twenty Dirham note.

The market continues with tables of spices piled into folded down burlap bags. The colors are amazing: red paprika, yellow curry, dark green powdered herbs like oregano, along with brown and white chunks of crystal salt, sparkling like rare diamonds in the sunlight. Burlap bags of pasta and beans fill other stands. I buy some dark ginger root to make some tea for my upset tummy.

As we leave the market, we pass a trickle of river on a rocky bed that extends past both sides of the road we are walking.

"To your left and to your right are the donkey parking areas," Ali jokes.

Indeed, there are donkeys standing in the sun by the river on each side. We pile back into the van and watch the people as we pass through the village once again. I notice a man in a brown robe with a brown dusty hat. His skin is weathered, his face has a grizzled beard, and he pushes a cart laden with rusty tools; a study in browns and greys. In the basket at the front of the cart, however, is a splash of color: bright plastic flowers in orange, yellow, and pink.

The final part of the tour is a visit to a Berber family house. The animals, a cow and her calf, are kept just inside the house, as if they are the official butlers to welcome visitors. They regard us passively as we walk through. The house is made of a type of mud that is similar to adobe, and the center, including the kitchen, is open from above. The Berber mother makes us mint tea, known as "Berber whiskey." Ali explains the process as she does. Her hands and feet are covered in henna.

"This means she is happy," Ali says. The designs are beautiful, and I decide I want henna hands before I leave Marrakech! The little boy who was blowing kisses when we entered now has his hand out for money as we leave. I have already tipped his mama, so I give him a high five.

We make our way up bumpy red roads into the beautiful mountains to a restaurant called Amnougour, cradled in the hills with panoramic views. I am unable to eat. I sip water and nibble on melon for dessert.

On the ride home I lie down in the back seat and take a nap. Upon the return to the hotel, I promptly heave all of yesterday's food into the toilet. I throw up violently several times during the evening and go to sleep early, alternating between freezing and roasting, kicking covers off and pulling the blanket up as needed.

⸎⸎⸎⸎⸎

By the morning, I am feeling better, and I take it easy. If I have to be sick, I am glad to be in a nice hotel instead of a gritty hostel room with a shared bathroom. I spend the day relaxing, writing, and napping. Wednesday I wake up feeling normal again. All is now right with the world, and finally – finally- I can shop. I meet Isa and we take a cab down to the medina, through the doors to the old town, surrounded by a red wall. I fairly hum with excitement. I am no longer ill, the day is bright and sunny, I have Dirham in my pocket and I have given myself permission to spend it. Let the haggling begin!

We browse the stores of the souks, a network of shops, and I am drawn to a pottery stand where little bowls are displayed. The shopkeeper tells us they can be used for olives, spices, water. I think about the table I will someday have to lay out small bowls of olives and sea salt along with lovely dinners I have prepared for hungry guests, and someday if I am lucky, my adoring lover. I hold a black bowl in my hand. It is trimmed with silver. I think of all the things I can use it for, always remembering Morocco when I touch its shiny glaze. I choose two, Isa chooses two, and we haggle for a good price, which ends up being only a few dollars for each bowl.

Back in the street, a woman in a black robe and headscarf holds out three bracelets to me. "Oooh, pretty!" I know they are not real silver, but they are beautiful, and I don't argue her price. I feel high, elated. The tiger is out of the cage! I am shopping!

I walk slowly, admiring the colors of the streets and hidden marketplaces. The rose-pink buildings hold small and interesting little stores filled with bright fruits and vegetables, bags of spices, handcrafts, small paintings of Moroccan scenes, silver jewelry, woven rugs, and much more. We wander and take our time, snapping each other's pictures as we stroll.

We follow a street that leads to a dead end in a lovely courtyard. Palm tree sentries flank an ornate wooden door of a plain building. Window casings in carved wood jut out on either side of the front door, and greenery peeks out from a rooftop garden. I gasp and reach for my camera. A man is leaning against a nearby wall with his scooter.

He stands. "This is a guest house, Madame. Isn't it beautiful? Where are you from?" We tell him, and he gives us both friendly hugs. "Brother, sister, welcome. I hope you are finding Marrakech well. Are you wanting to buy spices? I can take you to the very best place!"

No, we tell him, no spices, but we are trying to make our way back out to the main street.

"Follow me, brother, sister." As we walk, he asks me if I have children, and tells me he has five, one very small. We smile and laugh together – five kids! He points us to the street. "Sister, before you go, let me ask you a little favor."

My eyes narrow. Here it comes. "As I told you I have five children, one is on dialysis, do you know what this is? I am taking her tomorrow to receive this treatment, and I don't have enough. Please, if you could give something?" he smiles entreatingly. I tell him I cannot give money, but I do give him my blessing.

Isa and I talk about how disappointing it is that everyone here always asks for money. I feel bad saying no, and I want to tell them that I don't have a job, that I'm doing volunteer work to support my travel, that I don't even have a place to live right now. But I know none of this would matter to them.

We decide to get lunch. A taxi driver we flag down tells us he will take us to a restaurant. Cab fares are dirt cheap here; we spend ten Dirham, a bit more than a dollar, to go to the restaurant. Everybody scratches each other's back: the cab driver walks us in and presents us like a prize and walks away, I am sure, with a "bonus" from the restaurant manager for bringing us in. Upon entering, we see a tall white concrete fountain strewn with rose petals. Colorful orange and pink petals also decorate the tables. A duo of Berber musicians in robes are playing traditional instruments.

We order a fixed-price lunch to share for 120 Dirham and receive a wonderful "Moroccan salad", a beautiful platter of delights displayed on lettuce leaf petals, with the ubiquitous salty green and black olives in the center. There is Moroccan spiced potato salad, a stewed eggplant, a salsa-like salad with tomato and onion, and marinated red and green peppers. We are served round loaves of crusty bread, and the terra cotta tagine, the typical Moroccan cone-shaped cooking dish contains beef cooked with lemon and spices. I order a cold local beer, which is frosty and delicious. We lounge on the banquet strewn with red and pink pillows, and await our dessert, a plate of melon and grapes. As I drink my second beer and suck sweet grape juice from my fingers, I notice a sign directly across the street: Hammam. I bid Isa "au revoir" and go to check it out.

A hammam is something I have wanted to try. The word "hammam" means *spreader of warmth*. This traditional Turkish bath and massage is on the Must-Do list in Marrakech. I choose a combination of hammam (steam bath and scrub), clay body wrap, and massage with special oils. The whole treatment takes about an hour. First I relax in the reception area where they bring me tea. The whole room is pink: pink couches with pink pillows, pink paintings of typical arched doorways in the markets and robed men walking, all with a pink cast of light upon them, and even a pink "stained glass" (plastic) window bathes the reception area in rosy glow.

I undress and am given a very un-sexy paper bikini bottom to wear. I walk half-naked to the steam bath area, where the attendant unrolls a rubber mat on a marble slab of a table and asks me to lie down. She takes warm water and douses my body, then washes me with black soap. She puts a stiff exfoliating mitt on her hand and scrubs my entire body, then rinses me with more water. After this, she brings in a bowl of watery mud and covers me with a terra-cotta-ish coating. I lay in the steamy room a while, covered in mud. When the attendant returns, she gestures for me to stand under the shower, where she washes me off and shampoos my hair with a fragrant almond-honey shampoo.

This brings up childhood memories of bath-time, with my daddy washing my hair -he was quite the scrubber - and now I am purring, a contented and clean kitty. The attendant helps me into a terrycloth robe, and once outside the steam bath, I step into slippers and proceed into the massage cubicle. The massage is relaxing, with golden aromatic oils kneaded into my body. The whole interchange is silent; since I don't speak French there is no small talk necessary. When I am finished, I think the experience was well worth 250 Dirham.

But back in the hotel alone, the blues descend. I am listening to music on my computer when the radio station plays Adele's "Someone Like You." This is a song about heartbreak and regret, and it sucks me right in: "Sometimes it lasts in love, but sometimes it hurts instead…"

The tears begin to leak, then pour from my eyes. I clutch the counter in my mini kitchen in the nice condo in Marrakech that I am in all alone. My body is racked with sobs, the kind that threaten to choke off my very breath. I'm sobbing like the breakup with Brad just happened, knowing that I have to let it all go.

We're not speaking again – my choice this time – and I have vowed not to email him from Morocco. I curse myself for letting him reel me in to my old role of waiting and wondering – have I learned absolutely nothing in the year of grieving that dead relationship? Could I not have just been brave enough to tell him there were no second chances? Must I throw my heart at his feet yet again and watch him stomp on it? I know deep down that our plan to see each other when I get back to "see how we feel" is absolute and utter bullshit. Am I really so eager to give him more of my sweet precious milk for free when he obviously has no interest in buying the cow or even pasturing it nearby? Why does being an idiot hurt so much?

As the song fades, my tears subside. I want to sink down onto the couch, fold my arms tightly around my body, close my eyes and rock like a troubled child. But I have plans for this evening - alone of course - and I need to dry my eyes and get ready. One huge final sigh shakes my body as I go pick out something to wear.

<hr />

"Fantazia" is a dinner show with an Arabian horse exhibition for entertainment. This is arranged by the hotel, and they shuttle us out to the location, which is about twenty minutes outside of town. A double line of men on horseback pose regally for pictures with the throngs of attendees and then extend their hands for money. At the door of the place is a huge cobra fountain, two stories high, with glowing eyes.

Inside the entrance there are displays of traditional wedding dress from different parts of Morocco. I find it amusing and rather symbolic that the brides are behind bars. Each bride has the name of the area displayed. One is from a place called Ouarzazate, which makes me laugh, perhaps because of the two rum and cokes I downed before I left the hotel. "Where's it at?" is all I can think of. I take a picture to remind myself of my little joke, and follow our group farther inside the building.

It is a labyrinth of man-made red caves, complete with stalactites and stalagmites, which also makes me laugh because it reminds me of Casa Bonita, a cheesy theme-based Mexican restaurant in Denver that I loved as a kid! And in a sense, Fantazia is the same idea: a restaurant based on entertainment. Dinner is served in huge, open-air tents with wandering musicians and singers banging loudly on drums walking through the restaurant as we eat Moroccan soup, greasy roast lamb, couscous, and fruit. I feed a wandering cat and stash some mandarins in my bag for later.

The after-dinner show is outside; the audience sits on bleachers around an arena. The show is a spectacular event: a belly dancer gyrating on a float, horseman doing acrobatics as their Arabian steeds gallop in circles around the arena and the audience enthusiastically applauds. These brave souls do tricks such as hang upside down from one stirrup as the horse gallops, which I almost have done myself, but never on purpose! Later, a magic carpet with a sultan and his princess flies overhead, and everything culminates with a display of fireworks.

I wake lazily the next day and lounge in my room for a while to write. I consider the experience of Morocco: the lively markets and vibrant colors juxtaposed with the hard edge of people always begging for money.

Blog Post: White American Privilege

I am travelling through Morocco, struck by the aura of this place. Not Spain, but not quite Africa, Morocco has a distinct feel. Colorful buildings, markets, and people moving through the hustle and bustle of Marrakech give a pulsating energy to the city.

I am a white, blonde, American tourist. I stick out. Is this what it feels like for the occasional black person in my hometown of white bread Longmont? It feels curious, if not awkward. Along with the difference in skin and hair color between myself and the locals, there is the difference in religion. This is a Muslim country: mosques with tall minarets echo out the call to prayer several times a day, and shopkeepers drop to their knees and bow their heads on careworn prayer rugs. I watch, fascinated. I cover my curves and cleavage in respect to a culture where the women wear long dresses and headscarves.

But the biggest difference for me is not that of color or religion. It is the perception of my riches compared to people who live in poverty, or at the very least, people who have to hustle to make their daily bread. And who is it they are hustling? Me (and other tourists.) It's an odd feeling, being unemployed and homeless at the moment, yet being looked at as if I am a wealthy traveler. And perhaps I am, compared to the inhabitants of this country. I did afford a plane ticket to get here, and a hotel to stay in. Their assumptions are valid.

It is awkward avoiding the outstretched hands and plaintive eyes; I feel like a stingy and selfish person. Is it that I am only now waking up to what the rest of the world has long known: that Americans are born into a privileged status that people from other parts of the world can only dream about? It is called the American Dream, after all.

It seems unfair. I am blessed to be on the up side of the see-saw instead of the down end. But I did nothing to achieve this status; nothing more than any of my neighbors or colleagues. Perhaps this is the beginning of a lesson I am meant to learn. Even when I cannot easily share what I was automatically gifted with, I need to cultivate a never-ending gratitude for my privileges. When there is a time that I can help others, I hope to remember this lesson.

It is well into October now. Summer will soon be nothing more than a fond memory. It is my last full day here, and I decide to go for a walk to visit the famous gardens at the exclusive Mounmonet Hotel. I stroll along, not in a hurry, appreciating the quaint buildings on the side streets, shadowed by generous trees. I near the main boulevard that will take me to the hotel, and I see a slight-built man jumping up to pick an olive from a hanging branch.

"You must be hungry," I tease him as I approach.

"I am interested to know," he says, holding the black, wrinkled olive. "Why are some olives green, and some black?"

I know the answer to this one! The tour guide on my first day explained; it's the maturity of the olive, and they can be picked at three different stages to get green, red, or black olives. He is impressed. We fall into step together. His name is Jamal, and he speaks perfect English. I tell him I am going to visit the gardens, and that I have to return back and meet a friend later. He asks if I have time for a drink and I say I do.

He points out the Moumamet as we pass, and tells me he knows a nice place to get coffee, tea, whatever I like. Somehow, we get to talking about happiness as we walk along.

"What is life? What do you need to be happy?" He talks with his hands, gesturing with each statement. "I can make money, but money cannot make me. I can choose to be happy or sad. What will you choose?"

"Happy?" I venture, sure this must be the right answer.

We pass a hidden hotel, nestled behind a shield of green trees. Jamal points it out to me. "This is not a large hotel but it is nice. Five stars. You should stay here if you get the chance."

"Maybe I can find a rich boyfriend and he will bring me here." I joke.

"It's better to go with a poor one," Jamal assures me. I must look puzzled, for he says, "Let me explain. If someone has the money for nice things, fancy cars, expensive hotels, they can have this, no problem. But it means nothing. If someone can't afford a nice hotel, but they do this for you, to make you happy, it means more and you can both appreciate it!"

"Okay. I get it. I'm more likely to find a poor one, anyway."

We have coffee and I tell him I am leaving with my friends for Casablanca. He says he, too, will be in Casablanca this weekend, and we exchange numbers. When I go back to the Moumanet, I am told the gardens are only open to the public from ten until four. I have missed it. I take a photo from outside the gate, shrug (what can I do?) and start back to my hotel, admiring the sunset. A policeman is monitoring traffic and he smiles at me.

"Where are you from?" I tell him I'm American. "Welcome to

Morocco!" he says, beaming at me as he stops the traffic so that I can cross. I love the way the local people individually welcome me as if to their personal home. I doubt most Americans are this expansive in their hospitality. When it isn't accompanied by a hand out for a handout, it's charming.

When I return, Isa calls. Jose will be bringing him and Johnny back into town and they will pick me up. Jose drops us off at the square and suggests we all meet up in an hour. Isa and I wander a bit, lingering to smell perfumes at one stand, looking at earrings at another. We go to the juice stand and Isa buys me some fresh-squeezed grapefruit juice. An old woman walks up to us. She looks like one of the little apple dolls my daughter made in Girl Scouts, with a brown and wrinkled face.

She brings her fingertips up to her mouth, saying, "Mange, si vous plaît, madame…" I smile at her, but shake my head. She keeps smiling; she knows she's got me. She points to herself and says, "Mama." I nod. I think, *honey, you're a great grandma if you're anything!*

I reply, pointing to myself, "Mama." She nods in understanding and extends her hand again. Okay, fine! I ask Isa for ten dirham. He rolls his eyes at me but gives it to me. "I don't have any change!" I whisper.

I give it to her, she says "Merci," and toddles off.

I see two women set up at a makeshift station with crates for chairs, and one is painting henna. Henna hands! Remembering the Berber woman, I stop to ask how much and she tells me one hundred fifty dirham. Almost twenty dollars! I really wanted to do this, but it's a lot of money, way out of my budget.

"Sit, I do small flower." She gestures to the stool in front of her. "Gift." I look at Isa helplessly. He shrugs. I sit and she begins painting like mad. Small flower, my ass. Soon my hands are covered. She is masterful and the design is beautiful, but I try to protest.

"Stop," I say, knowing it's too late. "I can't pay one-fifty."

She shakes her head, impatient. "Money not important. You pay what you like." She keeps painting. Before I know it, both hands are covered and I am obligated to hand over the money.

I walk away, thanking her reluctantly. I feel steamrolled. I can't move my hands as the crusty henna dries. I walk along with a pout on my face. We wander the shops, but my heart isn't in it anymore. We sit and wait for Jose, who called saying he'll be at the square by the gas station in ten minutes, and he is bringing some other friends, two girls.

The two girls are in the back, along with Johnny looking like a Chinese jack-the-lad, all smiles, with Jose driving. I say hello but not much more. I'm homesick all of a sudden, and tired of the stress of this place.

The restaurant has a large gravel outdoor seating area with trees all about. We sit and tapas are served: the ever-present olives, some garbanzo beans, and potato salad. Dinner is some kind of bird; he calls it pigeon. The girls and Jose slip into Arabic to converse, which is fine with me. I'm too tired and grouchy for conversation.

Suddenly there is a small scuffle, and three black dogs - a mother and two waggly puppies - appear. My heart lightens. That's more like it! I miss Zepher, my daughter's dog who I helped raise when she left to finish her high school year in New Mexico. I always say he saved my life, greeting me as I came home from work to the too-empty house each day, sleeping with me every night. I miss his puppy energy. But here, suddenly, are some new puppy friends. I greet them like old pals. I wish they had come sooner, for I have eaten most of my "pigeon." I pick some meat off the bones and extend it to three eager mouths.

The puppies have bodies that go one way then the other like Slinkys. I reach out to pet one and he dashes off, scooting backwards away from my reach. Odd. I try again with the other one, with the same result. Soon the pups scamper off, and as they weave around the tables, I watch with speechless horror as a waiter forcefully kicks one out of his way.

"Did you see that?" I interrupt my dining companions' conversation, outraged. They look at me like I am a child having a tantrum. "He kicked the puppy!" The girls shrug. Johnny pats my shoulder. Jose throws me a bone, literally.

"Here," he says, pushing the rest of his pigeon onto my plate. "Give them this." I sputter. Does no one care about the abuse but me?

"Bones aren't good for dogs," I object.

He throws them down onto the gravel. "No, look. They eat." Of course they do. When one puppy is done, I put my hand against his side and he stumbles to the ground. I take the opportunity to caress him softly as he lies there for a second, but he whimpers as if I've hurt him and scrambles to get up. I am in tears.

I am trying so hard to be culturally sensitive. Muslim countries look at women differently, treat animals differently. But damn it, wherever you go, it just can't be okay to kick a puppy.

Blog Post:
Animal Love – The Musings of a Non-Vegetarian

Here is the wonderful part about being human: you can choose. Almost anything! You can choose to be married (although you may have to "settle") or choose to be single.

You can choose friends, a job, a car. You can choose clothes: skinny jeans, flare, or a boot cut? You can choose what to order off the menu. And, to take this a step farther, you can choose whether to eat animals or not.

So now here's where you go, "Uh-oh, this chick's on a vegetarian kick" OR "yay! One of us!" But truthfully, I'm neither. I am on the fence. I love a good steak once in a while. Yet I have looked into the deep brown eyes of cows and seen their beauty. I won't eat veal because I know how veal calves are raised. I am faltering about cows, but I'm okay with eating chicken. I don't much care for chickens; I am terrified of roosters. (And let me say here that I have never been scared of a big…. Well, never mind!) But chickens, as individuals, impress me as flighty and slightly suspicious. Is that like saying I would never eat human, except maybe Aries males because they really aggravate me?

I am definitely conflicted!

I was eating at a restaurant in Morocco when mother dog and two sweet black puppies appeared. I fed them scraps, but when I tried to pet them, the dogs fled. I soon saw why: when they waggled their way through the restaurant, they were kicked by the waiter. I was furious, but everyone else in my party was nonchalant (three Moroccans and two from Malaysia.) I held back tears and gathered more pigeon from my dining partners, who were busily having adult conversations while I was holding back puppy tears.

The next day, one of the guys from Malaysia (of Chinese origin) told me I'd better never go to China, where in the markets they display dogs you can choose to take home — not for a pet, but for your dinner. I'd spend all my tourist shopping money buying these pups and finding a way to ship them home, all the while crying inconsolably!

In France they eat horse. I love horses; I have spent the equivalent of at least a small one-family house over the years on my horse habit, boarding, riding, taking lessons, and showing. Horses have taken carrots from my lips. My tears have soaked their manes as they have listened to my sorrows, their strength and beauty has also brought me tears of joy. I've eaten with them, sharing sandwiches. But I've never eaten horse.

Can one be a selective animal lover? Can I assume that the steak I am enjoying was a cow living happily and then killed humanely? (Giving his life for his country, as it were?) Is it simply convenient for me to ignore what I know: that chickens are crammed into cages (much like veal) and raised until it's time to butcher them (humanely? Right?) I've never spent much time with pigs, either, but I enjoy pork from time to time. Bacon is yummy! If I take cows off the list because of their big brown eyes, is it okay to keep pigs on it if I don't think they are all that attractive?

These, boys and girls, are the musings of an animal lover/non-vegetarian! And I'm afraid there are no easy answers. Your comments are welcome, but please don't yell at me; I'm a sensitive Pisces! (That's the Fish, and yes, I do also eat fish....)

Monkey in the main square, Marrakech

At Fantasia

Moving On Through Morocco: Where's It At?

The next day I get up early to pack and shower. Jose is picking me up at – yawn- six-thirty! I get everything together, checking for left-behind items. All of my gifts, an explosion, it seems, are packed into one of the square plastic zip-up totes I have been seeing for months, and now I am privileged to have one of my own, brimming with goodies. And it's heavy! I haul it down the stairs, say good bye to the morning clerk, and off we go. We pick up Isa and Johnny and we are off on the six-hour drive to Fes. I lazily watch the scenery slip by; lots of red earth, donkeys in the countryside carrying large loads or people. The highway is amazingly smooth.

We stop for breakfast, which is coffee, juice, and a choice of bread. Why is there always so much bread? I sigh and select one, apologizing to my inner South Beach Diet coach. We chat and eat, and I find out that Jose is from Ouarzazate. I tell him about my little joke, "Where's it at?" and bless him, he finds it funny, too.

For the rest of the trip, we will occasionally riff on Ouarzazate, to the dismay of our traveling companions.

We get back into the car, and a few hours later, I wake from a car-nap to find we are driving down a side boulevard of a clean and shiny city. The center of the boulevard is a grassy park where people are strolling. Tall palm trees tower above us.

"Are we in Fes?" I ask sleepily.

Yes we are! We are going through the new part of town, Jose explains. Fes is home to the oldest University in the world. It has a young vibrant population. The boulevard seems to extend forever, alternating with ornate fountains that perch in the center of traffic roundabouts.

Finally, we leave the new part of town and we drive toward a keyhole-shaped doorway made of gleaming wood and blue tiles. Two openings in the center straddle the road to allow for cars, and smaller keyholes are at each end for pedestrians. It's the old Fes. We drive through the doorway.

Before long Jose is turning up a narrow street and slowly navigating the uphill climb, waiting for young boys to move as they walk down the road. We pull up to a carved wooden door and he hops out and rings the bell. We are escorted in while Jose parks the car. This is our guest house, a traditional riad. In the middle part of the riad, the customary fountain sits in a tile courtyard. The walls consist of the elaborate Moorish décor that I have seen in Spain at the Alcazar in Sevilla and the Alhambra in Granada; tile mosaic patterns alternated with carved white plaster. The entire room here is made of these tile and plaster designs. Three floors above, a skylight lets in the sunlight overhead. A few tables flank the fountain, and directly off the courtyard on either side are doors leading to bedrooms. They open one door and show us. The floor here is also tiled. A king-sized bed with an embroidered white

130

spread is in the center of the room, with a bathroom off to the side.

I realize that they intend to give this room to me and Isa to share.

He and I have already had a conversation in which he told me his wife has gotten fat and "closed up shop," and that they sleep in separate beds. I told him we are friends, but just friends, okay? Jose is trying to keep the trip budget down; Johnny snores loudly and will get his own room, and, while I am okay sharing a room with a gentleman, I am not okay with sharing a bed. I attempt to gently bring this up and see if they have a room with two beds, but instead I sputter and burst into tears.

Through my sniffles I say to Jose, "We're not sleeping together! I can't… it's not fair…" Isa looks perplexed and embarrassed.

Johnny puts his arms around me. "It's okay." He tells me.

But it's not okay. So not okay! I think of how long it has been since I've made love with someone I care about. I think about the false starts and disappointments on this trip. I think of all the men here in Morocco fawning over me, and how I really want a lover, not a one-night-stand, not a weekend with someone else's frustrated husband; I want a man to call my own, who can call me his own. Someone to share my dreams with, to walk hand-in-hand with, to eat fruit off his naked body if I want! It seems a cruel joke to throw me into a bed with an old Asian man (no offense Isa) – as if God is pointing his callous little finger and laughing at my predicament.

And what do these men think I am, the Sex Fairy? They put their marital problems, horniness, sexual frustrations under the pillow at night and I fly along on my gossamer wings, flitting from bed to bed, and leaving a big dollop of steamy blonde sex for them to enjoy, then disappear before morning so they can wake up with a smile? No thanks, buddy. I am sick of being looked at like some piece of candy you can suck on for the sweetness and then spit out when you go back to your real diet.

Now, truth be told, I know I invite some of this response: I dye my hair, I wear makeup, cleavage-baring tops at times, tight jeans that display my large round ass. I know this is waving a flag in front of a bull, or a corral full of bulls. But other times I walk around in modest clothes, no makeup, hair still blonde, but in a right mess. And in places like Morocco, this still draws attention. I can't help the way I'm built, 40's curvy va-va-voom, or that I have a friendly, open smile. I'm not the most beautiful girl (ahem, old woman) on the planet. Neither am I hideous. Okay, some mornings after an evening with too much wine, maybe then.

But in general, I'm pretty average. Plump. A nest of blonde hair that won't behave. Forty-eight years old, and I no longer can pass for thirty let alone twenty. But I am damned sure doing something wrong in this world, because I "pull," as the Brits say, foreigners, young boys, and dirty old men like nobody's business. I can't meet someone who is a real prospect, especially in my own country. I suffered through fifteen years of married hell and stayed faithful the whole time. I gave my all to Brad for five years and came out empty handed and broken. And now I am faced with the prospect of sleeping with a little old Asian man!

Dude, where's my karma?

Jose helps fix the room problem and arranges for them to put us in a room with two twin beds. Sniffling and embarrassed, and afraid I have hurt my friend's feelings, I get into the car and we begin our tour of Fes, visiting the leather tannery and factory, walking through winding streets. Then Jose takes us on a driving tour of Fes. We see the mellah, or Jewish area, then up a hill with spectacular views of the entire city, where we see a mule and an egret walking up the road together.

"Look," I wisecrack as I snap a photo. "He says, I have but one egret." Jose, the only one who gets my humor, laughs.

We go back down into the busy part of the city. People are teeming around us: women in headscarves, young people, families, and children running through the squares. We drive by the blue gate to the city, and past the University, where hordes of youths are hanging out, horsing around, looking like kids in any college town.

Jose takes us through the new city along the boulevard. We pass a car and the song "Party Rockers" is on their radio, and I start seat-dancing. The guy driving the car notices, smiles at me, and turns the music up. We stay beside him until the next round-about, then Jose finds Shakira's song, "This Time for Africa" and blasts it out. I am grooving along, singing loudly. Johnny smiles indulgently. Isa in the front seat is tolerant, or at least he doesn't complain. *I'm in Africa!* I think. I really am. Just the northernmost part of the huge continent, Morocco, but here nonetheless. It has taken me so long to get to see this.

Not that I would want to go back and re-shape my life. But I have seen so little of the world, and I'm edging up on forty-nine. I am making up for it now. We cruise down the boulevard, music blasting, heading back to the riad.

Back at the room, I say good night to Isa and have no problem sleeping all night, man in the room or not! At least he is over there, and I'm over here.

The next day we hit Rabat. We stop off at the old mosque, where nothing is left but pillars, and behind that the minaret still stands. On this sight there is a mausoleum containing the remains of

Mohammed V and two of his brothers. There are guards on horseback in full costume flanking both gates. Inside, more guards are at the four open doors of the mausoleum, wearing bright red capes. I walk in and see the coffins displayed below. In the inner corners are four more guards, dressed in green with white gloves and holding flags. When I snap a photo, the guard puts his gloved hand over his face.

Rabat is a clean modern city. I like it. The King's palace is here. His picture is everywhere and I think he is sexy with his full lips and slanted eyes. I wave as we drive by the palace, as we leave Rabat and are on the way to our final destination, Casablanca.

We stop at a rest area and gas station. The restrooms at these gas stations are usually filthy, and they have an attendant who gives out toilet paper and expects a tip. There is always a prayer room where men leave their shoes outside and go in to pray. In the café my travelling companions will be eating more damned bread. I use the restroom and decide to skip the meal to do some yoga. I tuck myself behind a building on a grassy lawn. The restroom attendant looks on, amused. I hear some Arabic music from a truck behind me, and I smile. Public yoga in Morocco. Look at me now, Mom!

After a few more hours of travel, we enter the congested city. Our hotel, the Morocco House, is elegant and rich in décor. It is tucked into a corner of an unassuming street just across from a pizza place. As we check in, I joke that I should get my own room, too.

"I snore," I insist to Jose. "I snore louder than Johnny!"

"You can have your own room. No problem. You just have to pay more!"

"Fine, then I want a bed like a princess, with a draping canopy!" When we are shown to our room, I am surprised to see that the beds in the room are exactly to my description. A filmy gold canopy hangs from the four posters of the bed. A print on the wall depicts exotic belly dancers swaying for a sultan.

We go out for a tour of Casablanca. We shop a bit in the medina, but the main attraction here is the majestic plaza and mosque by the sea. The minaret is the tallest I have seen; it stretches into the sky with accents of teal decorating the circumference of the tower. It is breathtaking. Many people are walking in the large plaza: couples holding hands, the women wearing headscarves. Two young boys are playing soccer and the guards drive up in a small white vehicle, scold them, and take the ball away. Small children run around chasing pigeons and laughing. It is a lively place. By the seaside there is a stone wall. Large boulders stretch out between the wall and the water, and here is where the young people gather.

Jose and I walk over and look down upon the rocks. The acrid smell of marijuana drifts up from a trio of young boys perched upon the litter-strewn boulders. I gaze out at the far-reaching sea as the setting sun glints off the water, turning it into a shimmering expanse of molten silver.

I am not returning to Marrakech with the others, so I say farewell to my friends and I get in touch with Jamal, who picks me up to go to dinner. We drive by the sea and I am amazed at all the restaurants and discos that I had not known were there.

Casablanca is the biggest city in Morocco, with a population of over three million, and the business center of the country as well. Afterwards, he takes me to the hotel to reclaim my bags, then to the train station. He urges me to buy a first-class ticket so that I will be assured a seat, and for about eight dollars more, I do so. I wave goodbye and settle in.

The train to Tangier takes six hours. I sleep through much of it. It is hot and stuffy, and there is no air conditioning. The toilets are disgusting once again, even in first class. I spend the last part of my trip talking in Spanish with to a gorgeous young man. He says I am the first extranjera (foreigner) he has ever spoken to. He is twenty-two and studying law. He mentions that the only way for Morrocans to get out of the country is to marry, and for a moment I entertain this fantasy, but I know it isn't how I want to attain the partner I desire. But damn, I am very tempted.

When we get to the Tangier station, I see that the connection to the ferry will be tight, so I flag down a cab. Despite my efforts, I still miss the ferry. I have not heard from Ralph, so I am not even sure he will be there to collect me. I sink down into a hard plastic chair and without warning, my eyes fill. I'm hungry, dirty, and lonely. Now I must wait two hours for the next boat. I take a deep breath and still my tears. I will be okay.

And eventually I am. The ferry slogs into Tarifa, and even though there is a two-hour time difference which means it is midnight in Spain, Ralph is there waiting for me. I am so happy to see him! We drive back up the bumpy road and I crash in my loft bed, my temporary home sweet home.

Making "Berber whiskey"

The minaret at Casablanca

Snake charmer

Return To Spain, And My Week As A Hermit – Or Not

I am in Bolonia at Ralph's place, alone, as Ralph has gone to Germany for a week while I care for his house. Of course, I am not completely alone. There are two horses, one who keeps knocking down the electric fence and getting into the grass on the other side. There is Romeo, the black donkey stallion. There is Filu, the elderly terrier, and Mitzi the cat.

All the animals are scruffy except for Mitzi, who stays scrupulously clean, as cats often do. My days now are self-orchestrated. After doing a little cleaning, I have a clear sunning area. I have aired out the house so it smells less like cigarettes each day. I plan to groom and lunge the horses today, then go to town to use the internet café and post a blog.

True to my word, I have not contacted Brad in over two weeks. I am glad I have withdrawn from contact. I know we are not right for each other; experience has proven that. But why is it so hard to let go?

I try to envision the man I will be with someday. I once read an

Oprah magazine article about listening to your inner voice. But it is hard for me, because I really don't know what I want any more. As I explore who I am, I am also thinking about the person who would best complement me. And along the way I am picking up tidbits from my travels that I can digest and incorporate into the next part of my life, whether I'm part of a couple or not.

For now, this is my relax and re-focus week. Morocco was hectic. Up here in the hills above Bolonia, it is anything but hectic, apart from the Battle of the Electric Fence!

There is a move called Dolphin that I learned in a yoga class. This pose is meant to prepare you for headstand. You clasp your hands (as you would to cradle your head) and use your arm and body strength to do mini-pushups touching your forehead to the floor in front of your clasped hands, then behind, and keep repeating. The next preparatory move is one I call "Toe Dance;" in this dance you place your head on the floor in the cradle of your hands and arms, and walk your feet up closer and closer and then gently (and preferably gracefully) pick up one foot and balance on the other toes for a moment, then quickly switch, transferring weight from one foot to the other, but shifting most of your weight to the front of your body – head and hands.

Not only is this the week I would like to start in my journey toward headstand, but I see a metaphor here: Dolphin and Toe-Dance are also what I'm doing in my life. I'm practicing being my authentic self through removing all the disguises I've put upon it – the career, the place I lived, the relationships I've had. All had their own elements of truth, certainly, but now I am seeking a new truth, a new me. An evolution, better late than never.

Fear and Faith are opposite sides of the same coin. Fear of the Unknown is a real and powerful force, but it is not a good place from which to operate. Faith is not knowing and still forging ahead with the feeling that whatever it is that happens next, good or bad, is right and true and necessary. I am trying to edge away from the Fear in my life- for I am afraid of my own shadow at times – and toward Faith.

The best way I have found to do this is to truly live in the Now. I plan a little of what's next, because of course it is foolish not to plan at all! But I cannot orchestrate my future. I cannot make other people do my bidding: not my kids, not Brad, not even this little grey horse. You can't row someone else's boat; you go gently down the stream, not against it. Life is but a dream.

So now, I row my own boat, a poor little beat-up dinghy, down the stream of a peaceful contemplative time in the hills above Bolonia. The week spreads out before me: unstructured time held together by meal times for the animals. I can write, do yoga, go to the beach. I practice yoga in a patio-like clearing that overlooks the horse paddocks. Unfortunately, this means the flies do it with me, so I don't do as much as I would like to. Ralph has a workshop that is basically spread throughout his outdoor space. The house is cluttered and I feel claustrophobic inside. Outside, though, it is hot and there are lots of insects. The horses need more care and attention than I can give; they are both scabby and itchy and covered in bot eggs. I can work them in their pens, lunging a bit, but they are basically prisoners. Without the truck Ralph has graciously left me, so would I be.

My saving grace is meeting up with a lady from New Zealand with whom I have exchanged some emails on Help-Ex. She was in Morocco at the same time as me, and is coming back to Tarifa. We are unable to connect directly by phone, but continue by email. I tell her when I will be in town but I have no idea when her ferry will be coming in.

So I go to Tarifa, park downtown and wander. In the Chinese

store I purchase some hair dye; my roots are starting to show again. When I come out, I see a tired-looking lady, slight of build, with a huge blue back pack strapped on her back, hunched over from the weight. Our eyes meet. I say hello.

"Catherine?" she asks. It is indeed Jo-anne.

In the next week we get along just fine. For three days we hang out, drive down to the beach for walks, and generally just relax. We share dinners together and she cooks and washes up, grateful for a place to stay. I feel a little guilty for inviting her without permission, but what Ralph doesn't know won't hurt him, and I was dying of boredom. Jo-anne is just what I needed! She has the ingenious idea of cutting most of the bots or fly eggs off the horses with scissors, so we do this, and I use the baby oil I found by the computer (which we joke madly about) to rub down their legs so no more eggs will stick.

One morning at feeding time, I spot a black hen hopping along. She has string wound about both ankles tying her feet together with about an inch and a half of string between them. How she managed this, I don't know. I am scared of chickens, so I tell Jo-anne, who is not. She goes outside and comes back with the hen held in her hands.

"Do you have the scissors?" she asks. I cut the string between the feet and then proceed to carefully cut the pieces that are wound tight around the scaly claws. The chicken is docile.

"She's not scared," Jo-anne tells me. "She's just a baby." Emboldened, I reach out and touch her shiny black feathers. Soft. I finish unwinding the string. "Do you want to hold her?" I nod. "Here," Jo-anne instructs. "Their breastbones are really fragile, so just put a hand on each side, over the wings."

I hold the hen, marveling at her soft feathers and her bright, blinking eyes. The feet are reptilian and scary, but her body is warm, her feathers silky. My heart melts a little; why have I always been afraid of chickens? I add chicken to the list of beings I might not want to eat anymore. I hand her back nervously to Jo-anne so she can let her free. She hits the ground skipping, lifting her newly-freed legs high, and runs to join her little poultry friends. Jo-anne and I grin at each other. Good chicken karma!

⁂

On our last evening together, we have a barbecue of fresh veggies sprinkled with olive oil and sausages, paired with the box wine that I have been buying for 55 centimos a box. Then we go down to the internet café to check email after a walk on the beach with Ralph's elderly dog. Tomorrow Jo-anne will stay in Cadiz, then make her way to Portugal. I will miss her but I, too, am ready to move on again.

It is our final day, the day before Ralph gets back, so we take the bus to Cadiz, or, more accurately, we miss the bus to Cadiz by about five minutes. We are able, however, to catch the next bus, going to Sevilla, and transfer to one getting to Cadiz, thanks to the helpful driver. It is so useful to know at least a bit of Spanish.

Jo-anne and I find her hostel so she can leave her backpack. Soon, I realize, this will be me again, struggling with a heavy bag, and now the addition of my Christmas shopping in Morocco! – and trying to find a place to leave it. I think I might need a valet.

We go down to the main square and find an outdoor place to have a snack.

"Well, I'm off again on my own," Jo-anne says.

"Yeah, but you'll meet people." I assure her.

"I'm not like you," she says. "You're more outgoing than I am, and speaking Spanish helps, of course. People tell me I'm so brave to travel alone, but it's not like I have a choice. When I'm home, it's a lonely life, and when I travel, it's also lonely, but in a different way. It's not like it's easy. I would rather travel with someone."

"Me too," I agree. "But admitting it makes me feel like some sort of wimp, so I'm glad to hear you say it."

I think about my parents and my family in Colorado, and the new community there I want to join. I think about my kids, living their lives in Washington. I wonder if I will ever get to have them close by me again. I can't think about it too much or I get inconsolably sad. But most of all I think about having someone special by my side: someone to travel and share it all with. Someone to make a home with when we are not traveling together. Someone to miss me, someone who wants me as his partner. Will I ever have this? I think I will start by appreciating the people I have now, pulling them close before I take off for more travel. Regroup, refocus, relaunch.

The following day, Ralph is due back. We have only talked once, for Ralph the worrier is too busy in Germany to worry about his place here, which makes me feel trusted. In the morning I clean a bit, mop out the shower, and do yoga in the sun. I get a call from Ralph, who will take the bus part way and let me know where to come and get him. Fine, I think, I can do that!

But when I get into the ancient truck, with the finicky locks, the missing gas cap, and the key that needs "a magic touch," the steering wheel is locked and the ignition key will not turn. I go on an inner rant. I have dealt with this problem on ancient cars before, when I was in my twenties and could only afford a bucket of bolts. But now I am forty-eight years old. Ralph is fifty. At this age, haven't we earned the right to have things around us that actually work, for God's sake? Ralph calls and I tell him about the truck, and then I flag down the neighbor, another German, and persuade him to help me pick up Ralph from the road to the beach.

At night I start making plans to get back to Madrid quickly, but I can tell that Ralph is upset with me. He doesn't want me to go so soon. I say I can stay one more day to help him with the fence or whatever he needs, but then I need to get to Madrid. I tell him how beautiful his area is, how I've enjoyed the sunsets. But I can't live like this, I would go crazy. He admits that sometimes he feels crazy as well. That night we get drunk and talk about ex-wives, ex-husbands, and sex. Ralph and his lady were swingers, and ran a swinger's club. He offers to give me the name of a woman in Madrid if I want to try it; she will take me to the club and I can indulge myself.

I laugh; thanks, but no thanks. Even in my crazy New York stripper days I didn't go to the sex clubs, even though I had friends who went and was often invited to one or the other. Back in those days, people did not seem to worry about STDs; promiscuity was de rigeur. I was promiscuous on my own, without the assistance of special sex clubs. I satisfied that part of the bargain. But I have come to realize that even in that era of one-night-stands, the prince on the white horse fantasy was always dormant, waiting to be fulfilled.

So many damned obtuse princes have totally missed their chance with me! The fools.

Back To Madrid, Third Time Is A Charm!

On the road again. How I wish someone less twangy than Willie Nelson had recorded that song, if it must be stuck in my head!

I am on the bus from Bolonia to Sevilla. From there I will take another bus to Madrid, and Nica will collect me. Last night, for lack of anything better to do for dinner, I made a tuna noodle casserole for Ralph. It's something I swore I would never cook! But he loved it and ate the whole pan. He told me last night he wishes he had someone to live with. I can relate. This morning when I got up, Ralph was also awake. He was walking around nude as he often does, but usually he waits until after I have retired to my own room. He was in the kitchen, and I really wanted coffee, but how could I empty the basket of grounds when he was standing in front of the garbage can, naked, and I would have to bend over to dump them in? I'm no prude, but the thought of confronting a dangling penis while I nonchalantly went about my coffee routine stopped me. I couldn't do it. I waited for him to move and eventually I got my coffee!

We drove in silence to the bus stop. As always, it was a bittersweet parting – feeling anxious to move on, but sad to say goodbye. We exchanged the typical Spanish kiss-kiss, then I gave him a big hug. "American goodbye, "I told him. Ralph squeezed me hard.

I am glad to be returning to Madrid, since I haven't really gotten to see much of it. I am staying with my friend Nica, and hopefully will have the opportunity to practice Spanish, and help him more with his English. He says he doesn't cook, so I offered to make dinners while I am there.

When the bus stops for the rest stop, a man selling nuts out of the back of a truck calls out to me, tells me I am "guapa," and his two friends smile, amused. I tell him in America they like "flaquitas," skinny women. He gestures to me, appreciating my shape, and links his arm through mine as I walk to the bus, horsing around for his friends. I laugh and he goes back to his truck. I feel light-hearted.

⠿⠿⠿

It amuses me when people call this my "Eat Pray Love" journey. I admit there are similarities. I read and enjoyed the book. But Elizabeth Gilbert had a lot of advantages: first of all, she had no kids. No associated expenses or guilt! She was already a published writer and was not changing careers, and she had a book contract with an advance. She wasn't broke like me. She was also at least ten years younger. And the most important difference – the one that made that book a best-seller – was that she ultimately wrote a romance. It probably was not her intention when she made her journey, but that is what she ended up with, that is what sold a bazillion copies. She met her prince. We are all suckers for the happy ending, and the happy ending, damn it, always ends in romance.

Ahem, you might say to me at this point – the point at which I am stomping on my soap box, a single gal traveling broke and unencumbered – *wouldn't you prefer that this story end as a romance, too?* Well, maybe. As much as I also would like to find love, I don't want that to be the reason for my existence!

When my twenty-year old daughter, the romantic, laments that she will probably die alone, I reassure her. She is young, beautiful and talented, and she will go through a bunch of boys and decide on one eventually. But in the back of my head there is a little voice that is saying to me, *she'll be ok, but you, Mama, you will die alone. Cause you are gettin' old, girlfriend.* Shut up, Voice!

I want to be stronger than this. I want to give my daughters the same kind of emotional strength I wish I had myself. I want to go back in time and take away the Barbies and the Disney princess movies and teach them to be independent and strong and smart and not to feel they need to look a certain way or to find a man to be complete.

My younger daughter Veronica isn't struck with the illness that plagues her sister and I; she wasn't bitten by the romance bug. But when I think about this, I wonder if it's because she suffered psychological abuse from her father, who wanted a boy? He treated the girls differently, and they grew up wanting different things from men. I could psycho-analyze my kids here, I could shoulder the guilt I bear for being any part of damage to them, I could bring in astrology – a water sign and a fire sign – and I could go into the "nature versus nurture" debate. I will spare us all.

But I miss them. I miss my babies - they will always be my babies, no matter how old they are. My last month in Spain is ticking away, and then I will be on the way back "home", if I can call it that.

One thing that is difficult about traveling is not having a real home. But when I think of going back to Colorado, I realize I don't have that there either. Not yet. I am restless here at times, but I also know I'd be restless in the USA. Without a job to wrap my life around, it will take some re-adjustment. And it will take time.

≪≪≪≪≪

Today is my first day back in Madrid. I buy the boots I have been fantasizing about for two months. It's chilly here now and the nip of autumn is in the air. I am staying with Nica in his apartment.

It is a tall red-brick older building in the northern part of the city, surrounded by many other tall red-brick almost identical buildings. Most have a series of stores at the bottom, but this does nothing to help me distinguish one from another, as the shops are interchangeable. I resign myself to getting lost. The space between the buildings forms a plaza where families and youth hang out, and very noisy children run around screaming until late into the evening. Even on the fourth floor with the door to the balcony shut, we can hear them. Nica smiles indulgently, so I do too. When in Rome! It reminds me that it has been a long time since I have really lived the city life.

I wander around in my new boots. Nica and I are meeting at a tapas restaurant that has earned two Michelin stars. We get seated at a small table, and the tapas courses begin to arrive. Amid conversation, we eat. And eat. And eat. The food: a fluffy concoction with caramelized onions, potato and mussel croquettes, potato with caviar and a creamy topping, baked chicken, asparagus tempura, and Cava sparkling wine and tiramisu, is plentiful and wonderful. We stagger out and go back to the apartment.

As I waddle to the car park, I tell Nica, "This is why I can't go on cruises – no buffets, no 'tenedor libre!' I'm like a dog. You put food in front of me, I just eat and eat."

He grins at me. "No control?"

"Well, if it's there, no. I will eat what's in front of me. So buffets are bad! But I'm not hungry all the time or anything. I just want as much as I can have. Like a dog licking clean his food bowl."

Saturday arrives, and since Nica does not have to work, he is going to teach me to play padel, a game popular in Spain that is a combination of tennis and racquetball, played in a court with a back wall that one can bounce the ball off. We pick up his son Samuel, and I get to be the second person, first on Nica's team then on Samuel's. I don't do too badly for my first time playing, considering I am not very athletic. I proudly last the whole hour with Nica and his son. They encourage me when I hit a tricky shot and ignore when I miss an easy one or hit the ball to the bottom of the net. I also hit it outside the court several times – to both neighboring courts and to the sidewalk outside. But all in all, it is fun.

Afterwards, Nica and I have a leisurely lunch at the café across from his building.

"Nica, do you have a girlfriend?"

"No," he answers. "Just, you know, friends," he gestures, waving his hand in a circle.

"With benefits?" I prompt. "Female friends you sleep with?"

"Yes. Just this. It is nice, you know? It is better than picking up someone in a disco, it is someone you know, and like. It's like doing any activity; like padel, or going to the movies."

"Oh, no. I don't feel like that. Having sex is a way of connecting. I can't just have sex and not feel something emotionally for that person. I wish I could!"

"You wouldn't want to go to the movies five times a day, right?" I continue. He shakes his head, confused. "Well, remember the dog with the food bowl? I'm that way with sex, too. I want as much as I can get once I start. It's better to just not start."

He laughs. We go on to talk about other things, but then somehow the conversation comes back to sex. I'm explaining the words we use: dick, cock, pussy.

"And are these polite?"

"No. I mean, most people don't talk about sex in regular conversation. With friends or something, yeah. But not generally."

"So, then you use the real words? Like, penis? And what is the real word for the part of the woman?"

"Um, vagina," I tell him. Why am I whispering?

"Ah yes, same in Spanish. Vagina." Nica seems unconcerned to speak in a natural voice. I relax. After all, who cares?

Later I take a walk around the neighborhood, and I find a park on a hill where many people congregate. There are lots of dogs, mostly off-leash. I see an old man peeing on a tree. Honestly, why do men think they can just pee anywhere? Half of a birthday cake sits on a picnic table with a family around it. A toddler walks by shakily, his mother behind him. His shirt says "Big Guy." I see old men and women at the benches where there are foot pedals for exercising. Some are pedaling away, others are ignoring the apparatus.

As I walk along, two old men stroll behind me, and I hear one say "muy guapa." And "extranjera." Are they talking about me, or am I just self-conscious? I glance back quickly, but I can't tell. I hear "muy guapa" again, and this time I give them a radiant smile.

If they are talking about me, I want them to know I appreciate a compliment.

This has got me thinking: if I don't end up in love by the time I am fifty, I should return to one of these foreign places where the men love me. Spain, Morocco, and who knows about South America? If I can't have love in my life at home, I'll come to a foreign place where I am appreciated and found beautiful. I'll hang out where the older guys with money congregate. I'll meet one and make a deal: I'll marry him if he buys me two horses. The two horses will keep me busy enough and from them I will get my love, as well. There have been worse plans!

In the park I watch a huge glorious sunset that looks like a neon tangerine in the sky, hovering above the trees. I sit cross legged on a park bench for a few minutes, trying to absorb the feeling of just being alive now: the sun, the birds chirping, voices speaking Spanish, dogs barking. This is my life, right at this mo-ment. The tangerine sun glows brightly, huge at first, then smaller as it descends and I make my way back to the apartment without getting lost. Small victories.

The next day I set off to meet Cristina at the Sorolla museum. I am getting used to negotiating the Metro, starting to feel like a city girl again. Even though it was twenty-five years ago, New York subways have trained me well. I easily transfer between lines and get off where I can walk to the Museo Sorolla. I enjoy these smaller museums, and this one is in the family home of the painter which makes it more special. The garden is beautiful without being extravagant, and it is there that I find Cristina waiting.

"I called you…" I say apologetically, as I am twenty minutes late. We kiss kiss, cheeks touching.

"I know. I thought, I hope she isn't doing the American thing, calling to say she'll be late." I smile because that is exactly what I was doing. "This is Spain, darling. No pasa nada!"

I have missed Cristina and her outgoing energy. We sit in the garden and talk about her new apartment and roommate, and the search leading up to them. I tell her about my travels. We stroll through the museum, and are both drawn to the seaside scenes. Pastels, especially robin's-egg blue for the water, characterize these works. Sorolla's style captures the feeling of lazy afternoons by the ocean.

Later we meet Cristina's' friend at a place on Gran via, which, as a happy surprise, has a free flamenco demonstration. Afterwards Nica joins us, and the four of us look for a place to have dinner, which we find on a side street: a Brazilian restaurant that serves a set meal. They call the style rodicio. They serve us rice and beans, the ever-present French fries, salad, and then the meat begins to come. The waiter brings a long skewer of beef, charred from the grill, and hands me the tongs. I grasp the slice as he cuts it from the slab. This process is repeated about six times throughout the meal. It is all delicious but I feel a little guilty, since I have decided I am drifting toward vegetarianism. Oh well, I haven't made the commitment yet. I enter meat paradise.

These few days with Nica have been pleasant; he is a wonderful host. Nica loves to watch movies in English, and we put on Spanish subtitles. I have been helping him with the subtleties of the English (American) language, although his English is pretty good. This morning as I say goodbye for my day trip to Toledo he says, "Goodbye, honey," having picked up the endearment from the movie last night.

I originally thought I would stay overnight in Toledo, but the prospect of walking the legendarily beautiful streets, lit up in a golden glow, does not appeal to me if I am alone. I cringe to remember where my Sevilla fantasies took me! So this will just be a day trip and I will save money as well as pride.

In Toledo I get a map from the information center. This is a famously hilly city, and my muscles are gently reminding me I got my butt kicked by hot yoga yesterday. I wander around, map in hand. I ask a Japanese couple to take my picture with the statue of Cervantes. I stroll through stores. Toledo seems to sell a lot of pistols and swords for some reason. There are models of Knights of the Templar and knight helmets that remind me of a Monty Python skit.

There are several museums and churches here, but with these winding streets and my inability to read a map, I have found but one. I'm picky about museums, having discovered that I prefer the small ones. They are more intimate, and huge museums full of masterpiece paintings, like the Prado or the Louvre, blend into a big blur after a while. My favorite museum is the Rodin museum in Paris. It is intimate, telling the story of the sculptor's life and work. I found the Sorolla museum in Madrid to have a similar feeling. Perhaps I can also discover this in Toledo.

I wander about, taking photos and pausing to enjoy the sunny benches here and there along the charming streets and shops. The cathedral is large and dramatic, but the entry charge is steep. I think that God would want people to be able to enter his buildings for free. Instead, I continue to appreciate his real work: the sun, the breeze, and birds flying overhead.

I come to the end of town, overlooking the river Tajo, where there is a museum that I saw on the map: sculptures by the artist Victorio Macho. This is a museum that resides in the house that the artist lived in, and his workshop is also there. I enter and see the magnificent views of the river and the hills beyond. The museum itself is virtually empty, so I wander around the beautiful courtyard with its tranquil fountain, and up to the mirador with its panoramic view of the Tajo River and all the accompanying scenery. Off the courtyard is a room of sculptures in one direction and an exhibition of portraits drawn by school children in another room. In the room of sculptures, a drawing catches my eye. It is entitled "The Siren," depicting a woman with gentle curves. *This could be me,* I think, *if I get my yoga routine back.* I stare at the drawing for a while, admiring the shapely hips and generous round slopes of her body. I love it when real women's shapes are represented in art.

I am drawn to a pair of wall friezes which flank the entrance door. They are of bronze, and depict five nude men on each side, climbing a staircase. I notice that one is crumpled on the staircase, weeping. Of all the men depicted, this is the one I would have chosen to date in my past. A man with problems used to be very appealing; it made me feel needed. Which one would I choose today; which of these beautiful heroes, while I leave Crying Man to get his shit together? On the left, the hero I most like appears to be in a yoga pose; upward facing dog. Him. That's my hero. Yoga Man.

A throng of Japanese tourists has entered and my garden is no longer a peaceful place. I thank the docent and make my departure. It is time to get back to Madrid.

Nica and I watch another movie that evening. It is his favorite way to practice his English, even if the movie is bad. Tonight, it is

"The Wedding Planner", in which Jennifer Lopez falls for the man whose wedding she is arranging. Of course, he dumps his bride in the end (they mutually agree they aren't right for each other) and he and Jen get together.

Nica turns to me. "This," he gestures at the television, "is what is wrong with Americans. These stupid movies."

"Well, they're romantic comedies. They're supposed to be romantic."

Nica does not believe in marriage, so it stands to reason that he doesn't like big fluffy weddings. He scoffs. "You wait for the perfect man, to have the perfect wedding, and wear the perfect dress? This is not real life."

"I know," I say. "But I think that love can be romantic. Sometimes. Maybe."

He shakes his head. "You are waiting for, how do you say it in English? In Spain we say Principe Azul. The Blue Prince."

"I guess we say the prince on a white horse. But no, really, I'm not waiting for that."

"Oh, you don't mind if he's green?" Nica teases. I start to protest. "I'm fucking with you," Nica says proudly.

We spent a lot of time over dinner a few nights previously discussing the distinct difference between "I'm fucking you" and "I'm fucking with you." "I'm fucking you" is what he originally told me one day when he was trying to tease, hence the big discussion. I think he has totally got it now.

I smile sadly. Why can't I have a prince? Well, not a real one, of course. But why can't there be someone in my life I treasure and love, who feels the same way about me? I have seen enough of life to know this is not a given situation, in fact it is rare, but I still want it! Now I am not such a catch; unemployed and homeless, a wandering gypsy. But when I go back to real life, maybe I will be ready for this un-prince.

Although I will probably not find my prince here in Madrid, I love flirting with Spanish men. Cristina agrees that they are good at flirting, but laments that they don't follow through. She has a friend and student who she cooks with each week.

"I have been waiting for him to make a move for months," she complains to me. "I think, just rip my clothes off already!" I laugh at the image of her bra flying across the kitchen while the Spanish tortilla burns in the pan.

Tonight, I will move my things to Cristina's, and Sunday I leave for Denia. I am going a few days early so I can spend my last few days in Spain visiting Pamplona with Cristina. Nica has been a wonderful host, but jokes about sleeping together have been sprinkled throughout my stay, and that has been hard on me. I used to think sex was a good way to show gratitude, but I am trying to grow up. Of course, I don't want a life without sex, but I don't want a life of one-night-stands either.

I am once again emailing with Brad, but communication with him is disappointing. He led me to believe that he had changed with the death of his mother. I took that to mean he has started to value, if not cherish, important relationships. But I see no evidence of this. His emails are brief and impersonal. I told him he is still more guarded than Buckingham palace during the Queen's birthday celebration! I imagine that the things that were good between us would still be good, and the things that were missing would still be missing. I can't even tell if I still love him.

And yet, although traveling has taught me patience, it has also taught me to ask for what I need. And what I need in a relationship is a sense that I am important – no, necessary – to the other person, that he would cross oceans to be with me. I'm not sure Brad would even cross the street. He is too afraid of breaking out of his emotional fortress.

One of my male friends who helped nurse me through the break-up suggested that loving Brad was a bit like gold mining. You might suspect that the treasure is there, buried deep, but how much trouble do you have to go through to reach those depths? And is it ultimately worth it? For fifty-two years he has learned to hold his cards closely guarded, so why do I think he'll finally show me his hand?

I am tired of the guesswork. Nica's right, I think. I want my prince. Last night, which was Nica's birthday, we talked about people in their fifties having experience failed marriages, expectations and fears that make it difficult to make a new relationship work.

"We call that baggage," I told him.

"I am happy living alone. That's what you need to do," he points his fork at me as we share a plate of calamari. "I am social and I like to be with people. I can go out. But when I am alone, I am content."

I shake my head. After my daughter moved out to finish high school I took in a roommate, a friend of a friend, so that I could help her have a place to live as she got out of her marriage. I didn't ask her to pay rent. I had been relieved to not have to come home to emptiness each day, to hold my breath and hear the kitchen clock, tick-tick-tick. I hated living alone.

And maybe Nica's right; when people have been through marriages and long relationships, raised children, climbed their career ladders, maybe it is too hard to compromise again and make a relationship happen. But I don't care if it's not probable, I only know that it's possible. And that gives me hope.

Nica has plans for the weekend, and I am glad for this. It has felt too much like dating when we do everything together. Saturday he will be seeing one of his friends with benefits. He offers to drive me to Cristina's. Her apartment is cute and close to the Legazpi Metro, in the south part of Madrid. Her roommate, Catalina, is gone for a few days, attending a conference on motivational speaking. This is a good thing, I think, as the woman seems very controlling from Cristina's description, and probably not the type to enjoy a wayward American crashing on her floor for a few nights.

Cristina, who loves to cook, makes us pesto pasta. Nica has brought wine. We sit down to dinner. I talk about how nice it is to have generous friends, and how difficult it is to travel with limited money.

"She wants…" begins Nica. I know what he wants to say, a phrase I taught him only yesterday. He holds up a hand. "Let me think. A sugar… puppy?"

Cristina and I laugh. "Sugar daddy!"

Later, though, I think about Nica's phrase. I wish such a thing existed: imagine a sugar puppy, a puppy that gave you money! He would want nothing more than your love and cuddles, and for you to feed and walk him. Yes, I think as I drift into sleep on the mattress on the floor, I would love to have a sugar puppy.

We sleep late on Saturday and get up to explore areas of Madrid that I haven't seen. Cristina is a born tour guide. We grocery shop and cook dinner, then decide to go out for the night.

"You haven't experienced Madrid until you've experienced the night life," Cristina tells me with a grin.

Cristina's Brazilian friend, Adriana, is going out with us.

"You'll love her," says Cristina. "She knows all the clubs and she loves to go out and party."

I do indeed love Adriana when she arrives; she is warm and funny and vibrant. I make us drinks and we raise our glasses of rum and coke. It's actually my divorce-a-versary, seven years divorced, so it's a great night to go celebrate. I tell Adri my favorite joke about divorce:

"A man and his second wife go out for dinner. At the bar, a woman is laughing and flirting with the bartender, drinking wine and having a great time. The man looks, then turns away. 'What's wrong? Who is that woman?' the new wife asks. 'That's my ex-wife', the man replies. 'We were divorced seven years ago and she started drinking.' 'Wow,' says the new wife. 'Imagine celebrating that long!' "

Adri laughs and laughs. I decide to try my favorite Spanish joke out on her. I point to Cristina's roommate's fat black cat.

"Aranya? No, gato!"

She nods and laughs some more. We are practically crying.

Cristina shakes her head at us. "I just don't get why that's funny."

Adri explains, not knowing I have already told Cristina. "The name for scratch is the same word for spider! So, she asks if it scratches, but it's like she's asking if it's a spider. But no, it's a cat!" We look at each other and resume laughing.

Cristina gives us a scolding look. "Yeah. I know. Still not funny."

It is twelve thirty and it is October twenty-ninth. We put on the cheap Halloween headbands Cristina has bought for the occasion: Adriana has spiders, Cristina has little white ghosts, and I, of course, get the devil horns. We head for the subway, which closes for the night at two. Our ambitious plan is to stay out until it opens again at six.

The train is packed. As we exit at Sol, I see that a few people have costumes on, but most don't. Halloween is not the same here as it is in the US, an opportunity for people to dress up and get wasted. In Spain, they tell me as we walk towards Plaza Mayor, it is gaining in popularity every year, but it is mostly still for children.

We walk toward our destined night club, down a crowded street. A young man with a bald head and a big friendly smile is trying to get people to come to the bar where he works. He stops us and guesses where we are from.

With his arm around my waist, he queries Cristina, who is Phillipina: "Machu Pichu? Singapore?" she laughs and thanks him. "Women from Singapore have legendary beauty," she tells me.

My turn. "German? English? Irish? Swedish?" The blonde hair, I think, is throwing him off. Also, he appears to be bad at this game.

"Americana," I tell him. I don't necessarily say this with pride, it's a neutral statement, but at least I don't feel embarrassed about it as I did during the Bush regime.

We tell him we are headed to the Berlin Cabaret. "You go to the boring," he says, "then you will come back here."

We find our target club has a bit of a line, so we queue up. In front of us are a few guys, probably in their thirties. One turns to us and begins to talk. In fact, he will not shut up. He is personable, and he is making us laugh, so we let him rattle on. His name is Danny.

"What do you think of my English?" Danny asks.

"I think you're doing fine," I say encouragingly.

"I think you need classes," says Cristina. She whispers to me, "What do you think his sign is?"

"Hmmmm. I don't know. I don't think he's water. Which sign is a chatterbox?" I turn to Danny again. "When is your birthday?"

"April the seventeen."

"Oh!" I exclaim. "That's the same birthday as my daughter!" I have a pang of longing, so I send Veronica a text to tell her I am waiting in line for a club and met a guy with her birthday.

Is he hot? She texts back.

He's talkative! I reply.

We have now been waiting in line for over an hour. This club has a drag show two times a night, and we figure they are waiting for one to end and let people out first. A few more men have joined our friends, and now they are a group of about seven. Suddenly, four young girls appear, start talking to these men, and insert themselves into the line as well, cutting in front of us. It is clear they think they should not have to wait! Adri says in Spanish to Danny that we have been here forever and this is *not* going to happen!

He assures her he will take care of it, and moves forward to talk to them. But I eventually realize that we have lost Danny to young, pretty, and pushy! I reach out and grasp his shoulder to ask him what is going on, but he is deaf to my questions, and apparently has no feeling in the shoulder, either.

I approach one of the girls and tell her in my halting Spanish that we have been here in this line for over an hour and we know that they are cutting into the line.

She sneers and says, "Welcome to Spain."

The line is not moving. We decide to leave, as the whole experience has been a downer and we no longer want in.

Back through Plaza Mayor we make our way to another

nightclub that Adriana knows. I buy a beer for one euro from a Chinese guy on the street. The streets are full of people, some in costumes. There goes Elvis, a couple of monsters, and a few sexy nurses. Many young drunk people mill about aimlessly, drinking street beer.

"There are a lot of young people who cannot afford to go into the clubs, so they just hang out on the street drinking," Cristina tells me. "We call these the bottelon."

We get to the club, El Sol, which also has a line but it is moving fast. We pay ten euro, which includes a drink ticket. Adriana tells us this club plays alternative music, so I am expecting pop punk or something techno, but what they play sounds like music from the forties set to a beat. The place is crowded but nobody is dancing. It is one big open room with ledges along the side, and a raised platform where a few people shift back and forth halfheartedly. We get our drinks and move to one of the ledges to sit. On our way there, two guys comment on the devil headband I am wearing. They tell me they are Italian.

"I am Gian Carlo," says one.

The other is younger and has a beard and sleepy sensuous brown eyes. "I am Gian Luca."

We talk a while, and then he wants to kiss me. And kiss me some more. My goodness, I think, this is nice but very weird. It feels good to be kissed after so much time on my own, but it is like an out-of-body experience.

"Maybe we should dance," I say, gesturing to the floor.

We wind through the crowd. I find a place and attempt to dance. The music isn't conducive to a lot of booty-shaking, but I try my best. He sways a bit and then brings me in close to press his body against mine and starts to kiss me again. My escape strategy didn't work. "I shouldn't leave my friends alone, it's my last night in town," I tell him, and we walk back over to where Cristina and Adri sit, amused. I roll my eyes at them as I get pulled behind the pole for more kisses. Adri says she is tired and excuses herself to go home.

"I need to go to the restroom," I tell Gian Luca. It's time for this to end.

"Me too, let's go."

Oh, God. I ask Cristina if she also needs to go, my eyes insisting she say yes, so we all head down the stairs. When I exit the restroom, there he is, waiting. I tell Cristina we should leave. She agrees.

"Don't leave me!" Gian Luca says. I look at him, exasperated. "Don't you want to be with me?" *Not really,* I think. I wonder if he even remembers my name. I explain that I can't, I need to go. "Okay, you may go, but five more minutes."

I shake my head. I'm really too old to be making out in a club with some Italian guy that I know nothing about. I grab Cristina's hand, and Gian Luca sets off in the other direction, no doubt to make up for his lost time with me.

Cristina and I walk along. I marvel at the multitude of people still out at three in the morning. We have forgotten about the change in time for daylight savings, so we wander the streets until our feet hurt and catch the night bus, the owl bus, to her apartment. As we wearily head up the stairs, she congratulates me for having one night like a real Madrilena. Even though we didn't quite make it to six.

Toledo

Out for the night in Madrid

Denia: More Horses, More Restlessness

I leave my tote bag of Moroccan goodies in Cristina's apartment, since I am returning to Madrid to fly back. I catch my bus to Denia, which takes most of the day. They play two movies and I have seen them both so I am able to follow along. Finally, late at night, the bus arrives in Denia.

My hostess is a Swiss lady named Barbara. She has two other helpers here, but at the moment they are in Barcelona. Barbara and her husband have two children ages eleven and thirteen, who are sweet and charming.

Although she is busy socializing with her friends, Barbara shows me some weeds she wants me to pull, and I do so for hours. After lunch, I rest for half hour and go back to pulling the weeds, an invasive vine that grows large seed pods. My job this morning was to pull all the small ones and the roots of the ones that have begun to wind around the trees in the yard near the garden. After lunch, I am still hunting for more weeds to pull, and my attitude has worsened. I am getting frustrated with this. At dinner, the family speaks German to each other and I am alone with my thoughts and feeling homesick.

The second day I go out of the gate to find more of the pesky weeds that Barbara wants eradicated. The field is full of thick red clay that is trashing my expensive Ariat boots. The ones I bought for riding. And although she has five horses here, I have not yet been asked to do anything with them. I tromp around, searching for the damned weeds. Finally, I find some! They are thick vines, and even with gloves, pulling them is hurting my hands. As I make my way around the edge of the field, she yells to me that I am on the wrong side, not even on their property. Damn!

I stomp back through the thick mud, wondering what weeds to pull next. Of all the jobs I would like to do, this is not on the list. Horses, yes. Cleaning stalls? No problem! Cleaning a house, taking care of kids, whatever. No big deal. But I am obviously getting it wrong, and I simply cannot pull weeds for five hours a day. I'm forty-eight years old; I have a Master's degree. I don't want to fucking pull any more fucking weeds in this fucking red mud!

At lunch time the other helpers come back. They are younger than me, of course. Ana is twenty-three and from Sweden, and Amanda is twenty-six and from the US, Indiana. They are nice, and they take me out to the barn to explain the feed for the horses and talk to me about some of the other jobs around the house. For this I am grateful, for I have been given very little direction, and I keep messing up the weeding job. I want to be with the horses. Barbara has said that riding is part of the job and I am looking forward to this.

I have told Barbara that I prefer housework to weeding, and horse work to anything else! We have lunch and I find out they are all going for a nice ride on the beach. I am not invited; apparently there are only three horses that can make this trip and since Ana is leaving, she really wants to ride on the beach one time. I am devastated and feel like an outcast.

When they return, I am shoveling manure in the paddock.

"Hey," Amanda calls.

"Did you have fun?" I ask in what I hope is a cheery voice.

"Yeah, it was great."

"Did you gallop on the beach?" She had told me earlier that she was a little afraid to gallop, as she is a beginning rider.

"Yeah, I did."

"Good. I love galloping." I remember my Thoroughbred and the gallops we used to have on the old logging trails.

"If you stay through next week, you'll get to go," Barbara says.

I stab a pile of horse poop and throw it in the wheelbarrow. I am uncomfortable with this hostess and her brusque manner, but it's just a week. I begin to try harder to put things into perspective. Sometimes things just get off to a rough start. That doesn't mean they have to stay that way. I am feeling more relaxed as I settle in and get to know the other two helpers. I am probably experiencing my dreaded monthly premenstrual symptoms. My period starts in the morning and, hey, what was I all upset about?

One night after we clear the table, we are sharing some of our wild escapades and I tell Anna and Amanda about my New York days. I marvel at what I did at such a young age, and compare that to my own kids, worrying about the possibilities.

"But," I say to Anna, "you have to let your kids do what they will at a certain point, just like we did when we were young."

"Um," she points to herself, then to Amanda. "We're still young."

I crack up. Of course they are. "Yeah. I know." I forget sometimes that I am not really the peer of other Helpers. I pat the head of the elderly dog under the table. "We're old, girl," I say to her. Her brown eyes look full of empathy as she seems to agree.

On Ana's last day we each saddle up a horse to ride in the arena. I am on Muchacha, a big dun-colored mare. I get her going in a dressage frame, forward and soft. She feels good. She must look good, too, because Barbara tells me at the end of the session that she wants me to start riding one of her younger horses, Serafin, a pretty seven-year-old bay mare.

For the next few days, I get to play with Serafin, and although we have some trouble with the canter transitions, she has good steering and will seek contact in the bridle easily. She is fun. As I ride along, remembering my instructor's voice in my head (lean your shoulders back, where are your hands? Heel down, and keep your lower leg still) I take in the natural beauty of craggy mountains on each side, and fuchsia and white bougainvillea petals cascading on the breeze all around. Once again, I have the good fortune to be staying in a beautiful place.

Saturday is a day off, but Amanda and I still feed the horses and ride. After lunch I nudge Amanda into a walk to the nearby small town.

There is not much going on, but it's good to get out and see civilization. We have a tinto de verano in a café and talk about life and relationships. I am finding a similarity in all the long-term travelers I meet; whether they are my age or younger, like Amanda, they are seeking some answers to life's questions by taking a long journey. We talk about this commonality.

"I think," Amanda says, "that travel widens your perspective and makes you appreciate different kinds of people." She has been traveling for two years.

I counter, "I think what I am realizing is that Spain isn't magic.

I thought it would be. But people live here, just like the US. They have their lives, they go to work, they do their laundry. There's nothing magic about Spain."

"You have to bring the magic with you," she says with a grin.

I wonder at this. Do I have any magic left to give? I have become discouraged about love. Maybe all that romantic Disney conditioning was for naught; I will still end up a lonely old lady. I had my daughters. Was that all I was meant to do in this life? Was I just put on this earth to have a few kids, to teach a few hundred more, and to never find a partner in life? Was I only meant to be a nurturer to children?

I no longer get a cheap thrill out of the possibility of sex with a stranger. Not since Seville. And I am not going to meet anyone permanent while I'm doing so much traveling. So I need to resolve that this is my year to explore the world and learn about myself without intimacy in the mix; the problem is that I didn't know I would miss it so much!

The days tick by as I do odd jobs with Amanda. We pick up horse poop, feed twice a day, clean saddles and bridles, and sweep out the barn and the feed room. At last, we all go for a ride on the beach, and it is as wonderful as I imagined: hooves kicking up sparkling drops of water as we gallop on the sand, the bite of the fall wind chilling our smiling faces.

I have two weeks to go until my return to Colorado. Most people only have two weeks total for their vacation, I remind myself. I try to appreciate what I have instead of longing for what I don't. Soon it is down to a week, and Friday I will go to Pamplona for a last hurrah with Cristina and some of her friends before flying back home from Madrid.

One chilly day, eight days before I go home, I am in a

particularly pensive mood. The sky overhead is white with wisps of stringy grey clouds like an ancient pair of threadbare tie-dyed jeans. A single leaf falls dramatically from a tree as I watch, a suicide jumper plummeting off a building ledge. Water pools on the stone walkways. I go inside and huddle under a blanket on the bed, wanting to burrow and hide.

Then, miraculously, it is time to ride. I take out Serafin, whose bay coat is like the fuzz of a teddy bear. She nuzzles me as I brush her. We are still having canter issues – she scrambles into a fast anxious trot instead of flowing into canter. This unbalances me and I thump around on her, trying to get the canter by throwing my upper body forward instead of sitting back, and we become one giant frenetic mess. It isn't just my riding, though, she doesn't have a smooth transition with Barbara either. Canter is a problem!

I have decided to do something different this ride: ignore cantering all together. We will work on the small transitions from halt to walk to trot and back down. We will work on an essential tool called the half-halt, which is a moment of "pause" to rebalance within a gait, in a transition between gaits, or anytime that the horse needs to refocus and learn to listen to the subtle cues of the rider (a good rider can give subtle cues, mine are a little less refined!)

It occurs to me that I should be able to give myself the same courtesy I want to give Serafin. She is having canter problems but instead of dwelling on them, I am working on things we can do together. We will refocus on canter another time, but I am giving us permission to scrap it for a while.

Could I do this with my own problems? Could I just work on the things that I can reach easily right now that get me ready for my "canter"? I can work on my smaller transitions, doing yoga, writing, being mindful in my interactions, and preparing myself for the next steps of my journey. I can accept the fact that right now I just can't canter! I will be kind to myself and build up the muscles and balance that will make it a breeze when I am finally at the time in my life where I am ready for love. I know it is not now. Why obsess about it? Just trot, baby, trot and walk and halt with perfect harmony. Cantering will come!

On my final day here, the sun is shining once more. Later today I will have horses to prepare for lessons, but for now I am lying in the sun by the pool, memorizing this feeling of lingering summer. It has snowed several times already in Colorado. I will be unpacking winter sweaters and boots upon my return. Here, the sun shines brightly and bravely over the pool. Palm and yucca trees wave their fronds in the whisper of a breeze. The dogs bask in the sun on the patio and birds sing faintly in the garden. My tan has faded. I know it's not really summer any more, but give me just one more day of delusion.

Speaking of deluded, I finally decided that I will not be stopping to see Brad on the way back to Washington. My daughters have been missing me, and I would like to get to them as quickly as possible. There are two routes to take from Colorado, says Mapquest, and I will take the one that does not lead me past Brad's door. I have found myself slipping easily back into the pattern of being the one who is longing, the one who will make the effort, the one forever asking, "Am I good enough?" I am determined not to be that person anymore!

I don't mind reaching out to someone. I think that in a balanced relationship, both parties must do some giving. But if someone is confused about the situation, even after they have "changed," then perhaps that person is destined to remain confused for a lifetime. I am not confused. I know I want a partner in my life. I feel like I have not met him yet. I don't think it's Brad, because the partner I want is a willing participant, not someone I have to convince to love me.

I am planning the South America leg of my journey now, piecing together volunteer and helper work with the places I want to see. There are so many alluring countries in the world. Amanda is heading to Australia next, and then New Zealand. I have never been to Australia. I have never been to Asia. I want to see Bali, China, Thailand, India and Malaysia. I have new friends in different parts of the world now; I can put another trip together. I want to explore as much as I can!

But the other part of me, the homebody, needs to move into my own house in Colorado. One where I can have a meditation and yoga space. I will completely design and plan the gardens and yards. But there will be that pesky mortgage to pay! So eventually, I know, I will have to get a job.

Early on my final morning, Barbara drops me off. We say a hurried goodbye as I jump on the bus and prepare myself for another long day's journey to a new place.

With Amanda

Riding horses on the beach (finally!)

Pamplona: The Running Of The Vikings

The bus to Pamplona is an all-day ride; I get on the bus in Ondara at 8:30, switch in Valencia, and arrive at 6:30 PM. On the bus I write and re-write an email I intend to send to Brad telling him I have changed my plans to see him on my way home. I have felt guilty about planning to resolve this relationship the second I hit the US and anxious about whatever the possible results of this meeting will be. Although Brad and I had great times together, I remain frustrated with his inability to express his feelings – terse responses to emails, ignoring anything I say about my worries. When we were together, it was the same song and dance. Do I want to reopen that door? I am not that person anymore. I feel strong in this decision.

If this trip has changed me at all, I realize, it's that I have gained patience and perspective. I am now a person who can take most small setbacks in stride, although I still have moments of total freak-out, and I insist upon my right to these. But I can take care of myself. I will never again be afraid to say what I want in a relationship; I will never wait in the wings and hope I'm good enough for someone to want me in his life.

Hell, there's always the green card marriage if I get desperate, and won't people be raising their eyebrows when I show up with a twenty-five-year-old Peruvian lad as a husband? I find the idea alternately appealing and depressing.

When the bus arrives, Cristina's friend Nacho sends me a text saying that he will be here in an hour, so I get on WiFi and send my message to Brad before I lose my nerve. It is time to refocus; I have a party to attend. Tomorrow there is a large group of people comprised of locals and couch-surfing visitors who are gathering for a Viking feast.

Part of the Basque region, Pamplona is famous for its San Feria in July, with the renowned running of the bulls. The street where they run the bulls is downtown and we go out, once Cristina has arrived, for drinks and tapas in this area, the Casco Antiguo. People spill from the doors of the tapas bars. We first go to the most famous one, squeeze in and order wine and tapas. I marvel at the women who wear heels all night and stand around at these places. My feet, in flat boots, are aching.

We go to three more tapas places, meeting the various Couchsurfing hosts and guests. Couchsurfing is a trend that has taken off, especially in big cities. People register as hosts or surfers, and match themselves up and, many times, make new friends. I meet a girl named Raquel who wants desperately to live in Seattle.

"Have you been there in the winter when it rains every single day?" I ask.

She admits that she has not. I smile knowingly. But she tells me Pamplona has this type of winter weather as well. We have hit a lucky warm fall patch.

Saturday morning arrives, or afternoon, I should say, as Cristina and I sleep in until eleven. We meet up with the Couchsurfers and we all walk over to the venue for the feast. Long tables are set up and the bartenders are selling cold beer to the gathering crowd. As the place begins to fill and we sit, Nacho comes out with coverings for us to wear, loose tunics of orange, green, or black plastic film. The food begins to appear: large gambas (shrimp) and gulas, jars of pickled white asparagus, and crusty loaves of bread. There are tins of sardines and smoked mussels. Cider and red wine are on each table. My seat partner, Romy, pours a mix of red wine and sparkling water into a cup, and makes one for me. On the other end of the table is a package of "salad," or mixed lettuce, a nod to the one known vegetarian guest. I grab a handful. There are no utensils. I have never in my life eaten salad with my hands!

Across the table from me is a very handsome man from France. He rode his motorcycle here. His motorcycle! He is ironic and adorable and I could be smitten if I thought he would be interested. But he is sitting with a girl who looks like Nicole Kidman. And he is younger than me, but who isn't?

Huge platters of meat are served. There are pork chops, sausages, clumps of blood sausage, some type of beef. I am a little full from the previous course and take it easy on the meat. When the plates are cleared, they hand us all long colorful straws.

"What are these for?" I ask Nacho

"You'll see!"

"Pajas, right?" I ask, trying to remember the Spanish name for straw.

He wags his finger at me with an evil grin. "Pajita. A paja is..." he pantomimes masturbating. "Don't ever tell a man he needs to give you a paja!"

The Viking waiter brings out a large metal bucket full of liquid and people descend with their straws. Someone tells me it is sorbet. Ew, I think, as I watch all the people putting their straws in. But gamely, I take a tentative sip. It is good, liquidy lemon, but I can't get past the Viking germs. One sip is enough for me!

Afterwards they bring out a karaoke machine. At the end of the night, I am asked to join a large group singing "We are the World".

"It's true we make a better world, just you and me," we all belt out.

People are singing, swaying, waving their hands in the air. It is a special moment, made more special by overconsumption of the free red wine.

After karaoke and the cleanup, we all hop a bus back downtown to an Irish Pub, where they have rented the downstairs to our group. A skinny and friendly guy from Africa dances with me and buys me tequila shots for most of the night. I dance and shake my groove thing and have a lot of fun. The French guy is getting ready to leave, and gives me the double-cheek Spanish kiss.

"American kiss now?" I ask. He's so cute! And I am a little drunk.

"I don't know what that is," he says, waving me off with a smile.

"French kiss then?" God, I must be drunk. He laughs, waggles his tongue at me, and beats a hasty retreat. Darn.

I go back to the dance floor and dance some more.

In the morning we meet the Couchsurfing gang for coffee at the famed Café Irunia, then Nacho walks us back to the bus station. Cristina has a wheeled backpack, and I am hauling Big Guy. Nacho does not offer to help with our bags, but lopes down the street as our guide. There is a definite lack of chivalry in the men here. I love Spain and the people, but culturally, they do not have the warmth I was hoping to find. It is still Europe, after all.

On our last night out, we meet with Nica for tapas and drinks. We end up at a bar called la Nus (which Cristina and I laughingly refer to as La Anus) – inside are draped banquets with filmy curtains and Buddha statues. We toast to our time together. We promise to all keep in touch.

Singing "We are the World" with Cristina

With Nacho at the bus station

Goodbye Espana!

I get up with Cristina, who has an early class, and we sneak out before her cranky roommate is awake. We grab coffee and pan tostada at a café near the Metro. I get a cab to the airport bus, and it drops me off at the terminal. Easy. I'm early. Which is better than being late! I have mucho tiempo.

When I get to security, my bag weighs 29 kilos and I must reduce it to 23. Hmmm. But with my newfound patient streak, I move it to the side and begin to select items I think might help. A pair of shoes comes out. My shampoo and conditioner get tossed. An Altoid box contains a lonely half Xanax. I pop it and put the tin in the throw pile. Finally, I remove my bulky toiletry bag, full of things I didn't need. I now must get all the things I pulled out of Big Guy into the plastic souvenir carryon with the questionable zipper or into my bulging shoulder tote! I lean my weight onto the plastic bag, praying the zipper won't pop, and shove the rest into my tote. A small bored audience of fellow travelers is watching. I get Big Guy shut, and triumphantly face my adoring public.

One man raises a congratulatory eyebrow, and I encourage him to applaud so I can bow.

I return to the agent and load Big Guy onto the belt, which shows 22.9, and I nod to him with a satisfied smile. I know he does this all day long, but he plays the game and smiles back, *good job*. Now it is time for Security. These guys are tough. But security in Spain, like many things, is a bit more relaxed. I breeze through, and now I have an overstuffed tote bag to deal with, and almost three hours to kill.

I am ready to go home to my family. I smile, recalling the trip back from Pamplona.

"If one more person gives me a dirty look because of my big bag, I'm going to punch someone," I complained to Cristina as we changed busses after Pamplona and two Spanish women look put out that they must move from the middle of the narrow platform where they are chatting, pulling their own smaller, chic bags.

"Breathe, darling," she advised.

"I think it's time to go home," I admitted.

Now, in the airport, I eyeball other travelers' bags. I need lots of room, but I can reduce what I packed in Big Guy by half. I examine the dirty red duffle. I have a tender spot for this piece of luggage that has been my constant companion for almost four months. *Maybe I'll keep this bag and just not pack it full...* but I hear Cristina's voice in my head. It's too big! In South America I will be working in rougher places, travelling larger distances. I need luggage I can manage more easily. I need to pack less crap!

The flight is nine and a half hours from Madrid to Chicago. I feel fortunate that the seat beside me is empty so I can stretch out, but I end up not getting any rest as I shift one way and another, head resting awkwardly on the armrest and my feet getting knocked into no matter how hard I try to fold them up. The flight leaves late, which makes my connection to Denver tight.

In Chicago, I run through the airport after going through customs and immigration, and security once again. I re-pack some things hurriedly into Big Guy, check him in, and then I am rushing with my bulky carry-ons, shouting "Excuse me!" as I stumble through the corridor, running, then pausing to catch my breath (and cursing my out of shape-ness.) Why are there no clocks in airports? Isn't that kind of stupid in a place where everything is on a tight schedule? I'm late, but how late am I? My gate is the last number in the concourse. Wheezing and staggering, I finally approach, only to see the sign that directs me down another escalator to the gate number.

"Fuck me!" I exclaim. Heads turn. Ooops. I forget that these people all understand English. Sorry, Chicago business men. I feel like commenting snidely that it wasn't really an invitation, but I won't kid myself: I am a mess. Sweaty, in baggy dirty clothes and furry boots, and wheezing like the intake of an accordion; I am sure no one is remotely tempted.

I do make the flight on time, though.

Home Again Home Again, Jiggety Jig

I think that people who travel extensively are either looking for something, or escaping something. In my case it is both. But now that I am back home, it feels like I never went anywhere. I am back in my parents' house. I can't explain the things I went through while I was traveling. Nothing phenomenal happened, and yet I am not the same.

Living out of boxes and suitcases even at home, I am eager to hit the road once more in less than a month. I am planning my next adventure, vowing to take lessons I learned from Spain and apply them to South America. A nagging depression looms over me, but I push it away, trying not to succumb to it.

I'm in a place of limbo between the life I used to have and the life I want to create. Am I really going to survive living in my parents' house while I look for a job and a place of my own? And although I am here to help my them, when will I feel like I can take care of myself? And how will I fare being so far away from my own children? I feel torn, but I know it is time to let them figure out things on their own.

Blog Post : Empty Nest

I have just completed Phase One of a longstanding dream – to travel without a time limit. I spent a little over three months in Spain, zigzagging from North to South, East to West, with a side trip to Morocco. It was wonderful and difficult and scary and relaxing all at once.

Now I am celebrating the holidays with my daughters, back in the USA for a month. As good as it is to be here with them, I sense that things have shifted and it makes me melancholy. My babies are now young women, living their lives. They have jobs I don't drive them to. Friends I have never met. Adventures that I am not sharing in. Hopes and dreams that are their very own.

My kids have grown up.

And now I will have a chance to grow too. Although being a mother to two spectacular girls was my calling, and I will never stop being their mom, I need to look into my heart and determine what I want to do next with my life. They will always need me, but not in the way they once did.

It's a bitter pill for a mom to swallow. But it can also be healing.

As parents we give so much of ourselves to our children, so much that sometimes we lose ourselves in them; they become our identity. I am somebody's mom. But who, exactly, am I?

It is my quest to find that out. I am lucky enough to be able to do it through travel, whereas not all empty-nest parents have that opportunity. I will traverse parts of the world I have never seen, but my daughters will never be far from my thoughts.

Life is learning to let go. A friend with three teenagers once told me that she believed the reason God made some teens so nasty is to help us prepare to let them leave and begin their own lives.

In fact, sometimes we are more than ready for them to take that step by the time they are eighteen! But in other cultures children don't leave the moment they reach eighteen; daughters stay in the home until they are married. Sons stick around to help their aging parents. I wonder if I can reach a compromise where my daughters and I are close in distance, close in our hearts, independent yet intertwined?

I will ponder this when I get back from South America!

I have had almost two months – November through January – to prepare for the next leg of my journey. Reuniting with my daughters in Washington was joyful and comfortable. Christmas was much more peaceful than I had imagined; I also spent much more money than I should have in my month in Washington. As much as I'll miss my family and friends, I am anxious to get on the road again where – paradoxically – I spend far less money!

Back in Colorado, I prepare myself for the South America journey one step at a time. I have bought a bag that is a foot shorter than Big Guy. I call him Buddy. I initially thought about buying a giant backpack but I had to admit to myself that I am just not a backpack girl. It has no wheels, after all. And Buddy, a blue duffle, has wheels and straps to throw it on my back should I need to.

I alternate now between joyful excitement and paralyzing

fear. South America is a daunting prospect, huge and unfamiliar. My plan is to start at the southern tip of Argentina and traverse four countries, working for room and board with hosts I have contacted through Help Exchange. Although I am striking out on my own, I long for a guide of any sort: physical, metaphorical, spiritual! Anything!

After my email to Brad, I got a reply that was indignant – "I really wanted to see you! Why are you doing this?" Soon another lengthy response came from him: emotional, distraught, once again wanting to sever all contact, as he did when we broke up a year and a half ago.

My immediate reaction was relief. That says a lot.

Now my waters are no longer muddied by a dead relationship that was never authentic in the first place. Although it saddens me that he needs all or nothing – either we are in love or incommunicado - I now feel free to go on, but to what?

I know I do not want to pursue one-night-stands; my failed attempt at romance through Spain has shown me that. Nor do I want to live without love and companionship. But for now, I can't have what I want. No more sexual misadventures on the next leg of my journey. I am seeking clarity, not confusion. I will take a temporary vow of celibacy. For the moment, I decide I just won't canter.

The last few days here are enjoyable. On New Year's Eve I talk my sister and her husband Paul into going to a black and white ball at the art museum, co-sponsored by elephantjournal, the online magazine I occasionally write for. Paul is my midnight kiss. My sister nods approvingly, then gets her kiss. It's now 2012. I am gearing up for a four-month trip through South America and my two-hundred-hour yoga training in Costa Rica. Who knows what this year will bring?

Argentina: El Calafate, And My First Stay In A Bunk Bed

It is snowing in Colorado. The week has been emotional – waking up in the middle of the night, my head spinning about this trip. The continent of South America is so very large! And I don't know how in the world I'll get from the bottom to the top, then to Costa Rica! Never mind that I have three months to do it. Never mind that I have done a lot of research and scheduling. Nothing will calm the doubt-monkeys in my mind.

On the morning of my flight, I wake up more excited than scared. It is finally time. And I feel prepared. I successfully packed my smaller bag and found a secure way to strap my yoga mat to the outside. I swapped my zebra tote for a backpack. I have Argentinian pesos in my wallet and a shuttle pick-up scheduled at the airport in El Calafate. Yep, I think I'm ready!

My dad drives me to the airport. His presence is steadying. "I wish I was coming with you, Katie. You'll have a great time, have a few mishaps, and make all the right decisions. What an adventure!"

I am still anxious, but it's not paralyzing. I am on my way!

I love airports. I enjoy people-watching the most: seeing how people are dressed, smiling at the children pulling pint-sized luggage, and wondering where everyone is headed. I cruise past podiums and imagine I am going to places I've never been, or some I've never even heard of. Or I see a flight to Cleveland and feel a little smug that I am going to Buenos Aires.

However, it's a scramble when we land at George Bush International Airport in Texas. I have no time to waste! My plane to Argentina has already started to board. I am suddenly one of those people who runs up the aisle as soon as the plane lands, nudging fellow passengers out of the way as they unload their roller-bags from overhead bins. I try to have patience, really, I do, but I cannot miss my flight! I race-walk through the airport, remembering my last time running and wheezing with asthma. I huff and puff to the intersection where Concourse C becomes Concourse E. It's much farther than it looked on the map!

A cart-driver takes pity on me. "Need a ride?" he asks. Thanking him, I get in and he rushes me to the gate. I tell him it's my first trip to South America.

"Thank you so much!" I exclaim as I hop down from the cart. The kindness of strangers has begun early on this journey.

I am seated in the back of the plane among a group of German nuns. This makes me smile. Is someone trying to send me a message about the trajectory of this trip? I sleep on the ten-hour flight as best I can.

The final flight will get me to El Calafate. It is a three-hour plane ride from Buenos Aires. It would have been thirty-five hours by bus. I peer out the window of the aircraft, enchanted by sunshine playing in the summer-blue sky. I left Colorado in winter, but it is summer in Argentina. My final vehicle today will be a shuttle to take me to the hostel I have booked for two nights. For the first time, I am staying in a shared room. Four beds, three of them occupied by strangers. This type of arrangement has always made me uneasy; what better reason to try it?

We fly over clouds that stretch out like quilt batting, giving only glimpses of the terrain below. Sunshine, beaches, the Andes, glaciers… I packed lighter this time, but did I pack right?

I close my eyes and thoughts of Brad invade my mind, but it is like poking at a faded bruise that doesn't really hurt anymore. I just sometimes remember that it is still there. Even though he let me know in no uncertain terms that he never wanted to talk to me again, I feel free and mentally unencumbered. Perhaps we needed to revisit everything that was wrong in our relationship to truly end it. Opening up the old wounds and discovering strength in myself has made me more independent. Humans leave parts of ourselves behind all the time; shedding the skin of the past and moving into the future, and it is bound to hurt sometimes. Ultimately, the growth achieved is worth the struggle.

When I leave the airport, I easily find my shuttle to the hostel. The bus fills with passengers and off we go. As we enter town small guesthouses and hostels dot the landscape. Many are made of logs in a rustic mountain style, others are constructed with tin siding. Two by two – for everyone seems to be part of a couple – the shuttle drops off guests at various hostels or hotels. The younger ones have huge backpacks and hiking gear, but there are also some older European couples, one of which gets dropped off at a five-star hotel with a golf course. I gaze at it longingly, wondering what my cheap hostel will be like. I am the only solo passenger on the bus, as well as the last one. The driver flirts with me as he brings my bag up the stairs to the reception desk. My brain is tired. My

Spanish is tired. I'm not sure of everything he says to me and perhaps it's best not to know!

I find that I am sharing my room with three young girls – two from Germany and one from England, but all live together in Buenos Aires now. The worst part of the hostel is that the beds are bunks, and since these girls checked in ahead of me, I am left with a top bunk. The frame is wobbly and there is no ladder. Oh shit! Fortunately, one girl takes pity on me and offers to swap. The best part of the hostel is the price – about seventeen dollars per night. The staff is friendly and helpful, and there is a small breakfast each morning.

In the morning, my alarm wakes me. It is already light outside. Today I will visit the famous blue glacier known as Perito Moreno. I have booked a tour so I wake up early and pad downstairs for coffee, trying not to wake my roomies. All is quiet. It's eight on the dot. I am anxious, have I missed my bus? The desk clerk assures me that I have not. The eight o'clock pickup finally happens at 8:40. Argentine time is, apparently, similar to Spanish time.

The region of Patagonia encompasses the southern part of South America and is shared by two countries: Argentina and Chile, with the Andes Mountain range dividing them. The Calafate area of Patagonia is the Wyoming of Argentina – wide open spaces under an expanse of blue sky with a backdrop of craggy mountains. The bus travels through grassy farmland. A herd of horses run through a scrubby field on my left. It is a rainbow of horse colors: bays, whites, chestnuts, and blacks, herded by a man on horseback. Is he a gaucho, an Argentine cowboy? On the right, Lake Argentino stretches out at the base of the mountains, the color of sparkling turquoise. Our tour guide tells us that sometimes chunks of ice break off the glacier and drift down to the lake. I picture it like a giant blue margarita.

Chamomile flowers edge the road like a sprinkling of snow. Hundreds of sheep roam around an estancia, or farm, to the right. They, too, are like patches of snow over the dry landscape. The land stretches on and on out the bus window as we go along the desolate road. Patagonia is an expanse of dry plains that goes on as far as the eye can see. We enter Glacier Park and catch our first view of the glacier, with a rainbow arcing perfectly over it.

At Glacier National Park I board the boat takes a group out to see the glacier up close. The wind takes my breath away and spumes of ice-cold water fly up from the lake. Large chunks of ice, cartoonish blue, float nearby. After the boat ride, we are free to walk among the pathways that have viewpoints of each face of the glacier, and wind around through the forest back up to the parking area and snack bar.

The Perito Moreno glacier reminds me of a huge blue and white phyllo pastry, with flakes of ice slabs and deep azure gaps in between its layers. Every once in a while, you hear a sharp "crack" like a gunshot, and a slab or a chunk comes cascading off the wall, falling into the waters below. It is impressive and impossible to capture with my camera.

Some people say, when they witness this type of natural wonder, that they feel insignificant. For me the opposite is true. When I gaze out over the expanse of glacier, its peaks and blue swirls like crazy icing on a giant's birthday cake, I feel at one with the universe. There is a sense of being part of it all: the German, Japanese, English, and other languages eddying all around me, the sun warm on my back, the mountains, the trees, and the glacier itself. It makes me feel connected to the world, and, more importantly, to myself. I'm not really alone in any of my experiences, after all. For the moment I am right where I should be.

The second night at the hostel, there is an asado, or barbecue. I sign up, as I want to experience it, but I have mixed feelings about the whole "eat a bunch of meat" thing. My aversion to meat-eating is becoming stronger, and I know that there are some things I will phase out soon. Eating meat is one. Drinking too much is another. But by the end of the night, I will have done both of these.

As I sit down at the table inside, I ask to join my young roommates. Samira, the youngest, is the same age as my Emily. Sometimes in these settings I feel so out of place! But we sit and await the meat fest, talking with two young men at the table as we wait. As the first pieces are placed on the wooden plates before us, I bow my head to thank the animal that sacrificed its little furry life to feed us tonight. Charlotte, one of the German girls, tells me that Samira and Alice have both been vegetarians. Alice says she grew up that way, and that meat used to make her sick. She digs into her chorizo with a smile.

"What about you?" I ask Samira. "Why were you a vegetarian?"

"My sister said she wouldn't play with me if I ate meat."

I laugh. "That is the best reason I've ever heard!"

After dinner, we drift outside to sit on the wooden porch. I chat with a Swiss boy and a local Argentinian one. They are so young, so beautiful and unfettered. The part I love about meeting fellow travelers is hearing their stories and sharing mine, making friends for the moment, and some that may last beyond the trip. Thank you, Facebook. The hostel environment is conducive to new friendships; it's a hip, social atmosphere. Maybe I have been missing out on something by not staying at hostels while traveling alone!

This year I only made two New Year's Resolutions: a daily practice of writing, and a daily practice of yoga. Yoga is harder to do while traveling, I can write on a plane, train, or bus. The yoga teacher training that awaits me at the end of this trip is both exciting and scary, for it signifies a possible career change. And I know that I don't feel fit enough right now – the ten pounds that found me in my Spain travels have been joined by five more Christmas pounds. Now I need to lose that weight and do a daily practice to be strong enough to take full advantage of the training. Of course I know that a person does not have to look like the cover of a yoga magazine to teach a class. But I also know where my body feels best, and this ain't it! I love my curves, but I love them more when they are a little less, well, curvy.

In the morning I check out of the hostel at ten and I will catch a bus at four o'clock. My next stop is Puerto Madryn, a coastal town halfway between Calafate and Buenos Aires. I have plenty of time to do some yoga. But where? I psyche myself up as I haul my wheeled duffle and its attendant yoga mat all over town. On the main street of El Calafate there is a grassy area, park-like, between the lanes. Perfect for yoga? Maybe. I can totally envision it. The problem is, the girl doing yoga in my vision isn't me. The me doing yoga in this public place with cars going by at an alarming rate might be getting rotten veggies thrown at her from a passing remise (taxi) or getting hauled off by disgruntled policia. I chicken out.

I walk by a place I saw yesterday as I strolled through town – a collection of shops with a garden and deck behind. I peer around. It seems to be part of a cute but empty café. I find some courage and ask the woman at the counter in my substandard Spanish if it would be all right if I did some yoga on her deck. She agrees, I roll out my mat and do about half an hour. Rejuvenated, I stroll to the bus station.

After a twenty-hour bus ride, feeling tired and dirty, I find the hostel I booked, which is close to the bus station. I am dismayed to see that the shared dorm is dark and smelly, with ugly metal bunk beds and a bathroom that is musty. The owner, a stout and serious woman, explains that the five of the six beds are taken, and the girl who remains sleeping in this dorm has claimed the last bottom bunk. (I had previously emailed requesting a bottom bunk if possible!) Taking pity on me, the owner's husband asks if there are rooms left in the main house. There is one, and it's completely empty, so they put me into it with no extra charge. The room is clean and bright, with a shared bathroom. Score!

The next day I take the tour to see Magellan penguins at Punto Tumbo, one and a half hours from Puerto Madryn. The tour includes an optional stop on the way for a boat ride to see dolphins, but I decide not to go; I want to save money. I walk down the road to see the beach, but this is a port, a fishing village, not a pristine cute beach town. It smells like fish or cows, something vaguely pungent. I see an interesting monument – a lady with hands in prayer, her eyes cast upward, and a star above her head. Behind her is a ship's mast. It is a memorial to los desaparecidos – the disappeared sailors. I try to read the plaques dedicated to the lost men. Their pictures adorn tablets saying that their families will never forget them, will always be waiting. I am moved, almost to tears. I don't know why, but I accept the emotion, glad to be able to feel this kind of empathy. Perhaps it is because I am a mother. I send out a prayer for the families of these men, wishing my children were here for me to hug.

When the dolphin-watchers return, we continue to Punto Tumbo. I befriend my seatmates: a young woman from Sweden and a Chinese-American from Texas named Jenny. When we get to the penguins, Jenny and I walk together, finding the cutest penguins to take pictures of. These penguins in this arid landscape, not an ice floe in sight, are a bit disconcerting to us at first. They dig burrows in the ground under the scrubby bushes. The babies are a few months old, almost the size of the adults, but still covered with fuzzy grey down. They help each other shed the fluff with their beaks. By the time we have walked to the end of the road we have seen thousands of penguins. They dot the landscape like black-and-white rocks, standing in the sun, lying under the buses, solo, in pairs, or in family groups. They sleep in the shade of the raised walkways, feather to feather like an overcrowded kids' slumber party. Jenny takes a video of a baby flapping his wings and me encouraging him; teaching a penguin to fly.

I have a date tonight. He is a friend of the hostel owner who was visiting last night: a boisterous man who entered the house singing loudly. He came to the table and met the group of us who were sitting there. I, the fool, said something slightly coquettish and he zeroed in on me like a jovial predator. He tells me there is a point at the top of the town, El Indio, where I can see the whole city and take a picture. Then we can go to dinner. Upon my return from the penguins, the hostel owner tells me that this man, Roberto, has been by already. I was hoping he would forget. I'm a bit nervous. However, it will be great practice for my Spanish.

We go to El Indio that night and I see the lights of Puerto Madryn spread out below. The casino hotel is lit up with blue lights, the flag waving on top of the hill echoes the colors of dusk, and city lights sparkle along the sea.

Roberto chooses a restaurant on the beach and he orders for me, which I don't mind. I told him I am on my way to being vegetarian, but not quite there yet. He gets me a steak. It comes served with eggs on top, and he tells me that they call this style "caballo", which means horse. I pale and drop the knife until he assures me that it is not horse, promise! It's because the eggs are "riding" on top. Was he positive? Yes. Okay. I'm really going to quit this soon, but the steak is delicious: Argentina is known for its meat.

Afterwards he wants to park and look at the ocean, and I humor him with a few tepid kisses, but I explain that I am not here for this kind of thing. Just what I told the bus driver the night before! It seems to be a convincing argument. He takes me home without dispute.

I am beginning to feel stronger in these situations; feeling that I can speak up for myself. I don't owe anybody anything! My company is gift enough.

Perito Moreno glacier, El Calafate Argentina

Penguins at Porto Tumbo

Buenos Aires: Hot In The City

On the bus to Buenos Aires, I am sitting across from two children aged eight and six. We talk a bit; they are adorable. I think of how nice it will be to teach again. I hope I will be teaching yoga, but I also miss classroom teaching. I love the wisdom of children, the sincerity of their questions and their honesty. The kids ask me where I'm from and we talk about the places they have heard of in the United States: Hollywood, Nueva York, Miami. The boy asks me if there are sharks where I live.

"Not in Colorado," I assure him.

"I've heard, but I don't know if it's true, that there is a boy there who was raised by wolves!"

I smile. "I think," I tell him, struggling for the Spanish words, "that is a story, a book." I hate to disappoint him.

I wake to Pink Floyd over the bus speakers in the morning. After an eighteen-hour bus ride we are finally approaching Buenos Aires! And of course, I get off at the wrong bus station. But all for the best, because I get a cab for about eight bucks right to the door without having to worry about hauling luggage on the Metro.

My host here is Juan Carlos. He is friendly and mellow. I will work for my bed and supper, but he has nothing for me to do the first day. "Relax" he says. So I do. I check my email, write to my family, take some dirty clothes to the lavendaria, take a siesta, go back and pick my laundry up, hang it on the line – just normal stuff. Taking care of business. I will begin to explore Buenos Aires in earnest tomorrow. It is very hot here, and stores close at mid-day like they do in Spain. I will have to re-institute siesta time in my schedule! Back in Washington they are having record snow.

The house is like a large puzzle. Walking in the front gate from the street, there is a long narrow walkway to the gate at the back, which opens up into the main courtyard. Off the courtyard are several small rooms, not connected: the kitchenette, the bathroom, Juan Carlos' study, and his bedroom. Up the narrow concrete stairs, there is a rooftop terrace. My room is up here: small, but comfortable. There is a large child's wading pool on the roof. Wow, I think with a smile, I scored a place with a pool!

There is also a Siamese cat – Tato the Gato. We have bonded already and Juan Carlos warns that the cat will probably be in my room now. And indeed, he does sit on my lap while I check my email. It's almost too hot for this, but I let it slide. Kitty love is good.

In the evening I spread my mat on the tiles of the courtyard to do an hour of yoga. Then I make pesto, Juan Carlos makes a salad, and we dine together and converse in Spanish. This is nice!

In the evening as I go to retrieve my laundry from the line, I startle a woman who is also at the clothesline. She is a houseguest staying in the other little apartment, but she is leaving in a day. Pity, because I like this gregarious woman, who is Spanish.

"Do you like Buenos Aires?" I ask.

"No. Not much. I miss Spain."

I agree, Spain and my Spanish friends have been on my mind lately. I ask her for her recommendations of what to see while I am here. The subject of men eventually comes up. It begins by talking about sunbathing, then our bellies (which we both wish were smaller) then motherhood and divorce. She tells me about a man she is dating. He is nice, short, with beautiful eyes, and he treats her well when they get together. There is only one problem – he is married.

Who am I to judge? But I tell her I think it's not good, that it causes such harm when someone cheats. I tell her that my husband cheated on me, and she confesses that hers did, too. She claims that her boyfriend is unhappy in his marriage and that his wife does not want to do things with him. She met him when he was on a vacation that the wife did not go on.

We part, and I am left to reflect on the conversation. I get it, I know that it is tempting to meet someone new and keep the façade going at home. It's an adrenaline shot. I remember Brad saying that much of the appeal of his big affair was the forbidden fruit aspect of it. I tried to not hold it against him - the fact that he cheated on his wife for over a year - but I think it says something about the character of a man. Men, when unhappy in their marriages, find someone else to have sex with, while maintaining the lie of their union at home. Why? For the kids? For appearances? Women, on the other hand, find something else to do, not necessarily an affair. In my case it was college and riding horses. Others find new hobbies.

The old adage goes, if he'll cheat with you, he'll cheat on you.

So many women are "waiting for him to leave his wife." Are we so desperate? What if, in a show of solidarity, all women refused to sleep with married men? We would cause a revolution! Think about it; if no one would sleep with married men, they couldn't cheat! They would have to work out their problems in their marriages and become single without the safety net of someone else's arms and bed to immediately crawl into.

As for me, I admit to not being perfect. I never cheated on my husband, but I did cheat on a boyfriend when I was in my 20's. And at the end of my relationship with Brad I fooled around with my sexy handyman, who had been my fantasy to take my mind off the fact that the man I really loved "wasn't sure" about me.

Giving in to temptation makes a person realize how easy it is to do. It makes me wonder if there is ever such a thing as a loyal and true relationship. I will have to remove these barriers to trust if I am ever to have a successful partnership in my life. I know this. I will work on it. But for now I will remain an unenthusiastic celibate.

The next day Juan Carlos and I do a little work around his house, trimming and watering plants, and then go to San Anselmo, where his other house is. I scrub the kitchen walls while he does some repairs, then I am free to explore. The day is hot. I grab some empanadas and a drink while I examine my map, then I head down the street to Calle Florida, where artisans spread out their wares for sale. I stroll along, trying to get a feel for this big city.

For me, Buenos Aires lacks the charm of Spanish cities. It is bigger and dirtier and feels in disrepair. The sidewalks buckle and you have to watch your step for the dog poop that no one ever picks up. The subways are ancient. The bus system is difficult to navigate.

I am trying to feel happy and fortunate that I can explore and travel, but I miss having company to do it. I miss nice hotels, at least a little. I have lost my motivation to explore on my own. I walk around for about five hours until my feet and even my hips hurt, and then make my way home for a siesta. After I, the lady of Perpetual Lostness, walk blocks out of my way trying to find the right street.

I think the lonely part of solo travel is what's making me reminisce about a time when I did not travel alone. For most people, trips are a respite from real life- brief vacations -and they are lived that way: dinner out, lying on the beach, sight-seeing, museums, and shopping. But this is my real life, at least for now. And it would be nice to have someone to share it with, someone to chat with as we stroll around or do our work-trade, gardening, cleaning, or whatever. I miss having company. It doesn't need to be a lover, though, does it? Sex complicates things, and I surely don't need complications. Maybe, then, it's time to find a Buenos Aires friend.

I remember the Couchsurfing network, which connects travelers to hosts all over the world through their website, but also provides social opportunities for travelers and those new to a city. I decide to check out some of the Couchsurfing events. I find a listing on Couchsurfing for a group doing yoga and slack line in a park today – what luck! I check with Juan Carlos for directions, and after a morning of helping him fix some things in his car, I'm off to find the event.

I scold the Disney Princess in my head, who is trying to tag along. I clicked the organizer's profile, and found him to be, well, male, for a start, as well as really buff, not too young (mid-thirties) and from Vancouver, Canada. We have a lot in common. Princess has him falling in love with me immediately, and me taking him back to "my" place to cook us dinner. Juan Carlos will smile on affectionately and, of course, allow my prince to stay so he can make love to me all night. We continue to see each other this whole whirlwind love-affair week in Buenos Aires, he will accompany me to the yoga park next week, and of course, to the condo in Chile to celebrate my birthday. Sternly, I ask Disney Princess to leave my head. I remind her of my temporary vow of celibacy. She sighs, pouts her pretty lips, and goes. I shake my head and go catch the bus.

Blog Post: The Death of a Disney Princess

I need to commit a murder. Not an actual one, of course, but a metaphorical one.

You see, there is a Disney Princess living in my head. She has been there for as long as I can remember. I'm not sure which one she is, or if she is just a compilation of all the worst ones: passive, helpless yet optimistic, beautiful and fragile, golden or raven-haired, perfect lips and huge sparkling eyes, and waiting-for-a-prince. If I had my way she would be a combination of Belle (bookish and independent) and Mulan (tomboy and unconventional), but I'm afraid she is more like Sleeping Beauty or Cinderella. She lives her life waiting to be rescued.

She must die!

You may think me a bit harsh, but this broad is screwing up my life. I'm single and happy – most of the time. After some attempts at physical encounters in the past year that were unsatisfactory and boring, I have settled into a reluctant state of celibacy; accepting this temporary state the way one drives through a patch of thick fog on the highway:

mindfully, carefully, and with lights on. Right now I am focusing on creating a new life exactly the way I want it to be. But here comes Cinder-Beauty, just when I am feeling content, insisting that I am incomplete until I meet the Prince.

And then I start looking for him. In the grocery store, at the New Year's Eve party, even in fictitious places and dreams. I recently read a memoir by a man I admire. I read right up until the point that he met his wife-to-be, then I lost interest in the book.

Princess-projecting much?

So I'm printing a collage of all the Disney gals, folding it neatly into an envelope, and transporting it to Chile, my next stop on this trip. At sunset on my 49th birthday, I will shred her into pieces and burn them (in a fire-safe bowl of course.) And I will do this in front of Pablo Neruda's house, Chascona ("woman with tousled hair", which is a version of what my last ex-love used to call me.)   I may even read a piece of Neruda's poetry at this ceremony-for-one.

I think Cinder-Beauty, with her last dying gasp, will appreciate all the romantic irony.

Oh, Buenos Aires. There is no such thing as door-to-door service here! After I take the bus I walk about twenty-five more blocks. I assure myself that if I don't find the yoga group, I will lounge in a shady spot, read, write, and do my own yoga. It is good to have a plan B.

I wander by a group of three people lounging under some trees. They eye me as I walk by, looking curiously at my yoga mat. I wonder if they are part of the group, but I don't see anyone with a yoga mat or a slack line, so I don't stop to ask. How do you find a small group of strangers in a big park?

Soon a boy I passed earlier runs after me and asks if I am with the Couchsurfing event. I say I am looking for it; so is he and his friend, so I join them. Soon this young man, George, asks another person, who turns out to be the yoga teacher who organized the event. A few others join in eventually, and they play around with the slack line, which is like a tightrope that they stretch between two trees. I don't try it, but others do, and I enjoy watching them balancing precariously, then jumping or falling off. Eventually, we do the yoga session, and I find I have spent a luxurious four hours or so just lounging and getting to know these people and making new friends.

I shoulder my mat roll and walk out of the park, checking the map. There is an interesting bridge noted, so I find it and cross the river. The bridge, Puente de Mujeres, is like a sail to the sky, a graceful triangle that stretches over the river. There are numerous people out strolling, rollerblading, and walking on the bridge or the promenades on either side. An old sailing ship is docked at the harbor; it looks like a pirate ship. As I pass it, I hear music and see a couple dancing tango in the middle of the sidewalk. The man is elegant in a white shirt and dark pants, and the woman, her satiny black hair pulled back, has a black dress and impossibly spiky purple stilettos. A slender belt of silver links dangles around her hips, shimmering as she moves. A piece of canvas covered with chalk is spread beneath their feet. And, oh, those feet – swooping and bending delicately, as she moves her foot in an arc around him, stepping back, back, then a dip and a forward stride. They are so in synch! I imagine how I would be stepping all over, tripping, fumbling, and a general disaster at this dance. I watch for a long while, appreciating the poetry in their movements.

On the way back to the apartment I see the Casa Rosada, the Argentine president's mansion, beautifully illuminated at dusk by a series of pink lights. It looks magical. I take some photos and try to look at the city anew. I feel rejuvenated by my yoga day and exploration.

This trip feels different than my trip to Spain, and not just because I have sworn off sex. It comes with the heavy realization that, at the end of the line looms the obligation to actually do something with all of this travel and experience. To use my yoga training to start teaching. To sculpt and coax my words into something I can use to share my experience with others. To use my increased Spanish to assist my next career steps, and to find ways to keep improving. And, of course, if all else fails, to get a real job. It's a long way off, but as I have learned, it will be here before I can blink.

During the week, Juan Carlos and I go out to the Dragon festival in Chinatown, make some dinners together, and spend some time doing repairs in his house and his rental apartment. He is a kind and mellow host, content to speak English or Spanish with me, depending on my mood. He allows time for siesta, which is muy importante! Tato Gato often sleeps in my bed.

After a siesta one day, we take Juan Carlos' car, an old VW bus, and bring new sheets and towels to his tenants at the other apartment, which is near San Telmo. He tells me about the Sunday feria that spreads out through many blocks, so I bid him adios to go check it out.

I am still being careful with my shopping, so I wander through cautiously, extra vigilant about my backpack and its contents in this crowd. I have heard Buenos Aires has some talented pickpockets! I stroll and talk to some of the vendors, who are generally happy to let me practice my Spanish on them. As I walk around, I realize two things: that I am running low on money again and that I have a persistent ache in my lower back. Gingerly I walk back through the cobbled streets, protecting my back. Was it the yoga? The siesta? Either way, I'm a big baby about discomfort so I tread carefully so as not to pull it any farther out of whack.

At the ATM machine, I glance around. No one is there, and this one is inside the building, so I feel safe. Still, I separate the cash I withdraw, one thousand pesos, into several pockets and pouches so I don't seem rich if I buy something from a vendor. "Shit!" I hear a voice say and a girl peers around the corner from the second ATM. "Is that one working?"

I step away from the machine, tucking the money away. "Yeah, go ahead," I tell her. Ow, my back still hurts, maybe I should pause here and do some stretches?

"Wait. Is this your card?" she points at the machine.

Oh my god what an idiot I am! "Yes, thank you. I cannot believe I did that," I say, embarrassed. I retrieve the card and put it safely away, then go about my way. I silently berate myself, then let up. The worse that could happen, I guess, is that someone else would take it, but probably the machine would have eaten the card and I would have had to retrieve it at the bank. I would hate to lose my debit card on this long of a trip! All's well that ends well, I guess.

I do a little shopping, wandering into an indoor antiques mall. There is not much to see, but as I loop back through, I spot a café. I take a table.

At the next table sits an older woman, probably about seventy years old. She has flame-red hair, and the coral of her blouse is matched by the color of her lipstick. She begins to talk to me in Spanish. "What sign are you? Horoscope," she prompts.

Now this intrigues me. I love astrology. "Pisces," I tell her.

She looks at me and nods thoughtfully. "Yes. Small ears, blue eyes. You are very generous," she tells me, "but maybe too generous with your heart sometimes."

I nod. I am trying to decide if she is clairvoyant or just astute. Then she surprises me. "You hurt in your body. Your shoulder?"

I shake my head. "My back," I tell her.

"You are by yourself?"

"Yes."

"You should be accompanied by a Leo."

No, I think. This part she has wrong. Brad is a Leo. "No, I was with a Leo. We broke up."

She purses her lips. "Leos are difficult. They like to play." I agree. Her food comes and I take some time to write in my notebook as I sip my coffee. She points to my notebook. "What kind of paper do you prefer?"

I gesture and shrug.

"Plain, or with lines?"

"I like the lines."

"You are a person who needs a guide." She reaches for my notebook to look at the writing. It's sloppy, I know, but I'm just going to type it up later! " You are a little disorganized. You like to be led."

This rings true. I am learning how to muddle through on my own, but I would rather be taken around. I remember touring Madrid with Cristina and Nica. I prefer to have people show me the way. I like to believe I am getting tougher, little by little, when I don't have anyone to help me. I have been doing okay alone. Haven't I?

"You're a fortune teller?" She shakes her head, not understanding the word I used. I try again. "You guess the future?"

"No, I look at characteristics of a person. Only up there," she indicates the sky, "knows the future. Do you believe in God?" She looks at me sternly.

"Yes. In some type of God, anyway."

"I think you do not have children."

"No, I do. I have two daughters. They are my world."

"Hmmm. You seem like someone with no children." This disturbs me. Do I? "When you go traveling, you make up your mind. You go! You don't like to be alone, though." I shake my head; no I don't. "You have endured some suffering, and now you are going through a test. Many doors to open. You must be careful, open the door and look around before you step through."

"I will. Thank you." I gather my things to leave, turning back at the door to wave my thanks.

Back out at the endless street of vendors, I contemplate her words. I don't think I'm impulsive, but I am strong willed. It disturbs me that she did not sense that I am a mother, for it is the most important thing I am. Maybe it doesn't seem like it, since I am traveling and not home with my children. And maybe the suffering part was more correct than I would like to admit. It was the heavy sad weight of my life that made me want to escape it with travel. She may have gotten some things right, but she was damned sure wrong about the Leo!

I meander through the street vendors, buying a few presents for my kids, and some earrings for myself. I talk to a vendor of stone pendants from Columbia and with a seller of beautiful beaded earrings. It is so interesting to meet all the people from different walks of life. This is the nice part of wandering around in the big city. It also gives me the chance to practice Spanish with different people, getting used to different accents.

I stroll down the street and find myself in the square. At the café Arbol I order rum and coke and a hamburger. The burger is tasteless to me. I think it is time I give up meat altogether. I don't really enjoy it anymore. I push my plate aside, watching the night life begin. At the plaza, men are breaking down the booths and setting up tables. A few yards away, I hear music. I follow the sounds to a square on the plaza lit by shiny Christmas lights spreading out over a dance floor. The dancers are locals who come to the square on Sunday to practice their tango steps. Some are good, some not as talented. But they all look like they are having a great time. I notice many older couples. I wonder whether they are married, if they have been together forever. What's the story? I always want to know everyone's story!

The next day is hot. Again. Juan Carlos and I work in the morning, have lunch, and then I spend some time surfing the web. I feel lazy, but I have such little time left. I should go somewhere! He tells me what bus to take to go to La Boca, where I have been told to watch my bag carefully. When I showed my ingenious little clip (a large paperclip threaded through the zippers) to him, he warned me that I still need to wear the bag on my front, as the robbers will cut the backpack with a knife and just reach in, even with the zippers secured.

It is time to ask myself a very important question: What is my freaking problem? I have a bad attitude, and I feel like I can't get out of Buenos Aires fast enough! It is a hard city to navigate; the subways are archaic and very limited, and the buses, when I can figure them out, are hot and crowded. This city itself has scattered charm, but I mainly find it dirty and hot. I have met some wonderful and friendly people, but it just isn't my kind of place.

I have been overly alert (or tried to be) about my backpack

or purse, and this is stressing me out. I've had no reason so far to worry, but the vigilance makes me anxious, as if my pickpocket is waiting around every corner.

Riding the bus to La Boca, I caught a glimpse of myself in a window: a fat disheveled frizzy-haired blonde with a scowl. Is that really me? How do I fix this?

I am hoping that the next part of my journey - a week of yoga, meditation and working the land - will do the trick. I also hope it will not be quite so hot at the yoga park. And finally, I admit that I am tired of traveling alone. Yeah, I said it. I am sick to death of my own feeble company. I'm missing physical contact like an addict with withdrawals. This must be what it is like to give up a substance addiction – to walk around with cravings when you see others with a cigarette or a drink. That's how I feel when I see couples kissing or walking hand in hand.

I take photos of colorful houses, but my heart is not in it. I look at the map and note the nearest subway, a hundred miles away. By now it is dusk. Maybe I should just go home; do some yoga, cook some veggies, write… but no! I reprimand myself. Walk around! See this city!

I do my best to explore, but the blocks are long and I am tired. After another hour I get a bus and a cab to Juan Carlos' place. Minutes after I arrive, the sky cracks open and it begins to pour down rain. I fall asleep with the rain hammering the tin roof.

It is my last in town, and I decide to take the train to Tigre, a touristic section of Buenos Aires. Juan Carlos has given me specific directions so I don't get lost.

Tigre is lovely and picturesque, with a network of rivers running through. I take a boat ride on the river that will take me to a restaurant and a little pueblo. The boat passes private homes with docks naming their spot: Babylon, Nido (nest), Suerte Loca (crazy luck). I smile. They remind me of the island homes of the Florida Keys. In the town I explore the Puerto de Frutos – which is not a fruit market as I had thought but a large market with stores selling many things – mates and bombillas, children's toys, purses, leather goods, baskets, and furniture.

I return to Buenos Aires, finding the house with no incident, and go to bed early. I leave in the morning for Yoga Park, and I am eager to get out of Buenos Aires. This is not a city for a person with no money who does not like to walk until her feet fall off.

At midday I get a car service to Plaza Once to take the bus. I have to bring my suitcase on board, as there is no luggage storage like on the long-distance buses. I let the driver know where I need to go, and a kind man helps me hoist my bag past the narrow aisle and onto a vacant seat. I take a nap and look around when I wake. Where are we? The driver lets some people off but does not announce the stop, and a few moments later I figure out that I missed it. Frustrated, I take some deep breaths and berate myself for being too timid. I need to speak up! I take this bus to the end and get into the line to take the next bus back again.

One of the skinniest dogs I have ever seen is hanging around the bus station. I call him over. He's friendly and sweet. No sign of the bus yet, so I buy a sandwich, take two bites, and give the rest to my dog. I feel better. A sure way to forget your own silly problems is to help someone with bigger ones. Even, or maybe especially, if that someone is a dog.

Eco Yoga Park – Getting Down And Dirty With Hare Krishnas

When I arrive at the park, I sign the register and put my bags in a long wooden building with tables. The volunteer coordinator, Ashley, is an energetic British man with a monk haircut: the sides of his head are shaved and the middle part left long and gathered into a ponytail.

"You ready for yoga? Just leave your things!"

So I immediately go to a yoga class. There is a young man (a monk, I learn later) teaching. He begins with a spine twist and goes into Sun Salutations. He explains in English, but it is not his native language, I can tell. I glance around as we twist and bend. The majority of the people here look to be in their twenties. I am almost always the oldest person around, but I'm getting used to it.

As the afternoon turns into evening, I begin to meet people. There are a ton of volunteers. In fact, everyone here is volunteering; at the moment there are no true guests. Volunteers pay a bit for their room and food, but we work four hours a day as well.

The schedule is explained to me by a vibrant girl from New York who directs women's theatre. Another woman I meet is writing a book and a screenplay about a traumatic incident from her life. There are several women here who are teachers like me. It is an interesting mix. My roommate is a nineteen-year-old Danish girl who does amazing sketches.

We get up at six to work in the garden. The property is huge; it must encompass almost ten acres, several of which are devoted to an organic garden. Everyone works in the garden until breakfast. After breakfast, we work another two hours, some in the garden, some in the kitchen, and others at various tasks like building benches or making art.

The meals consist of vegan food, and they use no garlic or onions, so things are a little bland. Breakfast sometimes comes with what we call "pink goo," a rubbery paste made from corn flour, sugar, and strawberry juice. I skip the goo, but I like the homemade bread, the arugula salads, and lentils and squash. It is healthy fare. My goal is still to lose the ten pounds I gained in Spain (and did I mention I put on more over the holidays?) to ready myself for the yoga training in April, so this might help. A schedule of four hours of work, yoga and meditation, and veggie meals? This is like a detox center, but definitely not a spa!

Yoga Park is run by Hare Krishna devotees. They don't push their philosophy on us, but in the very first yoga class, the young monk explained some of their beliefs.

"We believe that it is not right to eat animals, because of karma. We do not do harm to others, or eat food that is full of torture. Some people say that we must kill a plant to eat it, but the fruit of a tree is our gift from nature. She says, take it. It is for you. If you put a young child with a rabbit and an apple, he will play with the rabbit, and eat the apple. He does not eat the rabbit and play with the apple; this would be unusual! That child would be..." he pauses, searching for the English word, "a freak." We all laugh at this.

Getting up just before six is difficult. There is no coffee. We harvest squash and watermelon, and then take out the weeds and remaining vines, reducing the back garden to a vacant space in two hours. Then breakfast, then more garden time. It is relaxed work, if not relaxing. I feel free to go slowly, as I see others half my age sitting on their bottoms pulling grass by hand. Volunteers chat with each other as we work.

Later, in meditation, I fall into an almost-sleep state. After lunch I lie in a hammock, reading. Then yoga, then more free time. I meet a young woman named Tess from Australia, who is just twenty-two and traveling alone. We exchange stories of our failed romances. A South African woman joins us. She tells us she came to Brazil to marry a guy who bamboozled her: took all her money and jilted her. We commiserate, and continue the conversation at dinner.

"I was dating this man for four years when I worked on a sailboat and then found out he was married," she tells us.

"Didn't anyone else know? No one told you?" Tess asks.

"They didn't know either!" she exclaims.

We shake our heads and raise our tea glasses to toast to our bravery in this world of trickery and devious men.

Days at the yoga park are calm and predictable: up at six, work two hours, breakfast at eight thirty, two more hours of work, meditation at 11:30, and lunch at 1:30. After lunch we have free time, and this is when we hang around in the sunshine and talk. Sometimes I slip away to a hammock to read, or hide in my room to write. At four-thirty there is a yoga class, and sometime a movie (often a documentary about food or politics) then dinner at 8:30 and bed shortly thereafter. It is a nice, calm flow, and all the volunteers are an amiable group.

We work side by side in the garden: weeding, harvesting, watering, and basically getting dirty. The work can be tedious, but everyone remains jovial. One morning as we are called in from our chores, Pepe, a Czech boy, looks around.

"Are there seven of us?" he asks. The group looks at him, puzzled. Slinging the hoe over his shoulder, he starts whistling and singing, "Hi-ho, hi-ho, it's home from work we go...."

One day I decide to skip meditation and work on mosaic art. I go find Vicunya, a Chilean woman with a glowing spirit and a gracious smile. She is the resident artist, who designs and creates all the mosaics that adorn the temple. We will be working on one that will go above the door. She lays out netting and we glue glass pieces to it, following the pattern that has been drawn in dark marking pen. I begin by cutting the glass pieces. Vicunya shows me how to gently squeeze the corner of the glass with the cutting tool until a piece breaks off, warning me to keep the glove on my left hand and watch for flying shards of glass. As we work, me cutting and others gluing, three small children mill about. They are Vicunya's children; she also has an older daughter who is one of the mothers (which is what the nuns are called) at Yoga Park. As I join the table and begin to help glue on yellow pieces of glass, one of the helpers asks about Vicunya's family. She tells us she was married and divorced very young, leaving her with a child to raise, and she turned her focus to spiritual pursuits. She no longer wanted anything to do with romance. But when she gave her life over to God, she met another devotee, a monk. They fell in love and married three months later. He gave up his vows to make a family with her.

"So the lesson is that when you give up on love, it finds you?" one of the other girls asks. I was wondering the same thing.

Vincunya smiles a secretive smile. "Puede ser," she says. Could be.

~~~~~~

Days pass in a comfortable routine. I do yoga every day, and I sometimes go into the theatre/yoga studio to do some on my own in my free time. Sunday comes and we sleep in until nine o'clock breakfast because, as Ashley says, "Even slaves deserve a day off."

At breakfast some of the girls are talking about their plans to go to Iguazu Falls next. That's where I want to go! I ask them when they are leaving, and since it coordinates with my schedule, I ask to go with them. They are two American girls: Holly, a perky blonde who is also a teacher, and beautiful dark-haired and long-legged Steph, both in their twenties. Another lady around my age is also going. She has been at the park a month. Her name is Mary and she is from Toronto. We will form a posse of four to take the seventeen-hour bus ride to Iguazu. Afterwards, we will part ways, as I make my way west to San Juan.

At least, that is how I thought it would be. As we were simultaneously booking our bus tickets from Buenos Aires online, even arranging seat assignments, mine went through without a hitch. I thought we were all set. But on this day off, the other three went to nearby town of Lujan to explore while I stayed at the park to do extra yoga and some laundry. They discovered that there is also a bus that goes to Iguazu from Lujan, and since their tickets did not go through on the spotty internet service here (no one told me this) they are now leaving, together, from Lujan, and I am leaving, alone, from Buenos Aires on the seventeen-hour bus trip. Alone again, naturally…

I am upset with this at first, but I cannot get through to the bus company to change the ticket so I resign myself to going alone. Stephanie eventually says how sorry they are, but I feel like a third (fourth) wheel now and I regret asking to go with them.

The Spanish word for fitting in is encajar, which literally means in a box. So it is an apt way to describe the feeling of not being part of a group, in their cozy box, being on the outside looking in. The irony of this simplistic theory is that almost no one feels that they are in the proper box, but we all think that everyone else is!

What I have noticed with this group of two sweet girls in their twenties and the older woman who hangs out with them (I discovered that she is my age and recently divorced) is that they talk about things like how hot boys are, who they have or would like to fuck, and exchange mischievous encouragement. I'm just not there. But it does not surprise me that Mary is; I remember my own post –divorce lustful craziness. She is in that stage. I, fortunately or "un," was in a relationship (with Brad) at that point, so all the renewed sexual energy went directly to him, do not pass go, no walks of shame. I try to send quiet compassion to her, but do I sense that she resents my intrusion into their cozy threesome where she gets to be the wise and brazen older woman, the MILF of the day? Or is this in my mind? I truly cannot tell. Anyway, we will all be meeting up at the hostel. It will be fine.

Before dinner there is a talk by one of the mothers, or nuns, on Oida Therapy. As an exercise she has us draw a "treasure map" of our own goals; something we want to accomplish in our lives. It could be short term or long term, but the point is to map it out with all the obstacles past and present, in whatever form we want.

Mine is a flower with the goal "peace" in the middle. It's what I constantly wish for. At some point in the past I might have had a material or career goal, but those things have fallen aside. I want to maintain a lifestyle and pay my bills, but I have broadened my idea of how I want to do that. I might have said I want to buy a house or have kids when I was younger, but of course I have met those goals and now I need something that will sustain me no matter what; whether I have a partner, a job, or a nice place to live. I write: "A peace that lives within me, glows, bathes others in its light, not dependent on having anything or anyone."

I list two obstacles: lack of focus and self-esteem problems. I list some strengths: resources such as my family, access to money through work, many blessings I have been given, and my talents. Then I begin to make big loopy petals to my daisy-like flower. Some negatives like fear and self-doubt adorn the petals. I list a few more negatives: my horrible husband, other failed romances, bad decisions, my wild youth. But then I reconsider. Beside the minus sign I put slash-plus. Because all those things have put me on the path to where I am right now. If I learned lessons from the bad things in my life, doesn't that put a positive spin on them? As further positive influences I list the fulfillment of raising my children, my education, my curiosity about life, and resourcefulness.

During the lecture, the nun talks about meeting our basic needs and then being free to give to others. Oida loosely translates as "I know." The premise is that we all know our purpose on earth in our subconscious minds, and our mission is to try to remember it so that we can connect and live it out. This process must be based in faith. We do a guided meditation about a time we felt deep faith. I connect with a memory of horses in my life; at these times I felt connected to a greater being and an inner peace.

That night brings strong pelting rain, thunder and lightning. The electricity shuts off. It is ghastly hot and humid. Mosquitos are buzzing. Grandpa, the old bony Irish Setter, trembling for fear of the thunder, scratches at the door of my room until I let him in. I do not sleep well.

The next day, because of the continuing rain, we don't have to work, so our time is free. At meditation I shift in my cross-legged seat, unable to get comfortable. I feel stiff and tired. When did this old-age thing hit me, and can I transcend it?

Meditation today is being held in the temple, which is a beautiful beehive shaped building of white plaster decorated with shimmering mosaic borders. Inside are more mosaic wall friezes, stunning in their beauty and detail, with lotus blossoms winding in the borders.

I sit, damp and sweaty. I feel my hair curling around my temples. But as I sit I become more relaxed in the hips and can remain cross-legged without moving and wiggling. And perhaps because of the caffeine I snagged when I went to town earlier, my mind is skittering about while my body is still. The instructor has us chant mantras and then do a visualization exercise: imagine yourself in a forest, with trees, plants, and fresh air. Feel the air, hear the sounds. I breathe in, green, breathe out, trees. But in my head, I am still wrestling with this personality conflict with the group. (Real? Imagined?) I try to send positive energy and compassion out, try not to be hung up on the cliquishness.

But still, this is thinking, this is mentally struggling with an outside problem. This is attachment. I breathe in, green, breathe out, trees. Maybe I'm just being overly sensitive. Am I premenstrual? Should this really matter to me? Arrgh! I'm still thinking, horrible outside thoughts! Focusing on negativity; this is bad, bad, bad!

The instructor says, "You are eternal souls, connected to God." I am stirred deep inside by these words. Tears well up in my eyes and spill down my cheeks. I observe the emotion, not sad, but deeply moved. I allow it. Because what matters is not the little conflicts, the difficulties, the discomfort of not fitting into a group. What matters is self. Not in the ego sense. In the sense that my soul is eternal, will overcome this small challenge and many bigger ones, will be forever a part of this terrible and wonderful, magical and complicated world. My tears are diamonds. They are snow-flakes, unique and individual. Like myself. Like Mary. Like my daughters and each person I have met so far on this journey. I feel, suddenly, so much a part of the whole, so astounded and pleased by my tears, so forgiving of my own flaws. I stumble out when the session is over, not speaking to anyone, not daring to. The sky overhead is painted with dark indigo brush-strokes of after-storm clouds. I look up and acknowledge it. I acknowledge my struggles, big and small, and the peace that a vast sky can bring. And I know that under this very sky, spreading out, changing colors and lights as it circles the globe, we are all one.

❀❀❀❀❀

The day comes to leave the Park. Fortunately, I am not alone on the bus. Swami, one of the monks from Yoga Park, is also coming into the city. He gallantly helps me with my bag. (Buddy is smaller than Big Guy but still difficult to haul up narrow bus stairs.) We stand together on the hour ride and talk about philosophy, life, writing, and kids.

He says that someone once asked him if his choice to become a monk was based on wanting to avoid the responsibility of having children. "I think he was angry, and that anger became directed at me." He shrugs with a shy smile. "I told him that there was no conscious avoidance of such a role, that I chose the path that seemed right to me. But in a way, instead of closing myself off to be part of a specific family, I open myself up to think of the whole world as my family. So instead, it is like being a parent to many, a brother of many."

"Imagine if everyone felt that way!" I picture a world where we all try to take care of each other as sister and brother, mother and father. Teaching was like this for me; I always felt like I was not only the teacher but a surrogate mother to all the children in my class. Expanding your heart like this leaves you open to more frustration and pain, but it also raises a deep compassion. Add the Buddhist tenet of non-attachment and the perfect formula for enlightenment is born. Easy to say; hard to do.

We arrive at the plaza and he helps me get my bag off the bus, then we part ways. I make my way to the subway, through a transfer, to the bus station, get my ticket, and have plenty of time to wait. Piece of cake. Why was I worried about this?

The bus ride passes lazily. They show mindless American comedies and sometimes a drama, in English with Spanish subtitles. The volume is low, so I practice my Spanish by reading the subtitles. Four movies play before bed time, and two meals are served. I cheat and eat a ham and cheese croissant, but I peel the ham off. I remember the moment I looked into the eyes of the red cow; the moment my soul became vegetarian. It is time for my body to follow suit.

I sleep fitfully, for the cama (bed) buses leave your body at an angle, slightly sitting up with feet stretched out on a supportive ramp. I manage to slumber until morning. As the sun rises, I look quietly out the window at the passing landscape; pine trees and jungle-like foliage. The earth is a deep red.

Iguazu Follies

The bus pulls into Puerto Iguazu, a cute tourist town with small shops and restaurants. I'm too tired to pull my bag along the streets so I get a cab for fifteen pesos straight to the hostel. I have breakfast, do some yoga on the little outdoor deck, and wait for my friends to arrive. When they do, we hug and flop into the common room couches to relax. Later that night I go for a walk with Mary while the other younger women go shopping for food so we can all make dinner together. Mary and I browse some shops and then go for a drink. It's nice to finally get to know this attractive woman who is so comfortable hanging out with twenty-somethings, or at least that was how it appeared. She, too, has kids the age of these girls.

"You know what drives me crazy? That I'm constantly comparing myself? Why do we do that?"

"Who do you compare yourself to?"

"Girls that age!" We both shake our heads at the foolishness of this. I do it too. They are young and idealistic; they think they know it all and yet have so many surprises in store. And of course, they are beautiful with their unlined skin and their long limbs. Mary herself has an athletic tan body. She is much darker than I, but also has more laugh lines. I guess I'm still comparing! She packed a blow dryer; I brought a yoga mat.

I find my priorities ever shifting on this. I used to spend far more time making sure I looked good, putting on makeup and sexy clothes. On this trip I have hardly touched my makeup bag. I'm beginning to feel like I'm okay just as I am, although sometimes when I'm around a group of younger people, I feel like I am right back in high school.

In high school I also felt like I didn't fit in. I wasn't part of any of the cliques. I had friends, but not enough to acquire one of the all-important labels. I was boy-crazy to the millionth degree; hormones were coursing through my newly developed body and I had no idea what to do with them all. My grades plummeted; I skipped school to hang out and eat junk food with a few other confused girls. In my junior year my parents allowed me to try another school at my request.

One night I went to a party with some girlfriends, drank too much and was sick, throwing up. One of the boys there took the opportunity to force sex on me. It was rape, but I thought I had somehow invited it. Maybe this boy, who was a football player, would want to date me now? I had confused emotions: horror, shame, fear and revulsion mixed with a hope that somehow, he would make up for it. But he announced the next week in our typing class, to the ex-cheerleader teacher who did little more than flirt with the jocks, that he would marry a virgin. Soon after that, I went to my guidance counselor's office and told him I wanted to drop out. He helped me arrange to take the GED test so I had a high school equivalency, and I was finally free.

At eighteen when I moved to New York and became a topless dancer, I finally got a sense (a warped one, but a sense nonetheless) that I could do something productive with this curvy generous figure I had been blessed or burdened with. But the emotional scars from high school linger on to this day, and are probably joined with some scars from eight years as a stripper loaded on top of them.

I wonder sometimes if I will ever find love for and acceptance of myself?

At the hostel I sleep well in our dorm where everything glows red: the curtains and the rug and the bedspreads, and the morning sunlight washes everything in a rosy light. We wake up to have breakfast on the deck and then catch a cab to Iguazu Falls.

At the falls we decide to go up to the Garganta de Diablo first – the devil's throat. The powerful cascade of water is a swirling deep circular drop, hence the name. We stand, fascinated, with hundreds of other tourists, taking pictures and trying not to let our cameras get too wet. The roar of the falls echoes all around like a pack of hungry lions, and a thick sheer mist hovers in the air.

We have brought sandwich makings, which are in my backpack. The day is brutally hot and humid, but we decide to hike to a secluded swimming hole to swim and picnic. It is down a red jungle path through the woods; maybe it won't be so bad. In any case, I don't want to be the only one whining about taking a long hike on this hot day. I square my shoulders, laden down by the pack. If they can all do it, some in flip-flops, so can I! We start down the path. It is almost one o'clock, and the trail is supposed to take about an hour. I bring up the rear, a reluctant tag-along.

At one point on the jungle path, a monkey appears in a tree. We stop to take photos as he is joined by a simian friend, and more. There are at least half a dozen monkeys waiting to determine if we are the type of tourists who will follow the rules and not feed them, or cave in and throw them a little snack. They are watchful but not aggressive. We say goodbye and keep going.

The path seems to go on forever. I am sweating and panting. My Keens are filling up with tiny bits of red dirt as I walk. Mary and I trade bags so that I am carrying her lighter tote instead, which helps. But this settles it: no way am I doing the four-day Inca Trail to Machu Picchu! I'd be   miserable!

I watch the young leggy girls walk, and athletic Mary keeping up with no problem. I think, when I was in MY twenties... but that won't fly. In my twenties I was not all that athletic, either. Sure, I danced in high heels eight hours a night, but that is different. Maybe this walk would be easier fueled up with tequila, as well! Knowing thyself is a powerful tool, and what I know for sure is that I am not the kind of woman who carries camping gear on her back and hikes for miles. I never was and I never will be.

Finally, we get to the end of the road. There is a series of steep stairs with crumbling wood slats. When we descend to the swimming hole, we find a few others there: intrepid travelers who have also made the hike. There is not much of a place to sit and picnic, only jagged rocks. We strip down to bathing suits and get in the water, which feels marvelous. There is a small waterfall trickling down into the waist high pool. I am a bit disappointed. It is a pretty spot, but my body does not feel it was worth the hike. We climb back up all the stairs to the overlook and make sandwiches of bread and cheese. We relax for a bit, but the park closes at six, so we begin the long hike back.

The series of viewpoints at the top of the main stretch of falls affords us some incredible vistas. Our group walks along, oohing and ah-ing. A rainbow lingers above the pools, suspended in the mist. I marvel at the shallow, slow-moving pools that somehow make the transition into a huge cascade of raging water. It looks like one could frolic and play at the top of the falls without danger of being pulled over. I'm not going to try it, though!

In this part of the park, we are treated to sights of large lizards and long-nosed coatis. It's still roasting hot, we are all tired and weary, and it's time to go. The last train is packed, so once again we begin to walk. I'm on auto-pilot, one foot in front of the other. As we pass through the park and towards the entrance, a large herd of coatis passes by: there are dozens of them. Mamas and daddies and babies, going who knows where. They cross the path single-file, waving their raccoon-like ringed tails in the air.

Back at the hostel, we shower to get ready to go out, taking turns in the single bathroom. We will be going to dinner when everyone is clean, and I am looking forward to that. I put on lipstick and try to tame my frizzy hair. All my other clothes are dirty so I don my jeans, knowing I'll be hot. Is it possible they are a tad looser than when I bought them in December? This thought cheers me.

That night we all go back to the room, tired. Most of us go straight to bed. Mary, however, has met a guy and does not come back to the room until three in the morning. One of the girls saw her kissing and groping with him. I shake my head and smile, so glad it isn't me!

Overlooking Iguazu Falls

Iguazu

San Juan – Plays Well With Boys

The morning dawns hot and humid. The ladies and I exchange email info at breakfast, and then off I go to the bus station. I am ridiculously sweaty by the time I have walked there with my luggage. This bus ride is twenty-two hours, followed by a nine-hour one tomorrow morning. Finally, I will arrive at the hostel in San Juan where I will be doing a Help Exchange. Since the hotel internet has been down, they do not know about my arrival. I hope they will still have a space for me!

In San Juan I quickly find the hostel, walking only about five blocks. The boy working the desk has no clue who I am or what to do with me. The owner is on vacation in Mexico, and he and I were corresponding about my stay, but he has not yet returned. When the other owner, Gimena, comes in, she finds a dorm room for me with two other girls staying there. Meanwhile I have been practicing my Spanish with the boy at the desk and two others who are sitting in the lounge.

After a walk around town to get my bearings, I return. The

hostel is well-appointed, with a mixture of room types, big and small, dorms, doubles, and quads. There is a kitchen for common use and a small yard in the back with trees and grass. They tell me there is a rooftop patio, but I will wait until tomorrow to see that. I sleep well, having not slept much on the bus, but I feel sticky from perspiration all night. The air from the fan in the room does not reach my lower bunk. When I wake up, I take a quick rinse and have coffee. Then I help clean a few rooms and bathrooms. One room I clean is in the back of the hostel. I ask in my vastly improving Spanish if it might be available and if I can move. It has an air conditioner and big closet-like lockers, ideal for my stay. It is a room with four bunks. Gimena tells me that there are two chicas coming in later who will be in that room. That's okay with me. I can handle girls in my room. A bit later, though, a young bearded man with a glorious smile comes in, and Gimena puts him in the room. Hmmm, okay. He seems nice. I tell him that there are two girls coming and he looks surprised.

"My two friends are meeting me," he explains. "Boys."

"But she said there were two girls coming!"

We go to check, and Gimena clarifies that she said chicos, not chicas. Uh-oh. Me and three boys in the bunk beds. Ok. I can do this! I will just have to change in the bathroom. I'll be fine.

The three guys are Emiliano (the dark bearded one) Max and Daniel. Daniel reminds me of a hobbit, short with curls and pretty green eyes. Max is tall and funny. They are all from Buenos Aires. Yes, I do like these guys.

I wander around town, dropping off my laundry, exploring the streets, going to the grocery store. Each street I traverse brings a little surprise: a free cinema, an incense and herb store, a hidden mall between two shops, small boutique stores scattered through-out. I even find a yoga class nearby and decide I might try it out. I really like this town. It's big enough to wander about in, but small enough to feel safe. The people in the hostel are friendly, including my new roommates. When I get back to the hostel, they invite me to eat asado with them. I tell them I do not eat meat, but I will join them up on the rooftop terrace after I eat my cheese ravioli.

And when I do, they are gracious. The party on the terrace consists of my three roomies and two other men. I am the only woman. I begin to remember how fun it is to hang out with guys. They speak in Spanish and Emiliano stops every once in a while, to be sure I understand what everyone is saying. As they finish their dinners, we take the wine and move to the corner where there are lounge chairs.

We chat for a while. Daniel asks, "Por que estas sola?" Why are you on your own?

I tell him I don't know, and then I raise my eyes to the sky and ask God, "Hey? Why am I alone?" It's hard to explain in English, let alone Spanish. Not my choice, but it is how it is. Just for now. I hope.

Eventually we get into party mode. Emiliano plays the charango, an Argentine guitar-like instrument that is the size of a ukulele. He sings songs in Spanish in a low, lilting voice. He sings a Bob Marley one especially for me, since it is one of the few English songs he knows. I think I might be developing a small crush on him despite my best intentions. I just cannot help myself, no matter how strictly my inner nun scolds me. I've always had a thing for musicians.

I tell the guys I know a song in Spanish. I hum a bit for Emiliano and he strums some chords. It's a silly song I learned while teaching kindergarten: "Para Dormir a Un Elefante" – how to put an elephant to sleep. According to the lyrics, you need a giant pacifier and rattle, and you need to be a decent singer.

They sing along, laughing, and make me sing it again until they know it by heart. I feel like I have found another batch of cachorros. We stay on the terrace laughing and singing until the neighbors call to complain and the boy at reception comes up to tell us. We all stumble downstairs, and since they have to wash the dishes from their asado, I get a head start on brushing my teeth and getting into pajamas. I sleep well, but I dream about kissing Emiliano. Darn!

The next day I do some more cleaning. It is a hot, hot day. I try to nap a bit. Emiliano and Daniel are leaving today. I am sad but relieved. Daniel and I have had some heavy conversations about life, bearing in mind that I am not fluent in Spanish. He is a Leo, smart and surprisingly down to earth. Emiliano, I find out, is a Scorpio. He seems mellow for a Scorp, but then again, Nica is also that sign. Maybe it's just the females of the sign who are intense, like my own dear mama.

"I would not have thought you were a water sign, especially Scorpio," I tell him.

"I was once told that water signs have no shape of their own, they have to adapt to their surroundings and then take that shape," he says.

We are eating peanuts, mani, sitting in our little dorm room. I crack a peanut shell, thinking. Is this true of me? Do I morph to my surroundings instead of keeping my own shape? Or is it that I cannot morph successfully, and therefore feel like I am more or less shapeless?

"I never heard that. It's interesting."

"Translation please!" says Daniel, as we have been speaking English.

I am itchy that night; mosquitos? The boys have gone trekking.

Turns out they will stay one more night and take a morning bus. They invite me to go with them, but I decline. Instead, I go for a walk on my own.

I go to the Plaza 25 de Mayo. I expect it to be active, but there is not much there. Nothing save a few lovers making out on park benches. I try not to look. How long has it been since I had a man's hands wrapped around me and his lips upon mine? Too long. My Spain adventures fell short. I am not opposed to having some kind of fling in South America, but I don't want a one-nighter. No way. And I just feel so old right now. I would never approach someone young and handsome, like Emiliano, for fear of rejection, or worse – pity.

I take a roundabout way back to the hostel. The sunset is putting on a crazy show, illuminating the clouds in glowing pink. Another set of clouds is sending up what looks like searchlights. It is incredible. I look up to where the light hits the sky and disperses, half expecting it to start moving back and forth like a Broadway opening.

When I get to the hostel, I cook dinner. The guys are not back. I am itchy when I lay down, so much that I must get up. I smear myself with Caladryl that I purchased earlier and begin to look up bug bites on the internet. Is it bed bugs? The itching is driving me crazy. Midnight, and I am alone in the room still, and grateful for this. I take half a Xanax to crash, and it works. I barely hear the guys come in, and I miss their exit in the morning. I dream of Emiliano again, kissing and this time a little more. Seriously, what the hell is my problem?

Now I have new roommates to replace the old. Chicos again. Sleeping with different men every night has taken on an entirely new meaning for me. Rotating partners, here I am in Bunk A, who will be in Bunk B? I hope you like it on top, baby.

But in all seriousness, this week has really made me think about a lot of things. For starters, getting to know guys on the level where sex is not a part of the equation is an eye-opener. I ponder this as I sit on the breezy rooftop with my computer.

Blog Post: Who Am I if I'm Not a Sexpot?

It feels like my whole life I have been concerned about being attractive to men. Of course, as a stripper, that is part of the job. If they don't find you attractive, you won't make any money.

Being married changed the need to appeal to men, for I was in what I thought was a secure relationship; not a happy one, but one in which I had agreed to certain terms. So why try to be sexy to other men when I could not take advantage of it? Why flirt when my husband had a terrible temper and insecurities that caused him to fire accusations my way? And it wasn't like I didn't try for a while to be sexy just for my husband. But he liked me plain and frumpy. When I tried suggestive lingerie for him, even early in the relationship, he commented on my cellulite. When I playfully wanted to decorate the Christmas tree nude, he said to me, "Wow, those kids have really wrecked your boobs." I put my robe back on.

Even when I was at the barn with my horse, avoiding my marriage, he would accuse me of having a lover between the house and the stable. I became a female eunuch of sorts, detached from my own sexuality through marriage instead of blossoming in my conjugal relationship. A sad thing.

And in rediscovering this sexuality after my divorce, my pendulum swung the other way for a while until I found balance. I flirted shamelessly. My new blonde hair, yoga body and feeling of liberation made me like a libidinous teenager for a while. Brad reaped the benefits of my new empowerment, and had a secure (and then some) ego so that he didn't get jealous. Why should he be? He was assured of my love; I slathered it on him like sticky-sweet frosting on a child's birthday cake. Thick and rich and never-ending, or so it would seem. Too much sugar, however, is not healthy. I learned that the hard way when I discovered I was layering frosting on a cake made of nothing more than a few crumbs of sustenance and lots of air. It couldn't hold up. It was like McArthur's Park, a song I loved in high school-- "someone left the cake out in the rain."

So now, having endured my marriage, having survived the melting of my too-sweet cake, what is left? No matter what I do to my body (surgery, working out, mad dieting, piles of makeup), time will march on. I will be forty-nine in a matter of weeks. It is time to free myself from the trappings of being an insecure female hunting for a mate, searching for love, and allow myself to find peace as I am, with an identity that does not include being someone's other half. If I merely let go of that expectation, I am free in so many ways. Lonely, yes. But not constantly frustrated by trying to be a young sexy thing. Or even an old sexy thing. Or anything at all. I'm just me: quirky, funny, affectionate and warm, but not trying to achieve anything with all this. Just being me.

If I have learned anything at this week in the hostel (besides the fact that I don't like bed bugs, even though they like me) it is that I enjoy the company of men, especially for pure "amistad," or friendship. I have enjoyed bantering with them, even in Spanish, in which I can barely string the words together in a sentence sometimes.

My newest roommates are both very sweet. Julian is about twenty-five with a great sense of humor. He and I go one day to the winery and up to the top of the bell tower of the cathedral. At the church I see my old friend Jesus. Hey, Jesus, que onda? My other new roomie is Luis, who lives in Buenos Aires but is here for a friend's wedding. After I say hello and show him the room, I later find him on the terrace, reading. I ask if it will bother him if I do yoga, he says of course not. I roll out my mat and do yoga for forty-five minutes. He is still there when I finish. "Que linda," he comments (how beautiful.) I stop to chat with him, and he offers me mate. I have only tried it one time other than my first in Buenos Aires. Someone at the hostel is always drinking it. I have learned some traditions; for instance, you must pass it to the person who made it when you finish your turn, not to another person. If someone else receives it, they should kiss the bottom of the cup and pass it back to the original person. Who knew this bitter tea concoction had so many rules? I sip and talk in Spanish with Luis, and later he helps me to wander the streets in search of shrimp and skewers so I can put something on the barbecue while the rest of the hostel eats a meat-laden asado.

On my final day in the hostel, a huge group is coming in for the big futbol game (soccer to me) that takes place Saturday evening. They are a rowdy bunch of guys, eighteen of them. My two roomies and I move upstairs to a nicer room to make space for the group, and we now have a private bathroom and I have my own queen-size bed, not even a bunk. I'm in heaven. At least until I figure out that it will be a noisy location, because it is off the terrace, and the terrace is where people are gathering to drink all day before the game. I need to leave the hostel for a while anyway and explore the town. It is my last day after all.

I wander downstairs only to find five or six more of the futbol group. They chat with me on my way out, and one wants a picture with me. Three of them have the badge emblem of their soccer team tattooed on their chest. The tall one puts his arm around me and pulls me to him for another picture. I don't know how to react, my arm around this half-naked boy the age of my daughter. These boys are nice, but I am wary. They flirt and compliment me as we compare tattoos. Well, I am practically the only woman in the whole building, so their choices are limited. It feels good but awkward. I make my exit as quickly as I can.

On my own I wander, hitting the Museo de Memoria, which memorializes the earthquake that devastated San Juan in 1944. The museum is modest, and it has a simulator to demonstrate what the earthquake might have felt like. I sit and watch a short film, then the shaking begins. I gasp and hold on to my chair. The room rocks, first up and down, then back and forth. The man at the control tells me afterwards that the quake lasted forty-six seconds, but it was enough to destroy ninety percent of the city. I am impressed by the demonstration and grateful to not have personally experienced anything like it.

Next, I walk to a graffiti-decorated building that is also supposed to be a museum, but there is no sign that it is open or even maintained. The shop across the way is open, though, so I take advantage of the air-con and talk to the salesgirl. I meander through the store, cooling down. The shop sells silver jewelry encrusted with crushed rock, painted whimsical creatures in fired clay, and dangling wind chimes decorated with feathers. As I buy a few things, she tells me that the new museum of Bella Artes is just around the corner.

Upon entering the large building, I find that I have the place to myself. I wander around, killing time and gazing at paintings and sculptures. I do not want to return to the hostel until all the guys have gone to the game. My friend Julian is also going, but Luis is not, and we have plans to go out for dinner tonight together. On my way home, I stop to say hello to any dogs I see, as usual. I see a group of four, two brown and two white. They lurk at the street corner; what are they up to? I soon see that they are car-chasing tire-biters, as a red car turns the corner and they all chase after it, barking. It's like a little street gang of dogs, up to no good. A pandilla. As they cross, I approach, lecturing them in a kind voice. They won't come near, and are skittish when I hold a hand out to pet them.

I return to the hostel, which is quiet by now. Thank God. Luis returns shortly after I do, happy from a day of biking. I book my next tickets, to Mendoza on Sunday morning and then on to Santiago by night. Luis showers for our dinner. By ten we are both ready. I wear the fun earrings I bought at the artesenia shop: colorful swirls of bright thread shot through with silver strands, dangling enticingly from delicate chains. They swing pleasantly as we stroll and talk.

I have promised Luis some time speaking English, as he has been so kind and patient with my Spanish. I don't expect much, as he has not volunteered any English before, so I am pleasantly surprised at his level. I tell him this, but he demurs.

"No," he insists, "you do much better than I do. I have to think every single word." So do I, but I'm glad he thinks I sound fluid. As we cross the peatonal, I spot four dogs on the sidewalk.

"Hey! I'm sure those are the dogs I saw earlier. They were chasing cars. They're like a little street gang, a pandilla!" Luis

244

laughs, and as if to illustrate, the dogs take off barking after a taxi. "Bad boys," I scold them.

We decide to eat at the outdoor patio of the parilla. The garden has bright yellow umbrellas, wooden stepping stones throughout the grass, a huge fountain, and a fiery outdoor grill. It is a nice atmosphere for my last night in town. We sit, I order fish, and we get a bottle of wine. As we chat, moving back and forth between English and Spanish, I realize how much I am enjoying this quasi-date.

Luis is handsome and slim with a shaved head and beautiful eyes behind his wire frame glasses; eyes the color of honey-glazed jade. I lean forward, sipping wine and listening to him. His voice has a soft rolling tone. Am I developing yet another little crush? He is a music teacher and a pianist, so we discuss teaching. It turns out he also knows my pet song, "Como Dormir a un Elefante." Then we move on to family and relationships. He tells me that, when he was younger, he had the name of his girlfriend tattooed on his arm, and to cover it up took three sessions of ink! I tell him that my lion tattoo represents not just my Leo ex-lover, but also courage. And that most importantly, although that relationship is over, it represents that love is possible! And when I say this, I realize that I whole-heartedly believe it. I mean, here I am in Argentina, having dinner with a sweet and handsome man. Our paths may not cross again, but they did cross once. Who knows what else could happen; who knows what's next? Maybe love really is possible!

I explain how I feel about having the investment of time with a person, like my relationship with Brad, and how frustrating I find it that he wants all or nothing. After five years together, wouldn't one think that friendship is possible?

"No, you can't be friends with an ex," Luis says.

"But why not?" I complain, putting my elbow on the table with a little pout. "After all the time together, you don't stop caring. Why not be friends?"

"Because," he says. "It is too hard to close the door."

He tells me that a friend of his thinks love only lasts as long as a president: four years. Every four years, as it is time for a new president, it is time for a new lover. I consider this. The problem that I see is that every four years, we are four years older and less likely to appear young and beautiful, thus less likely to attract a mate. Four years, though.... Hmm. I could have done four years with Brad and avoided the painful last year. I definitely would have been better off with four years of my ex-husband instead of fourteen.

Luis insists on paying the bill. "So that you have more money for traveling." The restaurant, which was packed, is empty now save for us and one other table. We drift out, strolling down the peotonal, and continue back to the hostel.

Of course, the young boys are there, leaning against the front door in the street. Before we get there, I whisper, "Pretend you're my boyfriend!"

The boys holler at my approach. I'm sure they are all drunk, but Luis tells me their team lost, so don't ask about the game. They begin to call my name. "Come here, we want another picture with you!"

I know I look pretty good, but not that good! I'm no starlet. I look to Luis. "Un momento," I tell them as we dash inside. One pops his head around and I try to appease him with smiles. Luis watches cautiously.

Alberto, the owner, is there shaking his head. "You missed the quiet part of the evening," he says.

Luis and I go upstairs, where more boys linger on the terrace.

Soon the noise subsides; the young guys are going out dancing. I peek into our room, where Julian is already retired for the night, asleep in his top bunk. Luis and I go outside for a while, waiting for the others to leave. They wave to me as they head downstairs; the cutest and drunkest one blows me a kiss as he departs. I smile and wave back. Luis looks after him, then back at me. He tells me, "You are codiciana."

"What is that?" He shrugs, unable to translate. In my purse I rummage for the dictionario. *Codicia.* Greed. Greedy. I feel like the wind has been knocked out of me, because he's right. Even though I tried hard to be respectful to my date and not respond to the boys' attention, he knew.

After all my assertions to myself that I'm done with romance, that I can be just a friend with men and there's no problem, that I'm accepting my aging process gracefully, Luis saw right through me. It looks like I have more work to do.

"You're right," I admit to him. "I know that they're only paying attention to me because I'm the only woman in the whole place. Sure, I could sleep with one of these guys, whatever, but it wouldn't mean anything. I am so tired of that. They aren't paying attention to me because they really like me! I'm just here. It's like a game. It doesn't mean a thing, so why do I still crave the attention? Even when I try not to, I still like being noticed." I spread my hands in surrender. "But I know I'm nothing special!"

"You are special," he says. "Just not to these guys."

We retire to our room and Julian stirs, breaking the spell. I am relieved and disappointed. His presence in our room would prevent anything from happening. Do I want something to happen? Does Luis? I can't tell. I'm thirteen years older than him. Would that matter?

I am shocked to look at my watch and find that it is four thirty in the morning! I want to catch the ten-fifteen bus. We say hasty goodnights. Such a pity to waste this big beautiful bed by sleeping alone. But remembering my informal vow, I curl into a ball and fall asleep.

In the morning the sun wakes me and I stumble downstairs for coffee, then back up to shower. Luis remains asleep. Finally, I shake him gently by the shoulder. "I've got to go get my bus," I remind him.

"I'll accompany you." While I finish packing, he showers, then helps me with my bag. We flag a taxi because, even though it's pretty close, I don't have time to walk. Julian tags along. The streets are quiet on this Sunday morning and we get to the station, finding that the bus is delayed just enough to have time for me to make it. I exchange Facebook information with my roommates and hug them both goodbye. They wait until the bus leaves, waving as we pull out. I stand and lean over the aisle so they can see me.

Goodbye, boys. Goodbye, San Juan. I think regretfully about Luis, but shrug it off. So we had one nice date. That's a good thing! Not every date has to lead to something big. I have lots of friends from Buenos Aires, now – better late than never! If I visit again, I know I will like the city more.

The bus pulls out and I snuggle into the seat and try to snooze. After a stop in Mendoza, I catch the bus to Santiago. On to another new country. What will tomorrow bring?

At the hostel with my roomies

A little doggy street gang

Chile – Begin With The Beach

The beginning of this trip to Chile does not bode well for me. I paid an extra fee for "ejecutivo" – executive class. This meant, I thought, that I would finally get to ride in a bus with the seat that lies all the way back like a bed. I was excited! Tonight of all nights, I am super tired. But when I get on the bus, the seats do not lie back any more than normal. Not only that, but the bus is freezing with blasts of air conditioning, and there are no blankets or pillows. Usually when you pay more you get a blanket! And anything I would have brought to wrap myself up in is already in the luggage storage compartment: my big scarf, a long-sleeved shirt. All I have for comfort are my fuzzy socks. I go back out to ask the driver politely if I might please have a blanket. But my Spanish is tired. I tell him, "Por favor, no puedo dormir en el bus porque es frio! Necesito mantequilla!" He says no blanket, get back on the bus so we can leave.

I swear under my breath. Then I slowly realize that I did not ask for a blanket, or manta, but for butter! I can't sleep on the bus without butter? No wonder he shooed me away! I'm tired and grumpy and cold. Relax, I tell myself, and rummage through my bag. At least I have my inflatable pillow, and I pull out a plastic emergency rain poncho to cover myself with.

The bus attendant comes through with ham sandwiches, which I decline. I climb over my seatmate to use the bathroom one time before sleeping, and of course I forget to bring my tissues and of course there is no paper. They put on a movie, volume loud. I groan, grab earplugs, and burrow into my cheap plastic poncho.

At three-thirty, the bus stops in the middle of a dirty rocky road. Customs! Groggy, I grab my things and step out into the cold night, shivering. A German girl behind me offers her scarf. After customs, the German girl finds me and gives me her jacket for the rest of the ride. Again, the kindness of strangers comes to my rescue!

We get into Santiago, where the bus station appears to have outgrown itself; it is teeming with people, bursting at the seams. I put on my "no pasa nada" attitude and merge with the crowds. The bathroom costs money to get into, 200 pesos. But when you gotta go, you gotta go! I figure out it's only about thirty-five cents, anyway. After a minor mishap at the ticket window – reserving a ticket for the wrong bus, noting my mistake, and returning only to be told there are no refunds – I book the right bus to the town of my next host.

I get on the bus, having no idea what I will do when I get there, but I suppose I'll just figure it out. A young woman is assigned the seat next to me. I read for a while as we hit the road. Bye, Santiago. I'll see you again soon! I am sleepy and decide to rest a while.

When I wake up, we are driving through a seashore town. I'm excited; I love the beach. A gaily colored vendor's market is on the right side of the road, the ocean is on the left, and bungalows and cafes are everywhere. This must be the destination, or close to it. The bus stops and a lot of people are getting off. I ask the girl next to me if it is the last stop. She says it's not, and where am I going? I tell her my predicament; that I don't actually know where I'm going nor is my host expecting me at a certain time. I tell her I have a phone number, and she offers to make the call for me. She talks to Macarena, who tells me where to meet her in about ten minutes. Again, a kind stranger has come to my aid. We talk for the rest of the ride. She is a student who lives nearby. I tell her that it is my first trip to Chile and that I am excited to be by the ocean.

"I love the ocean," I tell her in Spanish, "maybe because I'm a Pisces."

"I'm a Leo," she tells me.

I show her the tattoo of the lion on my ankle. "My last love was a Leo. I guess he still is," I joke. "But now it means courage."

"Traveling alone, courage is a good thing to have!" she says. "And here is our stop."

We get out, get the luggage, and before I can wonder where the café is where I am supposed to meet Macarena, a lovely girl appears. "Cathy?" she asks.

"Yes!" We walk to the car with my bag after thanking my bus friend. A short ride up a dirt road takes us to the site of the cabanas. Macarena tells me their situation as we drive: she is a student in Santiago but comes out to help her mom, Ethel, when she can. She also has a brother in Santiago, and her brother has a couchsurfing friend who is staying at the cabanas at the moment, fixing up a van and helping Ethel work around the place.

I am introduced to Ethel, the jefa (boss), who only speaks Spanish. She is a tiny energetic woman with a sharp wit and an infectious laugh. I know right away that I will like her. She takes me to my room and we proceed to clean it together. Later I will wonder if this was a test, because much of my work here will be cleaning the cabanas as they empty and we ready them for the next client. It is high season, tourist season, and the place is busy. Ethel's phone is constantly ringing but she is never impatient with this. I would be likely to throw it across the room! But she answers in her sweetest voice, "Hola, Buenos tardes." And when she speaks to potential clients she uses terms of endearments like "mi amor" and "carin~a."

The cabanas themselves are scattered around the property, which is up a windy bumpy road from town. Ethel stays in the main house and her husband, Ivan, comes every weekend from Santiago. I will meet him this weekend. Together with their two children they have built most of these cabanas with little help, framing, laying tile, putting in the electrical. I am amazed. Each cabana is distinct and has special details. They are surrounded with natural grass and flowers such as bougainvillea and red geraniums, as well as green plants in pots. Part of my job will be to water these daily, as the summer is quite dry, and plants die quickly in the heat.

At lunch, which is at about three every day, I meet Ben, the other helper. He has a mass of dark curls and a slow, quiet smile. Macarena's friend is also with us for lunch, and they are planning to walk to the nearby beach afterward. "Do you want to come?" Macarena asks. I quickly agree.

Gringa, the reddish long-haired dog, follows us to the beach. We walk four blocks down a sandy road, turn, and are faced with a breathtaking view of the long expanse of sand spreading out below. The water sparkles in glimmering blue lapis waves. I am confronted with a huge stretch of staircase that leads down to the sand. Macarena grins mischievously. "Down is easy, it's up that's the hard part." The reward for the descent will be well worth it, I think, as we march down the stairs to claim a spot on the pale sand, Gringa at our heels.

In the next few days I work with Ethel cleaning cabanas. She has a high standard for cleanliness – she tolerates not a spot nor a smudge, but is patient with me. She is also patient with my Spanish, which is improving, I think and hope! The full-time cleaning person is Erika, and we work side by side during the week, getting each cabana spotless after guests leave and before new ones come. Sometimes it feels incredibly repetitious, as clients sometimes just stay two nights. Hey! Didn't I just do this one? And some days there are three or four to clean in a day, taking at least two to three hours for each one. Ethel manages one cabana in town, right across from the beach with a gorgeous view, and one day we are all out there cleaning. She takes pity on me and sends me to the beach for a look-see while they finish up.

There is plenty of work to do in this high season, but it isn't all work. One Tuesday evening Ethel, Macarena, and I go out to the feria, a market like the one I saw from the bus. There are three in the town, selling similar things: clothing, jewelry, kids' toys, and trenzas, which are hair decorations that you put into your hair like braids. They are decorated with shells, wooden beads, or plastic hanging flowers, and braided, woven, and macramé designs. I think Veronica might like this, so I buy one. I don't have much cash, but I spend what I do have in the market that night.

While at the market, a young tanned girl with a clipboard approaches us to sign up for a nature walk. I am assured this will be a family paseo, not a heavy-duty hike. Ok, I'm in! There are a bunch of cabanas to turn on Wednesday, so, with a nod of approval from Ethel, we decide on Thursday.

When Thursday arrives, it is a gorgeous day. The sky is

decorated with a few wispy clouds and the sun is already warm in the morning when we set off. Most of the walk is down the beach, where the guides stop occasionally to give us some information about the natural things we see, like the types of birds or seaweed. I don't really understand the lecture, so I happily tune it out, taking photos and feeling the warm sun on my body. The lull of ocean waves rolling in to lap at the shore is a soothing background. We take off our shoes to walk on the firm damp sand. Seagulls cry, zooming in, sparkling white with bright yellow beaks as if they were freshly painted; I think of the Sorolla paintings from Madrid. Families stroll along with us. One boy of about seven years old has a red t-shirt on that proclaims "I'll give you the ride of your life." Macarena and I laugh at this, and she tells me that American slogans on shirts are popular here, but most people have no idea what kind of statement they are making with them.

As we sit in a circle on the beach, the guide gathers up three sizes of crabs from the many dead ones washed up on the shore. Here they are called jaiba; Macarena tells me it is popular to buy crab and cheese empanadas. A few random dogs run by as we talk, and suddenly Macarena pops up. "Copito!"

A shaggy small white dog, wet and sandy, runs up to her. It is the other dog from the house. Apparently he likes to come down to the beach on his own sometimes. Happy to see us, he jumps and bites at my hand as we begin to walk again. Then he spies a gull and takes off after it, a white blur scattering foam as he runs into the water. He accompanies us for the rest of the trip.

We are faced with a hike up a steep hill. Hey, I think to myself, what happened to the gentle paseo? The warm sandy dirt and pebbles fill my shoes as I struggle and scramble up the hill. The lady in front of me has skiff-type shoes that are in danger of falling off. Panting, I keep my eye on her feet, thinking, if she can do it without a complaint, and if "the ride of your life" can get up this hill, well so can I, damn it!

We are rewarded with a gorgeous stretching view of the ocean and some rugged cliffs. The beach seems to extend forever, dotted with little people and dogs. Up here the terrain is different. Pine trees give off their Christmas scent, and the guide tells us these trees are not native to the area and have difficulty growing. Their sap excretes around them, allowing nothing to grow in their surrounding area. We continue down the path and find a huge cliff plunging down to the ocean below. On a fence across the way sit somber black vultures. Each has a splash of red under his chin. They perch, wings folded, each on a fence post like a sentry. Occasionally, one takes off flying, surveying the area, circling above us. The guide tells us that one of the main meals of these birds of prey is small dogs. We keep Copito close to us, although I'm sure he'd be a force to reckon with should one of these birds fancy him for a snack!

Finally, we descend the slope of shifting sands back to the beach. Macarena and I take the short cut: the hundreds of stairs up the hill to her house. I am hungry and tired, but it was a great day.

The rest of the week flows by, and most of my time is spent cleaning cabanas. I don't mind the work, but I crave a day to roam the beach and explore a bit. Saturday I get my chance. At breakfast, I meet Ivan, the papa of the family. Unfortunately, his accent is hard for me to understand, but he does have a great sense of humor. We are talking about homeless people in America, and I mention that some have mental issues or problems with alcohol. With a glint in his eye, Ivan adds, "And some just go traveling!" We all laugh. Ethel says that today I can have the whole day off, since tomorrow we have a lot of work.

Soon I am sauntering down the stairs to the beach. After laying down my towel, I run into the water. I plan to do some yoga for half an hour.

It is past ten in the morning, but there are still relatively few people out. The occasional family strolls by, or someone jogging. I stand, rooted in the warm sand, and begin a series of sun salutations, facing the ocean. At first, I feel self-conscious, but after a while I am in the rhythm of my practice. Gazing at the sea, my soul unfolds like a white hibiscus. All five senses sharply in tune, I listen to a subtle orchestra of crashing waves, rising and descending, spewing foam and rolling in to caress the sand. The sky is robin's egg blue and free of clouds, and the scent of the ocean is carried on the breeze that caresses my face. In triangle pose I sink deep, open my chest and heart, and look up, past my extended hand, to see a tiny white sliver of last night's moon, a shard of pearl on a baby's blanket.

My eyes fill with tears for the immense simple beauty of the world. I taste the salt breeze on my lips; feel my damp curls tickling my shoulders as my strong body bends. Five pelicans fly in formation; they skim the water and rise again, elegant for such strange birds. I want nothing more than this moment, captured in a memory so strong that none of my demons can chase it away. In this precise moment, five days before my forty ninth birthday, I have achieved a brilliant, aching perfection.

Balancing yoga postures on the beach on shifting sands is an apt metaphor for life. The body must adapt. Balancing in an asana, like tree pose, requires micro-adjustments to maintain equilibrium. Should we fall, we do so with a smile, even a laugh, and resume the posture. We don't berate ourselves for our clumsiness; we don't blame our body, our mother, our yoga teacher, or God. We simply acknowledge the fact and adjust. Balancing in the sand, I find such profound forgiveness for myself, such total acceptance. I am merely a human creature in a large and mostly glorious world. A grain of sand humbled by the tumultuous sea. Alone, yet part of the big picture.

⸙

I walk down the length of beach closer to town, where it gets busier and more crowded as I go along. A handsome father plays with his children by the water. He smiles at me as I pass. The beach is dotted with a rainbow cacophony of umbrellas. I could use a bathroom and a coffee. I turn toward the main strip and find a cute outdoor café. I sit and write in my notebook. A hammock is strung near my seat and a man plops his daughter into it, and begins speaking to me in English. It is obvious I am a gringa, I guess! His wife comes by and I invite them to sit at my table, since the others are full. They are Antonio and Cecily, and the daughter, Isabella, is two and a half. She is a precocious and headstrong child, and she begins following the waitress around to "help" her. It is adorable. We all go to the beach to play with Isabella in the sand. I find out that they live in Con Con.

"Hey, I'll be in Con-Con in a week or so."

"You must call us!" Cecily says, and gives me their number.

When I leave the beach, I am tired. I go by the feria and shop a while, then stop for ceviche at the restaurant by Ethel's town cabana. I use the waiter's phone to call and Ethel comes to retrieve me and take me back.

"I had such a wonderful day!" I tell her. I try to explain in my limited Spanish about my moment of enlightenment on the beach doing yoga, and although I don't think I am explaining it well enough, she tells me she understands. And I know she does.

Santiago – Big City Thrills, Big City Woes

The ride to Santiago with Ivan is a few hours, and I am nervous, wondering how the conversation will go. But one to one, we do ok. We leave at eleven-thirty at night, so we do not roll into Santiago until almost two AM. Fortunately, there is someone at the desk to give me my room. And the room is great! It has a single bed with a bright throw, a spacious closet, and bedside tables. The shared bathroom is clean. I am happy. No sharing rooms and no bed bugs!

In the morning I partake of the meager breakfast (instant coffee and bread) and prepare to take off to explore. People have told me to be careful; I remember Argentina. I opt to not take my backpack but to keep my purse close at hand, over the shoulder and neck; that should do it! It's my birthday week and I hope to shop, relax, and have fun.

I wander to the plaza of Armas, where I take some photos and get a map. I visit the cathedral which is, as always, impressive. I'm not a church-goer in my normal life, but I love churches while traveling. They fill me with awe. I walk slowly through the dimly lit building, noting statues of saints, the altar of the sacred heart, and my good buddy Jesus. Stained glass windows circle skylights above. A slightly musty smell mixed with lingering incense hovers in the air. People bow and genuflect before altars and statues. I look in vain for an electric candle box.

I meander through a street of shops – big department stores and drugstores, looking for a bath loofah. They don't seem to exist here. I stop for coffee to get my bearings. The waitress comes over to examine the map with me and point out where we are. So much is nearby! There is the Pablo Neruda museum, which I plan to visit on my birthday. Today, perhaps, I will go to the Museum of Bellas Artes, not far away. I will have to pass through the Fruit Market, where I'll shop later for my dinner.

Outside it is a beautiful sunny day, and I feel happy. A man is standing on the corner, passing out love poems on scraps of copy paper. I take one and give him some change.

"Un billete pequeno?" he asks, as I hand him some coins. He is asking for a bill instead.

"No tengo!" I answer. All I have is 10,000, which is like twenty bucks.

I stop to buy a slice of watermelon from a vendor. Strolling on, I cross the Puente (bridge) de Rio Mapocho, just before the main market starts. And there, to my surprise is a woman selling bath loofahs for only three hundred pesos! As I dig through my wallet, I can't find any change. But I know I have some loose pesos in my purse, so I start looking, the wallet still in my left hand, the watermelon tucked awkwardly under my arm.

Digging for pesos. It all happens so fast. Suddenly someone snatches what I was holding. What was that? Oh, yeah, my wallet!

I scream and give chase, yelling, running, screaming "Por

favor!" plaintively. He runs through the park, me in hot pursuit, but not close enough, not nearly able to catch him. Yelling loudly all the way. One man tries to trip the robber, unsuccessfully. Someone else- a friend of his? – throws a slab of board in my way. After a few blocks I lose him in the main market and remain, panting, panicked, in shock. Holy crap. That was all my money – close to a hundred and fifty dollars.

The afternoon goes by in a daze, me going to the police station to file a report, returning back to the hostel, making phone calls to my parents to help me cancel the bank cards. Fortunately, I have a spare credit card stashed in my luggage for an emergency. Although there are hefty fees, I can make cash withdrawals. I shop at the store for dinner items and a bottle of rum. Its name: Optimist.

I alternate wishing vast evil upon my robber and praying for his horrid soul. Neither of which is very satisfying. Three strong drinks in me, I go to sleep with plans to buy pepper spray tomorrow.

I check out of the hostel the next day, traumatized by my incident but determined not to let it get me down. Still, it's hard to walk around without fear. How easily one can shift from exploring, insouciant and smiling, to a paranoid stance of white-knuckle grasp on the handbag and a hand placed on the hidden picnic knife in one's pocket. What a difference a day makes! But I am reassured by the presence of policia and security guards in some of the areas I explore. I now know I was in a rough part of town that first day. One of the downsides of traveling solo, I guess. No one to discuss options with, no one to watch your back or your purse.

I make a conscious decision to stay positive. It was only money. A pain in the butt to lose the credit cards and my driver's license from home, but I needed to change it to a Colorado one, anyway.

The cards are cancelled. The residual stress is what I still need to conquer. But conquer it I will! He can steal my money but he cannot steal my smile! And, at least I've made one man very happy on this trip.

Blog Post: You Can't Rob Me of My Peace!

When a person is violated, it makes them feel vulnerable to everything. After my robbery, I couldn't look at people the same way. I walked around apprehensively, suspicious of even an old lady who brushed against me in a store. It is an exhausting way to live.

And who does it hurt, really? Not the unsuspecting passersby who are being silently thought of as potential hoodlums. It hurts the person being so guarded that she cannot live her life.

When you travel, it is wise to be on your guard – to assess new situations and to be aware of the people around you. Many cities are known for pickpockets and scams. When I first moved to New York City, I almost fell for an elaborate con involving a woman who had "found" a suitcase full of money with a non-existent address on the card. She approached me on the street to ask if I knew where the address was. The woman then called a lawyer for advice, and was told we could keep all the money if it was not claimed in two days, but we needed to give the lawyer a fee of a few hundred dollars to hold it until that time. Being eighteen, I had no access to the money she requested. I bemoaned the fact that I had lost the opportunity to score such wealth, only realizing later that it had been a scam.

I felt so foolish after my robbery in Santiago. I mean,

who holds her wallet up in the air? That guy must have thought it was his lucky day. Later, it would make a great self-deprecating story. "Hey, does anyone want this wallet? Because I obviously don't…" I would not tell people how angry I was. Nor would I confess that I ran after him so hard that I peed my pants a little. Funny sells. Pathetic is just, well, pathetic!

It could have been worse. He didn't hold me up at gun-point. He didn't make off with my passport, just some cash, my driver's license, and my Starbucks Gold card. Things I can replace.

The sense of insecurity he left me with is what I must now battle. I don't want to live with paranoia. I'd rather be the bubble-headed blonde who floats through the world appreciating its beauty. Not clutching my bag like it holds a hundred thousand dollars instead of five and some change.

So if you see me walking down the street in Santiago, eyes nervously darting around, please just give me a big friendly smile and whisper, "Relajate." Relax.

I take a cab to the address of my host, who is at the apartment for lunch. Paulo greets me cordially and shows me my room. He invites me to eat pasta with him. He introduces me to the cats and Maria, his maid. Although all our previous correspondence was in English, he is now speaking Spanish to me, and he is very hard to understand! I remind him that my Spanish is not so great and ask him to please slow down. He does for one sentence, then is back to rapid-fire and mumbled talking. Someone in Argentina had told me that I would have difficulty understanding the Chilenos; here is the proof that they were right. Still, he is sweet and welcoming, and I blame myself for not improving my Spanish enough in all my time traveling. I smile and nod.

I get settled in my room, fool around on the internet (that glorious time-suck), and then get ready to go to Bikram yoga, Santiago Centro. It's an easy ten-minute walk from the apartment. Once in class, my body kicks into memory mode; stretching, reaching, balancing. I'm pleased. Sweaty and worn out, but pleased nonetheless. I'm cautious walking there and back, but I feel okay. Maybe tomorrow I will venture out and sight-see again. For now I feel tender, recently wounded, and I am happy to take it easy.

In the evening Paulo and his wife Eva have a few friends over. I sit with them and try to chat, feeling awkward. Their friend David is nice and takes pity on me, substituting English words when I can't understand the Spanish. I blend into the conversation as best I can. They tell me that there is a traditional Chilean show at a restaurant, and if I have no plans we can go tomorrow or Thursday. Thursday is my birthday; I say let's go then! David asks if I like to dance; I say yes. He offers to take me to a club tomorrow where they have a lesson in salsa, machaca, and cumbia, then play music so you can show off your new moves. I tell him I would love it!

During the day I venture out and discover a cultural center with free displays. They are showing the paintings of Matta, a Chilean surrealist painter. There are other small galleries and a museum shop on the top floor and I visit, appreciating the boost of culture. I make my way down to the main display, which is spread out throughout three parts of the lower floor. The cavernous cultural center winds around an atrium with colorful art suspended from the ceiling like kites. I am impressed by the immense size of the Matta paintings. This is not my favorite kind of art; I prefer realism. Nevertheless, I enjoy Matta's playful use of color and shape. I come to appreciate the less realistic rendition of themes in his pieces as I walk among them.

In an adjacent room there is an interactive technology display. In hands-on exhibits I experiment with music and color. One display has a large screen and senses movement in a marked-off rectangle on the floor, where movement is translated to music and lights on the screen.

An old man with a crazy mop of white hair jutting at angles from a bald pate is standing in the rectangle. He waves his hand and some tones sound. I watch. He is curious, playing with the concept. He looks at me and smiles, so I enter the rectangle and begin to spin, arms out, which sets off a cacophony of various tones. The shadow image of my body flashes on the screen in red and yellow vague shapes. The old man grins at me and nods. We strike up a short conversation. I tell him, when he asks (they always ask) that I am American.

"Are you traveling with someone?" This is the other question that people always ask.

"No," I say with a smile. I have to smile when I say it so people believe that I'm okay. "Sola."

He comments on the beautiful blue color of my eyes, taking my hand. I can't help but be flattered. I tell him my birthday is this week and that I am going out with local friends. He says it's a pity that I have plans as he would like to invite me for a drink. I give him the traditional cheek kiss and say ciao.

As I go through the last sala de arte, I see some quotes on the wall. One stirs me and I reach for my camera, bringing a tight-lipped lady in a blue suit and severe bun scurrying over. "No fotos!" she scolds me.

I point to the camera, and to the quote on the wall, which is not even part of the artwork, for god's sake! "Sin flash?" I ask. Without flash?

"No!"

I tuck the camera away and pull out a notebook.

Saccharine sweet, I ask if I can copy down the words. She shrugs, gives one last chastising look and marches off, but stops about thirty feet away and watches me carefully as I write down the phrase:

"Hay que crear para creer." You have to create to believe. I have heard this phrased the opposite way; you have to believe to create, and both are true for me, but I like it this way. It stands logic on its head. Create first, then you will believe. I interpret that I need to be who I am, to find my own inner muse, before I can have the rest of the life I want. I snap my notebook shut and leave the room, careful not to make eye contact with the guard.

Back on the street my hand rests on the knife in my pocket from time to time for reassurance, but there is no sign of further trouble. When a man looks my way now I assume he's not looking because he finds me attractive, but because he wants to steal my purse. I try not to scowl; I hate this feeling. A man, crossing the street to beat the light, runs past me. I squeal and jump to the side, heart pounding. Time, I tell myself. It will take time.

At the artisan market there are uniformed security guards at the entrances, which makes me breathe a little easier. I browse, looking at the brightly colored display items in each stand. There are tourist t-shirts proclaiming "Chile" or "Santiago". I think of my own slogan, a shirt to buy for my girls: "My Mom was robbed in Santiago and he only left her enough to buy me this crummy t-shirt." Nah.

I find a little owl for Emily made of blue lapis, a popular stone from these parts. For myself I find a pair of copper earrings and a top in blueberry blue with a native looking design. It's demure, but cinches in at the waist, emphasizing my hourglass figure. I will wear it for my birthday.

It is hot out; I stop for a drink and an empanada of spinach, which is horrible. I have been good about not eating meat, and it really has not been difficult. But I'll bet the ham and cheese empanada was miles better than the soggy spinach one.

Back on the street I notice a hill with a large yellow building. My map says it is Parque Santa Lucia. I walk up and gaze at Neptune's fountain. A happy couple asks me to take their photo and I oblige. I don't feel like asking them to take mine, although I have very few photos of myself. Another down side of traveling alone.

The park is beautiful, laced with winding dirt paths that meander up the hill. It is studded with tall trees, regal and dark and beckoning with their shade. Vines and flowers languish on the hillsides: hyacinths of light purple and hot pink impatiens. I take a narrow path leading up. At the top of the hill is what they call the Castillo, or castle, with a large stone gate. Farther up is an old hermita, fenced off from tourists, and farther still, on the last layer of the wedding-cake hill, is a mirador, or viewpoint. I struggle up the stone stairs, stepping over the ubiquitous street dog (in this case, park dog) who is sleeping guilelessly, unmindful of visitors navigating the path. The faint murmur of British voices drifts behind me as another group is on my heels. Finally, at the top, I am treated with a view of the entire city of Santiago, its tall buildings and mountains in the distance. It was worth the climb. One of the British chaps takes pity on me as I extend my arm and try to get a selfie.

"Shall I take your photo?"

"Yes, please!" I keep my sunglasses on for the movie star look and smile brightly for the camera.

The heat is getting to me, so on the way down the hill I stop on a large expanse of lawn shaded by generous tall trees. A fellow being has also had this idea, so I lay down beside him and stroke his silky ear as we relax together. I stare up at the tree branches and canopy of star-shaped leaves, rustling faintly in the breeze. I feel content. The dog heaves a sigh under my hand. Later I will learn that this park, with its winding expanse of trails and hidden nooks, is also a haven for robbers, but at this moment I am blissfully unaware, and I would not have wanted to miss the afternoon out of fear.

I am tired when I return, so I take a short siesta. David is coming for me around nine. We greet each other and I put on a bit of makeup and a glittery top. Off we go, for my first trip on the Santiago subway.

We participate in the group lesson, stepping side to side, back and forth, hip-wiggling and dipping. There is a break and we get Coronas. When the music starts we dance salsa then machaca. It feels good to hold David's hands in mine, and he is encouraging and forgiving. I can be quite a klutz in dance steps; I'm better at freestyle. Still we manage to have fun, and I enjoy watching seasoned dancers on the floor when we take a break.

In the cab home I tell David that, long ago, I used to be a topless dancer. I guess it's my way of apologizing for my current clumsiness, and letting him know I wasn't always so awkward. I tell him about the dark café I passed when I went back to the apartment earlier in the day. Music was blasting from inside a café with painted windows. As I looked at the place, wondering what it was, a young girl in a hot pink bikini with vinyl high white boots opened the door and peered out. She gasped and shut the door, then slowly and shyly opened it again. I smiled at her. She gestured and invited me in. I entered, glanced around at the dark room where three or four bikini-clad girls were sitting on stools, bored. There were two men standing in the corner. I felt foreign and ill at ease, so I thanked her and ducked back out into the startling sunlight.

David laughs. "We call this café con piernas." Coffee with legs.

Thursday dawns; it is my forty-ninth birthday. Maria, the maid, offers to accompany me to the markets in town. She takes me through a market pungent with the smell of fish. The vendors and restaurateurs try to persuade us to stop and buy. I flirt with a fish man, telling him it's my birthday. He gives me a kiss on the cheek and starts singing Happy Birthday in English. A few of the other fish vendors come over to sing to me and I offer my cheek for more kisses. I am laughing. Maria looks embarrassed. I break away from my fishy fans and we walk on, until we tire and return to the apartment for lunch.

After a little siesta, I go back to Bikram yoga. I enter drinking coffee and am chastised by the teacher. The class is good but I'm a little worn out, so I don't push myself. Plus, there is more dancing to do tonight!

I dress in skinny black jeans and my new blue top, and off we go to a restaurant called "Los Buenos Muchachos." Our group is Paulo and Eva, David, and me. Paulo orders appetizers: a cheese plate and a bowl of ceviche – fish marinated in vinegar with onion and tomato. It's fresh and delicious.

The show begins with traditional Chilean dancers, the men dressed in black and the women in bright skirts. They wave handkerchiefs over their heads and dance in a circle, one hand on their hips. Audience members are invited to join, and Eva steps out.

"How do all these people know that dance?" I ask, puzzled.

"It's a traditional Chilean dance," Paulo explains. I watch the display. My country does not have a national dance I realize sadly.

Eva returns to the table, breathless. The next part of the show begins with women in grass skirts, the men holding wooden masks up. It reminds me of Hawaii.

"They are doing a dance from Easter Island," David says. How I wish that I could visit Easter Island! Next trip, I suppose. After the show we get on the floor to dance. David holds me close. I have drunk too much red wine; I'm letting my wild side have a go. I bump my hips back and forth, swaying. David matches my moves.

When we return home, David and I talk for a while in English. It feels like cheating but I welcome the break. We say goodbye with several long kisses. David hints at visiting me in Con Con next week. But I know I don't want to break my celibate streak for a one-night stand, even with someone as nice as this. Still, I let myself enjoy being kissed, sharing the intimacy that comes from all the dancing we did together.

Friday is my last day in town. I walk the few blocks to see the changing of the guard at the Palacio Moneda. There is much pageantry, complete with marching band and uniformed soldiers doing fancy moves in unison with their rifles. The horses march in; one is doing a hollow passage (a slow, suspended trot.) They stand by the palace. The band sounds all right, but someone hits a sour note occasionally.

After the changing of guardia I find the nearest subway and take the route I have decided on to get to Cristobal Hill, where a funicular will take me to the top for another view of the city. On the way there, walking a few blocks from the subway, I find myself crossing Rio Marapocho once again. It's not the same place where I was robbed, but I am still frozen with fear, eyes darting around as I walk. I take the picnic knife out of my pocket and clutch it in my hand, hidden but available. Available for what, though? I cannot even squish a spider - I coax them onto a magazine and relocate them outside. Could I stab a potential robber? Nah. But I might, dredging up my long-lost acting skills, wave the knife around like an insane person and scream in Spanglish. That is my strategy should someone approach me. It is the best I can do.

I find a little square with shops and restaurants, and the reassuring presence of security guards once again. Santiago is really trying to protect me, bless its little heart. I buy laminated fruit slice earrings for my daughters. The earrings are just unusual enough that they might like them!

The funicular ride to the top of the hill is fun; it goes straight up as it cuts a swath through jungle-like foliage and trickles of water. The zoo is halfway up, and I'm sorry I did not buy the ticket for this as well, but I must leave time for Pablo Neruda today! There are many stray dogs at the top of the hill. I pet one, and reach to pet his friend but he growls. Protecting her? I see that these dogs are an actual couple, as later they have moved to another spot, flopping in the sun together. It makes me wistful, briefly. Even dogs can find someone they love; why is it such a problem for me? But I chase the thought out sternly. None of that, little celibate-by-choice missy!

I go back down and set off to find La Chascona, just down the street. I opt for the English tour guide, feeling that my Spanish is not up to the task. La Chascona was the name Pablo Neruda, famous poet of Chile, gave to his lover Mathilda. He built this house for her to live in as his mistress while he was married to another woman. The guide takes us into the first room.

"Does anyone know what the name La Chascona means?" he asks. No one else does. But I do. This is what Brad used to call me, the woman with the crazy hair.

Mathilda did indeed have wild messy hair- tousled red curls. I smile at her picture, admiring her. Oh, to be the woman who inspired great romantic poetry! All I have ever inspired are a few drunk text messages. I guess it's a start.

We tour the house, which is filled with Neruda's own be- longings. Most of them were brought over from his home in Normandy, France, because this house was looted and destroyed by the Chilean army who disapproved of Neruda's communist ties. The guide tells us of Neruda's life and of Mathilda's dedication to restoring the house after his death. I examine pictures of him, a rotund man with thinning hair, a large nose, a big belly, and a kind smile. Looking at him, you wouldn't think Neruda was any more romantic than any average man. I know that somewhere at home in a box I have a book of Neruda's poetry, one page in Spanish and on the facing page, the English translation. I sigh. Someday I will get to unpack my books.

Back at the apartment I ask Eva to help me call Ivan for the ride back to Maitencillo. I'm more than ready to get back to the beach, to the calm environment, to the reassuring job of cleaning cabanas. On the ride back I tell Ivan about my Santiago experience. He tells me that this type of robbery, the quick grab and go, is called "lancado". I tell him I might get some pepper spray.

He laughs at me. "You wouldn't have time to use it! What are you going to do, insist that he stand there while you get it out and spray him?"

I laugh too. "Wait!" I call to my imaginary assailant. "I have one more thing for you, hang on a minute!"

As night falls, we head back to Maitencillo. Lights twinkle in the hills as we move out of town, through the countryside. I feel content to be going back to the beach. Much as I love a city, I feel like I can heal here.

The best rum to drink when you have been robbed

The beach at Maitencillo

Maitencillo And Con Con; Recovery

Of course, I have to relate the story of my robbery a few more times, and that is exactly what it has become: a story. I have not forgotten the feelings: the anxiety, the feeling of violation, the despair at my own naiveté, or the resulting paranoia. But each time I relate the story, it stings less.

Ethel shows me her left ear, which has a slot instead of a pierced hole. She tells me that when she was a young mother with a baby in her arms, sitting on the bus, a thief walked up and pulled her gold earrings right out of her ears. The right one popped out, but the left one resisted, leaving an irreparable tear. I feel lucky that I was not violated physically; all I lost was stuff, not my own flesh. I shake my head at the thought of thieves who maim mothers holding babies.

As a gesture to repay Ethel for all her kindness, I offer to take her to dinner one night. At the top of the stairs that lead down to the beach is a cute little café and bar that I have wanted to try. She tells me it's new and she has not yet tried it either. We sit and order drinks, which are delicious: mine, a margarita, and hers a mojito. We consult the menu and decide to share, ordering a shrimp quesadilla and macha (a type of shellfish) in parmesan. Both are decadently delicious; the quesadilla perfectly browned with the shrimp plump and bursting with flavor at each bite. The macha reminds me of lobster. Flakes of red meat are doused in a bubbling creamy parmesan sauce that we ladle onto chunks of bread. Each bite is a little treasure; I am practically purring. It's certainly not low-cal and for once I don't care. Later, when I stumble into bed, I am completely sated.

In the morning Ethel rouses me for breakfast and I stumble sleepily in to drink instant coffee with boiled milk. How I miss real coffee! Ben the couchsurfer is back and the three of us have been having interesting conversations in Spanish about love, relationships and life in general. Ben is refurbishing a VW Kombi to be ready to travel from South America to Alaska. Yesterday Ethel and I were trying to persuade Ben, the perfectionist, that it's okay if the Kombi doesn't come together as quickly or perfectly as he would like, but it is difficult to convince him. He's frustrated with the tools, with the project itself. There is lots of screaming and cursing as he works on the van. I think this must be the inalienable right of men when it comes to cars; I don't think I have ever heard a man quietly humming as he tinkers with an engine or tries to adjust a window crank. Maybe the swearing helps get the job done?

As I water the plants in the morning, there is a magical mist floating in off the ocean. It hovers above the trees; the branches shimmer in a shadowy cloak. It reminds me of San Francisco fog, without being heavy or damp. The sun is warm on my back. I bend to sniff the buried fragrance of a crimson rose as I water. It's such a tranquil place, especially after my experience in Santiago.

I am thinking again, as I have often, about having my own home. I crave it now. It is my carrot as this trip was once my carrot to get through single parenting. This doesn't mean I am not enjoying my time here. But I recognize that I am not necessarily a person who will crave traveling for months and years, at least not by myself. And even with a partner I know I would be missing my kids, my parents, my friends, my dogs. I think that is what this trip has taught me above all – that I want a home.

I am imagining a home by myself now, where I can be happy alone. The front room with its gleaming polished hard wood floors will be adorned with large floor pillows for meditating. There will be a wicker basket in the corner with jewel-colored yoga mats. It will be sparse and beautiful. In my bedroom I will have my Morocco theme – the camel-bone henna mirror, the leather lamp with its brightly painted red and orange design, and the wool and camel hair bedspread, also gay red and orange and gold. My daddy's oil painting of the ocean at sunset will hang on the wall. I smile as I decorate my house in my head.

And yes, someday I want to share it all with someone. But this is not my focus any more. I have shifted gears. I'm happily coasting in neutral. Neutral as in neutered, at least for the time being. I am holding on to my fire and light and energy and saving it for the right moment. No more will I open the treasure box for random pirates to pillage and loot and plunder and leave, waving their damned jolly roger as they go. I am going to be selfish. I am going to wait.

Finally comes the day to go to the resort hotel in Con-Con. I am excited to indulge myself and not work for my lodging. Ben and I rattle up the road in the Kombi; he has been nice enough to drive me so I don't have to deal with luggage on a bus. After a hug goodbye, I go to reception. Although there is a glitch in which they cannot find my reservation, eventually I get a room. I'm proud of my mellow new personality; I remain calm while we sort things out instead of getting angry or anxious.

The resort is beautiful, if a little careworn, and self-contained. It's not very near the beach but when I am shown to my fourth-floor room, my hotel guide points out the balcony. I look out on one of the outdoor pools, a little oasis on a green lawn. Directly below my room, hummingbirds dart to sip the nectar of a crimson trumpet flower bush. Beyond the pool, a stretch of sand dunes extends like a frozen beige ocean: cresting gentle waves which give way to a band of trees, then the actual ocean; a horizon of blue that rolls out to the end of the view, finally merging with a pale sky. I sigh with contentment. This will be my view all week.

My guide takes me around to show me the restaurant, the gym, sauna, massage room, two indoor pools and another outdoor one, entertainment area, a banquet hall, and an exhibition hall displaying artwork of Chilean painters. There are classes several times a day in the pool or the gym: yoga, water aerobics, and dance lessons. Every night there is an activity of some sort. I won't need to leave the place at all if I don't want to. There is even a mini market to shop for supplies for cooking in the kitchen.

I know that the beauty of travel is to experience life the way it is lived in each country; to get with the locals for language, food, and activities. But occasionally I like the kind of break that resort life affords: a touch of luxury, however faded, is welcome from time to time. Couch surfing and helping at farms and cleaning cabanas suits me fine. But this will be my spa week; my week to do tons of yoga, swim, lay in the sun, and write. I'm thrilled.

Days pass happily. I attend a yoga or Pilates class each day, go to the pool and swim, lay in the sun, hang out in my room, make healthy food and drink a lot of tea. I do yoga on my own, spreading out my mat and gazing out at the ocean sparkling blue in the distance. I sleep taking up the whole bed and let the sunshine spreading across my face coax me slowly awake each morning.

This is a time for processing my travels, and indeed I sometimes feel a new bit of growth, like a plant that is growing new tender green shoots, reaching up for the sun and drinking in the rain.

Blog Post: Dancing in My Tears

Today I cried.

I was in a stretching class. There were three participants and the teacher. I'm in Chile, and everybody speaks Spanish, so I keep my ears tuned to catch the words, straining to hear over the music playlist the teacher has selected. But it's not hard; I just copy what she is doing.

Suddenly a song comes on, and my eyes begin to weep. The song is "Dancing" by Elisa. It's about four years old. My soul shoots back to the past and everything that this song brings up: my then-16-year-old daughter Emily playing it over and over on the computer speakers. My own turbulent emotions that related so much to the angst and longing in the song, to love lamented.

Four years ago, I was firmly entrenched in a long-distance love affair; a relationship I knew would ultimately end, although it lasted five years. My heart resonated to the desperate pleading in the singer's voice; the knowledge and despair that love so strong and profound was not enough to change the tide. The hopelessness of loving someone incapable of loving you back.

All this comes rushing back to me and tears run freely

from my eyes as I lay back on the mat. The instructor, a young Chilean woman, looks at me with concern but wisely says nothing. I don't break down, but merely let tears stream unrestricted as I stretch one leg, then the other.

Then somehow the sadness morphs into joy. It's the joy of remembering the pleasure of what it feels like to be in love. The joy of missing my beautiful daughters as they grow and change and lead their own lives. The sweet ache of love reaching across the miles, across oceans and mountains, to hold them in my thoughts when I can't hold them in my arms. Missing my children. Missing not the object of my own romantic longings (for that ran its inevitable course and left me with the realization that it was better ended) but the expansion of the heart that comes with falling in love.

And finally, I relax into my tears. I don't encourage them, and I don't try to stop them. This is why singers sing. It is why songwriters write. It's why I write too, to connect through art with someone who feels the human condition the way I do; someone whose heart says "thank you" when they read my words. We live to be moved. I never want to close myself off to that.

I smile through the tears that end as soon as the song does. But I am changed, connecting and opening to my own tenderness. With gratitude, I welcome the sunshine of a new day.

I call Cecily and she agrees to pick me up and take me to Vina del Mar on Monday. She wants to introduce me to her uncle Marino, she tells me with a matchmaker glint in her eye. In rushes Disney Princess – I thought I killed that bitch - and my mind runs wild: imagining a sexy and sweet dark man who worships my body and becomes obsessed with making love to me for the next week. We swim naked in the ocean. I make food in his kitchen and feed him from my hand. He accompanies me on my next step of the journey and we explore San Pedro de Atacama together, awestruck at Moon Valley, holding hands as we stroll through town. Then, tearfully, we part: I move on to Peru, and he returns to work. We promise to remember each other always.

I have not even met this guy yet!

Turns out I don't have to worry about this love affair either. As Cecily and three-year-old Isabella and I drive in Vina de Mar, he calls her and tells her he must be in Santiago this week for work. I'm disappointed and relieved. Cecily has taken me under her wing for the week. She insists that she will find some way to get me exploring Valparaiso with a guide.

"Cecily, it's okay. I do a lot of things alone," I remind her. "And I don't want to take up all of your time."

While Cecily works at her computer, I hang out with Isabella. She is a bright and willful child, an Aries, who throws frequent fits to get her own way, and since this seems to work for her she shows no sign of stopping. I gently try to suggest that Cecily lay some ground rules before it's too late. Far from the perfect parent myself, I can sympathize. Cecily tells me she and Antonio have plans to have another child and I am glad to hear this, for every only child I know has difficulty negotiating social situations. They grow up thinking the world revolves around them, and in a sense it does. I relate some stories of raising my Veronica, also an Aries, to Cecily, letting her know that I have been there, and it turned out fine. I sit with Isabella and read fairy tales in Spanish, tripping over the big words. She turns pages before I am done. I learn the words for fairy, spinning wheel, spell.

On my last day at the resort Ethel comes to visit. We sit by the pool and converse in Spanish; I feel I have made another true friend here. Ethel has brought me a gift, a little mirror in a wooden frame engraved with my name. She tells me I am always welcome at her cabanas, and I know she means it.

I am starting to feel the creeping sense of anxiety that I always get when changing locations. I don't know why it hasn't gotten better for me. On my last night I am restless and anxious. Little things go wrong: the bank card that my dad sent to replace the stolen one has still not arrived. The bus reservation on the internet is not going through. The internet in general is slow, so it ceases to be entertaining and begins to be frustrating. I could go to the Casino Night at the restaurant, but I don't want to go anywhere. I eat popcorn and drink the rest of the rum I bought before my birthday – happy that it lasted so long! My yoga mat lays undisturbed on the floor. If it had eyes it would be looking at me with reprimand. I am slothful, slightly depressed.

The next day I check out of the resort and spend the day by the pool. It's a lazy day. Cecily picks me up and we go to her house. I do some yoga while she cooks for Isabella. My bus, which we found through another company even cheaper, leaves at eleven.

While Isabella naps Cecily tells me some of the woes of her marriage; she is afraid her husband drinks too much and he is negative about everything she does when they are together. I remind her of her secret weapon; the power of sex. I don't mean it in a bad or manipulative way, but the way to a man's heart has never been his stomach. It's a bit lower. When you are making love regularly with your mate, a lot of problems seem to fix themselves. She tells me she will try it.

It is sad to me that relationships are always fraught with problems. Shouldn't it be easier than this? I have been envisioning, a la The Secret, the relationship I want to find when I get home. But for a while, I am unemployed and homeless, a real catch. I might have to wait until I get my life back together if I don't want someone with low standards!

When I think about how difficult it is to strike a perfect balance in a relationship, I am reminded of how naive I have been. In our five years together, I knew that there was something missing for Brad. The fervor of my love for him could not make up for the fact that he never really loved me. He felt bad, ashamed, and tried to make up for it with fun dates and romantic weekends, which only served to cement my misguided adoration even further. But I was never really "it" for him.

It's not a crime not to love me. I can't blame him for that. But the lesson I learned from that experience is that it's not fair to do that to another person. And was the fault Brad's for deluding me, or mine for allowing myself to be deluded?

There is a meditation mantra, Hum Sa, meaning "I am that." It is recognizing in one's self the connection to the outside world, or that which is. It relates to the Buddhist principles of inter-connectedness and of seeing reality as it is, not as we wish for it to be, or is it might be in the future. In my relationship with Brad, I pulled the wool over my own eyes. It wasn't fair to either of us. I am determined to never do that again, even if it means never having a relationship with a man. Not having a relationship is better than having one that is not authentic.

Cecily drops me off at the bus with hugs and kisses and promises to keep in touch. Isabella, grumpy and sleepy, refuses a hug. Off I go to the next part of my journey, feeling very lucky indeed to have met such a good friend.

San Pedro De Atacama; The Desert

I'm sure I will sleep on the bus. A young man sits down next to me- a handsome Chilean boy who reminds me of a darker, smaller, Elvis. He is confident and chatty, and I take the opportunity to practice my Spanish. He tells me that he is going through a divorce, gives me a chocolate bar and flatters me by saying he just can't believe I'm forty-nine. Eventually, around two thirty, we sleep. His warm arm presses against mine. I've told him I'm una monja, a nun. I seem to be saving my energies for something almost holy. But still, the dark Elvis looks and the rapid teasing Spanish has got me thinking. I'm glad that he is getting off at Coquimbo. He kisses my cheek.

"Cuidate," he says. Take care. He will look me up on Facebook, he promises.

Bus life is weird. You sit, you sleep, you watch dumb movies. You sleep some more and eat junk. Some bus assistant comes through occasionally with cookies. This cheaper bus does not have a bathroom, so when we stop I always try to go. Sometimes there is not a place to use a toilet.

I gaze out the window as we move along. At about two thirty in the afternoon, we turn away from the coast and the rolling blue ocean. It sends up some splashes against a rock as we turn up a road, a wave waving goodbye. I'm done with my last book, so I stare out at the scenery, of which there is not much: dry cracked earth with faint tinges of red rock. There are a few cacti for a while, and some shrines. I suppose they are dedicated to people who have died out here.

I imagine myself walking, hot and tired through the arid land. There is no shade. Would I drink my own pee like the rock climber who inspired the movie 127 hours? I pray the bus does not break down. I think about that movie, starring the adorable James Franco, and its message. To me it was clear: we need people. No man is an island. We need each other; that's why we are all here. Me, my children, my new friends and old. My ex-husband and the creep who robbed me in Santiago as well. We all need each other. Maybe some of us, like the last two bad guys, need victims, someone to prey on. Others need someone to pray for. Still others need people to enrich their lives and connect with. I want to believe with all my heart that we are here for this.

⸎⸎⸎⸎⸎

I am on my way to the Atacama Desert, one of the most barren deserts in the world. It is a strip of land west of the Andes Mountain range that has been used for Mars expedition simulations. I will spend a few days exploring here, then make my way to Peru. Cecily helped me find a hostel with a private room; no more bunks! I'll be getting in late tonight, and tomorrow I will explore the desert by taking a tour or two.

The twenty-four plus hour bus trip, eating cookies and nuts all day leaves me feeling groggy. I disembark the bus around midnight, disoriented, and try to follow the little hand drawn map I made from the internet page directing me to the hostel.

San Pedro is a cute touristic town, very rustic with red dirt roads that must be charming while sauntering around shopping, but not so much when hauling a heavy bag that gets bogged down in the earth. I struggle the few blocks to the hostel, grunting and praying the wheels hold. At the hostel I wake the night worker, who shows me to my room. It looks like heaven. I flop into bed, exhausted.

The following day I consult with the hostel owner about tours. Fresh from my lazy yoga week, I gear up for excursions. I book four and take a walk to get the cash I need. Since my new debit card never arrived at the resort, I am using the credit card to withdraw cash, which is very inefficient because of the fees, but it is my only option.

On my first afternoon there is a tour at four o'clock to the Valley of the Moon, Valle de Luna. Once upon a time, Valle de Luna and the dunes were underwater and now the salt deposits remain in the earth. They have been washed up by all the rain to the top of the sand, our guide tells us, where the earth is frosted white like powdered sugar on a donut. Sand dunes stretch out through the landscape, mingled with rock formations, red and craggy. On the horizon beyond, under a lightning studded sky, the Domeco mountain range rises, indigo blue against a backdrop of silver sky. Our group walks to the top of the Duna Mayor, the main dune, where a trail takes us along the top ridge with magnificent views. I pant going up the trail, feeling the change of altitude now. The views are breathtaking and worth the hike.

Walking from the bus drop-off back to the hostel I am approached by a guy with flyers for a restaurant; full meal with drink and dessert for five thousand pesos, or about ten bucks. I decide to go for it. The meal is amazing. Restaurant Grado Six is off the beaten path by a block. It is small, and the ceiling looks like rock formations. A dragon leers from above the bar, its tongue jutting out madly. I order the soup of mariscos, salmon and potatoes, and red wine. The soup is delectable, served with bread and salsa. The salmon is a shimmering tender pink and incredibly moist. And the dessert, a plum custard, is wonderful. I leave the restaurant fully satisfied. The next morning, I must leave at four to go to the geysers, so I attempt an earlyish bed time, but eleven o'clock still does not give me much sleep.

The bus to the geysers is full of sleepy tourists. Our guide, a bearded skinny fellow, encourages us to get some sleep if we like. It is cold. Standing outside the hostel, a girl asked me if I had something warmer than my capris and suggested I bring more clothes. I grabbed my jeans, and added fuzzy socks and a scarf. Now I am glad for the extra clothes. We pass snow and ice on the hills all around, and a van is stuck ahead of us in ruts of mud. Our driver maneuvers around it and we pass a lake edged in ice as we continue up the hill, traveling through deep puddles and sticky red mud on the road.

We get to the top and enter the park. I change into my jeans at the bathroom, and Pato, our guide, links arms with me as I exit. "Watch the puddles," he says. Surprised, I take his arm and we return to the bus, which takes us a bit farther down the road to the main geysers.

The thermal activity happens at sunrise, which is why we had to get up so damned early. The cold night and the subsequent heating of the underground water by the morning sun makes the geothermal effect that causes the geysers to erupt. We walk amongst the geysers, and Pato introduces them with childish enthusiasm.

"Look, you can see and hear the water beginning to boil. Get your cameras out! Once it begins you will have twelve seconds for your pictures."

The geyser begins to bubble up. Pato begins to count. "One, two, three…" Sure enough, he was right about the timing. Twelve seconds later, the fountain of water quickly falls away, disappearing back into the ground.

We tour around the geysers. I have slipped the fuzzy socks onto my hands as gloves. I stomp my feet to warm them, then get the idea to stand in front of one of the steaming holes, letting the vapor warm me. Soon Pato calls that breakfast is ready.

When they said we would have breakfast on this tour, I assumed there was a little restaurant or café at the top of the mountain. But the breakfast is made by the bus driver, who has boiled eggs and heated milk in the water of the geysers as we were touring around. There is instant coffee and sandwiches of ham and cheese. I peel off the ham and cut my egg open to put it on the sandwich. It is surprisingly good. I pour geyser-warmed milk into my instant coffee.

We have more time to walk around, taking pictures, then it is off to the hot springs to soak. First, we stop again at the bathrooms. "You can use the bathroom, or take pictures," says Pato. "but no pictures of the bathrooms!" he teases, wagging his finger at us.

The landscape is beautiful, with plants and grass wearing crystal crowns of ice. Mountains watch over all. Here and there, wild vicunas, pale creatures that look like a cross between a deer and a goat, wander the hills. They are protected, says Pato, because of their valuable fur, which is used for textiles.

We bathe in the hot springs, which are not very hot in some places, with pockets of scalding water in others. There is squishy mud all through the bottom. We change, shielding ourselves with towels, and back on the bus we go.

The final stop is a little town called Machuca. There I buy more instant coffee and two cheese empanadas, warm and crispy from the fryer. I walk around a bit, but decide not to walk up to the little church at the top. The altitude, four thousand meters, is still a little difficult for me.

My next tour is that same afternoon. On this tour, we go to the salt spring laguna to float in the water. I lay on my belly, my legs turned up behind me. I try to grab my ankles in a floating version of bow pose, but I capsize, falling face-first into the extremely salty water. I give up floating yoga and just enjoy the experience. For days afterwards I will be scraping salt crystals out of my ears.

On my last day in San Pedro, I take a final tour. This tour will take us to a flamingo reserve and then up into the mountains to visit two turquoise lakes, splendorous in their natural beauty. The day is lovely and sunny, and we end with a late lunch at a local restaurant. Most people are eating llama, but I, of course, order the vegetarian option, which is a quinoa dish. Afterwards, we go back to the village, where I take my time packing and get the bus to Arica at 8:30.

At the bus station I meet a young English couple. They are taking the same bus as I am. We strike up conversation, and get on the bus, where I hope, once again, to sleep. This bus goes to Arica, at the northern end of Chile. From there I take a short trip across the border to Tacna, Peru, and from there to Cuzco. I have optimistically booked a hostel. I say optimistic because I have no bus tickets beyond this one. I hope I will be able to buy them as I go.

To complicate matters, the bus stops for a while at about three AM. The bus assistant comes through to tell us that the bridge on the only road to Arica is out and that we will have to reroute to Iquique to wait. I drift into sleep, unable to arrange my body comfortably, but still tired. My seat mate snores slightly. The man in front of me has reclined his seat all the way back. I shift around but can barely move. I wake up at around eight and my ankles and feet are swollen from being unable to move or elevate them. Damn it.

We sit on the bus at the station for a long time. I wake up, disoriented and feeling confined. It's like a horror movie: trapped on the bus! But then I think about it as my mind clears. We are at a bus station. Bus stations have cafes and bathrooms. Surely, they are letting people off the bus, if we are stuck here indefinitely. Yes, the door is open. I stagger off and ask the driver how long he thinks we will be. It is eight in the morning. He shrugs.

"Quien sabe." Who knows?

I get coffee, use the bathroom, and wonder how to kill the time. As I wander outside, the couple I met earlier are sitting on a bench. We chat a while until I spot something: just outside the small station there is an interesting spot by the back door with a tile floor, cordoned off by fake wrought iron that borders the sidewalk. The floor is dirty and probably slippery, but at least it is tucked away with a little bit of privacy. I go over and do about half an hour of bus station yoga, garnering surprised looks from the passersby.

Yoga in a place like this has some disadvantages: my mat is stored with my suitcase under the bus, so I have to deal with the dirty floor and I can't do poses where my body touches the ground, because that would be disgusting. The public aspect of it means that I must focus and concentrate. It also makes me feel a little accountable for some reason. I want to represent and show yoga as a flowing physical task rather than a few simple stretches. I avoid the stares and grins from passing people. When I am done, I feel good and my ankle swelling has gone down.

The bus is still sitting there. I ask again about the departure time, and get another vague answer. As I get back onto the bus to grab a cereal bar from my bag the man in the aisle seat in front of mine asks me in Spanish if I know anything about our timetable. Of course I don't, but we talk about the bridge being down and how frustrating waiting can be. He tells me he works seven days in Calama and then has seven days off, when he goes home to Arica.

As he talks to me, his eyes keep flickering down my body in a creepy way. I wish I had the guts to be just as impolite and say, "Hey! Pendejo! My eyes are up here!" I inquire about his poor wife waiting for him in Arica. Then I go back inside to buy another cheap coffee from a machine.

Finally, after waiting a frustrating six hours or so, we are told that the bus is ready to leave. After a twelve-hour delay, we will finally get on our way! People clap at the announcement, then we board the bus. But for another half an hour we sit on the pavement, waiting. Finally, we are told we must go to Arica on a different bus. We get our luggage out and wait. No one seems to know what bus we are supposed to get onto. People push me out of the way to line up at the baggage storage under the bus. Worse than Spain, many of the men here are happy to push a woman out of the way. I finally snap at one and he apologizes quickly.

"Estamos todos en el mismo barco!" I remind him. We are all in the same boat. Or bus as the case may be.

Other buses are coming and going. It is past noon. Finally, at about one thirty, there is an announcement: our bus is ready.

We load onto a smaller, single floor bus. Not everyone is allowed on, hence the pushing, I guess. A huge sumo wrestler of a man is in the seat in front of me. He must not be Chileno, as they are generally small in stature. This guy must weigh close to three hundred pounds, and as my luck would have it, he enjoys leaning his seat all the way back as far as it goes, then pushing his bulk into the reclined seat. He is now pretty much in my lap. It's going to be a long four hours. I stare at the roll of fat on the back of his neck, trying to think compassionate and peaceful thoughts; everyone has a right to comfort. But if I wanted a Saint Bernard to frolic with, I would do it outdoors, not in a cramped bus.

Flamingo in the Atacama landscape

Salt flats in the Atacama desert

Peru, Not Without Much Ado!

The bus pulls into Arica and immediately up pops an agent who sells us bus tickets to Arequipa for my English friends, and to Cuzco for me. Another traveler on our bus asks about the Cuzco ticket. He is a tall bespectacled Englishman named Gavin. We all pile into a car and miraculously fit our luggage into the back, and off we go to the border.

We cross the border into Peru, parking on one side and walking through customs, where our driver meets us on the other side.

As we enter Peru the sun is setting magnificently: a glowing orange orb slowly sinking on a desolate horizon. We drive into Tacna, where we will depart. When we get to the office that sells tickets to Cuzco, we learn that the road is blocked; what is it with that? So Gavin and I decide to go on to Arequipa with the other two and find our Cuzco ticket once we get there.

The bus arrives at a crowded bus station. People are lying on the floor sleeping. We step around them to find the ticket window, where we splurge the extra few dollars for the bigger seats on the lower half of the bus, and I reserve a seat in front so I can put my feet up on the glass. After a breakfast of toast and eggs, (we all open up our electronic devices, comically hungry for internet connections) we say goodbye and Gavin and I grab our bus. It turns out we paid that helpful agent Chile prices for a bus that is about a third the cost; but at least we had help across the border and did not have to worry about where we were. I guess it was worth it.

The bus ride to Cusco is one of the best I've ever spent. My feet are up, Gavin is good company, and the countryside is beautiful, with rolling hills and luscious grass so green it almost hurts my eyes to look at. There are animals peacefully grazing everywhere. I see more wild vicunas, tan colored and agile. There are flocks of white sheep that look brown due to large patches of mud, with one or two black sheep to round out the herd. Usually, they are tended by a solitary woman in a long dark skirt who sits among the flock. The bus rumbles on. We see cows, taupe in color, munching grass. They do not raise their heads to note our passing. The occasional dog lopes among the livestock.

We pass big lakes, nestled in the bottom of hills like a secret stash of jewels. As we rumble through small villages, Peruvian women in typical dress walk by wearing colorful striped blankets around their shoulders. They carry mysterious bundles, sometimes babies. The women with seem old enough to be grandmothers; their skin is leathery and their gaits are slow and steady. Many of them have hats on their head in the characteristic style of their culture. These ladies are known as "las chisperas," the gossiping ladies. The hats vary; there are bowlers or tall top-hats, just perched on the heads of the women. Why don't they tumble off? If I moved to Peru, would I finally learn how to rock a hat?

Sometimes the bus stops and women walk past the windows holding up wares they are selling: food items such as bread, cheese, and sodas, or trinkets like keychains and dolls. I buy a baggie of bread rounds for a dollar. Sometimes local people get on the bus and are herded up the stairs. Gavin and I have the lower part almost to ourselves. As we near Cusco, the bottom fills with people too.

"They all look happy to be let on," Gavin whispers. It's not clear if the locals get a free ride or not, but it's cool either way. This was a cheap ticket for us; about twelve dollars.

The busses through Chile and Argentina have been close to a hundred dollars each for long distances. I think I will like Peru!

I have read some warnings about fake taxis and kidnapping. These bandits take you to an ATM and force you to withdraw money, steal your bags, make you take off your clothes and leave you stranded. Although I take these warnings with a grain of salt, I am always a little scared when I get to a new place, especially after Santiago. I grill the driver who picks us up to make sure he seems authentic. He takes Gavin to his hostel, then me to mine for ten soles each, a little more than three dollars. (I later pay three soles for the same ride.)

The hostel is clean, open in the middle, which makes it a little cold, but my room has two beds. I take a hot shower and take the blanket off the other bed to pile it on the one I will sleep in. Tomorrow I will explore town. Today I am tired from the long bus ride. I cross the street to buy a cheese and avocado sandwich, then return to check my email, and sleep deeply.

The following day I do a bit of yoga in the hallway outside my little room. It feels good to get the bus-kinks out of my body. I plan to meet Gavin in front of the cathedral in the main square.

I venture out to get real coffee and meet an art student carrying a leather portfolio with paintings. He asks me to look at his work. I notice as he flips through that many of the paintings have different styles to them; they could not be painted by the same person. I ask him about this, and he says he and fellow students trade paintings to sell. There are a few watercolors I like; one depicts a llama gazing over the Machu Picchu ruins.

Curious, I ask him how much. "One hundred twenty soles" he tells me. Forty bucks. I don't really need a painting. But he bargains as I decline, finally going down to thirty soles. I wonder if he really painted it after all. I give him the money and he rolls the art into a cardboard tube.

I weave my way through persistent vendors: the gossiping ladies with their colorful blanket shawls, selling dolls, earrings, blankets, slippers. Three ladies with lambs in their arms ask if I would like a photo. I hold the lamb, docile and sweet in my arms, its long legs dangling free, and a crocheted hat fastened to its curly head. I pass restaurants and shops. More boys with leather portfolios try to convince me to look at their work. I wonder where all these paintings come from? A lady selling dolls talks to me for a while as I wait on the steps. We discuss how many children we have and how old they are; the theme of motherhood is a universal one. Finally, Gavin lopes up the stairs. I am happy to see him. We walk through the square to Avenida Sol, where he needs to go to the bank. I go along to help with the Spanish.

Afterwards we stop for lunch at one of the outdoor cafes that face the smaller square with a fountain in the middle. Everywhere there are security guards, which makes me feel more, well, secure! As we sit at the table we are bombarded by vendors. Gavin smiles, amused at my inability to turn anyone away. I think of Brad, who would get mad, both at the vendors and at me. I smile appreciatively at Gavin as I look through more paintings. I buy an alpaca sweater from a gossiping lady. She tells me it is her first sale of the day, and it cost me the equivalent of twelve dollars. I shoo the vendors away as our lunch comes: a lemony fish ceviche that we share, and big bowls of soup. When we finish, they descend again. One little girl of about ten is selling dolls. I tell her I really don't need one.

"Where you from, missus?"

"Estados Unidos."

She straightens and casts her eyes up, concentrating hard. "Washington DC, capital. Barack Obama, president…" she begins to rattle off facts in stilted English.

Amused, I point to Gavin. "He's from England."

She switches tracks. "Margaret Thatcher, prime minister. Elizabeth, Queen of England. Capital, London…"

"That's great, but I still don't need a doll, mija."

"Me invitas un gaseosa?"

I pour some of my coke into my glass and give her the rest of the bottle and she thanks me and scampers off. I explain to Gavin what that was all about- that since I did not want to buy her wares, I could at least invite her for a coke - and we laugh and pay the bill while shooing away more vendors.

Next, we go to the Chocolate Museum. It is well organized and clean, and admission is free. There we sip some cocoa tea, taste the types of chocolate, and learn lots of facts about the history of chocolate as we walk around. I am impressed that the government has implemented a successful program encouraging farmers to switch plants from coca, which produces cocaine, to the cacao, which produces chocolate.

Gavin is taking the Inca trail tomorrow, and is attending a meeting at seven thirty to advise him of the details. But we have just enough time to go buy the boots I admired earlier in a shop window; in fact, they are in several windows and I went into shops until I was convinced I had found the best price. For ninety-five soles, or about thirty-two dollars, I buy a pair of tall suede boots decorated with bright strips of woven fabric. They come in many colors; bright orange, turquoise, pink, yellow, and more traditional brown, black, or grey. Gavin steers me away from turquoise and I choose the grey. I also buy a colorful fabric tote bag. Although I have not gone crazy with purchases, I do have a half shopping bag full, and with the addition of the tall boots, I am going to need another carry- on for the airplane.

I go back to the hotel for an hour while Gavin has his meeting, and we rendezvous for a pizza dinner. I tease him about how tough the Inca trail will be. Truthfully, I did think about doing it. It is a once-in-a-lifetime experience, trekking through the Peruvian jungle for four days, sleeping three nights in camps set up by the rugged porters that come along on the journey, and finally coming upon Machu Picchu. And paying about five hundred dollars for the privilege. But I am not a hiker, and the altitude messes with my breathing. I do not sleep well on the ground, and I really can't afford it. Earlier in the day we walked into a tour office and I found a reasonably priced package to take me to Machu Picchu with a group. Sorry, Inca Trail. I wish Gavin luck, we promise to keep in touch on Facebook, and I begin the walk back to my hostel.

There are a few persistent late-night vendors still out, and they call out to me. "No, gracias," I wave them off. One little boy follows me, though, showing me first his finger puppets, then clay pipes.

"For your collection!" he says.

I look at the pipe and shake my head. "I don't have a collec-tion," I assure him. "And I don't smoke."

"No problem, missus. Look," he pauses by a ledge and places the pipe on it. "Very nice!" I shake my head and keep walking, but like a puppy he follows along. "Where are you from?"

"Estados Unidos."

"Washington DC, capital. Barack Obama, president. Before that, George Bush…"

"Ugh. Don't talk about George Bush."

He pulls another object from the bag; a knife sheathed in decorative leather. "This is my father's work. For your collection!"

"I don't have a knife collection either." We pass a store, a mini-market closing for the night. I get an idea. "Would you like some cookies?"

"Thank you!" he says. We enter the store, where two other chil-dren linger. I tell them I have five soles to spend, they can all pick out something. The shopkeeper, a young girl, helps them choose and collects the money from me. They all shout their thanks and I walk the rest of the way to my hostel in peace.

The next day is Saturday and I am on my own again. I go to the tour office to pay for my trip to Machu Picchu on Sunday, and I join the tour to an archeological site called Moray, and the salt mines at the mouth of the Sacred Valley.

As the van makes its way out of Cuzco I get my first real view of the city. We pass more women in typical dress, going about their day. Dark-skinned children play in the streets, boys running about as boys do everywhere. I look down upon red terra cotta roof tiles as we wind up narrow streets and make our way out of the city. I notice as we pass that there are weathervanes or crosses on most of the roofs, and on either side are small pink clay bulls. I later learn that the bulls represent success in the endeavors of the family.

In the countryside are more animals tethered and grazing: sheep, pigs, cows, and donkeys. Dogs and puppies run about. Women are usually caring for the animals. I see one woman walking and spinning a small spindle as she tends her flock, a hat perched on top of her head, her dark blue skirt grazing the grass around her ankles.

Farther into the lush green country side we go. Blue skies are dotted with cotton clouds. The hills roll alongside us like waves of some celestial painter's brushstrokes. Tall trees border the roads, bark hanging in strips from their skinny trunks. As the bus labors up a hill, we come to the town of Chincharo. Here there is an artesan market where we have been promised a bit of shopping. First, though, is a weaving demonstration. Several women are demonstrating their crafts while one speaks, switching easily from English to Spanish in practiced dialog. All the women are dressed in long dark skirts and flat hats with red designs and flowers on the top. Their shoulders are draped with colorful woven shawls. The tourists sit on a wooden bench covered with fluffy sheepskin while they show us spinning, weaving, and dyeing wool with ground plant extracts. One woman takes a cactus, plucks off a parasitic insect, and squishes it. The red blood runs into her hand, then she adds lemon and uses the resulting tint to paint her cheeks and lips. She grins mischievously at our surprise. I buy a peacock-colored scarf for my daughter Emily, but we are rushed back to the bus before I can do any serious damage to my wallet.

More gorgeous scenery awaits as we make our way back down the mountain. Yellow flowers dot the landscape, mixed with yucca and blue agave cactus with their shadowy blue-grey spikes. I see potato fields and corn crops as we go through more small farming villages. Two small boys herd half a dozen pigs up the road with sticks. Mountains loom ahead, and our tour guide tells us that the tallest mountain is called Veronica. My eyes fill with tears. I just let the feeling wash over me.

We arrive at Moray, an archeological site with a circular spiral shape, carved with terraces for crops. There are stairs built into the terraces for farming. I climb down slowly, descending using the rocks that are positioned like stair steps on each level. They jut out from the side, staggered just right, but are still difficult to navigate. When we all reach the bottom, it is time to go back up. Snap, snap, snap – I take some pictures and off we go again.

⟪⟪⟪⟪⟪⟪

The day finally comes to begin the trip to Machu Picchu. I get up early and leave the hostel with just an overnight bag; the rest of my stuff is stashed in the locked storage closet. I walk down the narrow sidewalk, cut through the alley, and go to the cathedral square, where the tour office is located. From here the shuttle will take a group to Ollantaytambo, the town where the Peru Rail train transports us to Aguas Calientes. Once there, I will stay in a private room in a hostel. The next morning I will take the bus up to Machu Picchu, and meet the guide to explore the ruins.

It is a bright sunny day, and I load into the van with others from various hotels. A family takes up the back seat: Mom, Dad, and two kids. On the way, they are counting the dogs they see.

"Two hundred seventeen, two hundred eighteen!" the young boy proclaims.

"Look, there's five! How many is that?" his sister asks.

I am rooting for them, looking out for dogs myself. As a Talking Heads song plays on the radio, we make our way out of town, passing a fruit and veggie market, the produce in old wheelbarrows, piled to overflowing. I watch the scenery go by; glad my trip is all mapped out for me for once. At Ollantaytambo, the shuttle stops in a parking lot and our group disperses. I get coffee while I wait for time to pass, then make my way to the train station at the end of the street.

The Peru Rail train, elegant dark blue with a bold gold stripe on each car, awaits on the track. When our boarding time is called, we file on and take assigned seats. I order a cold beer and relax while I watch the scenery roll by.

The train rides its tracks close to a chocolate brown river, which tumbles, turbulent and churning, over large rocks, then widens and calms. More tall trees flank the river, while plump cactus and their cousins, the spikey agave plants, line the passage. Wooden flute music is piped in, background music for the beginning of our journey.

I think of my friend Gavin, somewhere on the Inca Trail. I sometimes wish I were an intrepid hiker, but why? Four long days hiking is an amazing experience, I am sure. But I will be able to walk all around Machu Picchu and be content with this. I earn no bragging rights to get there by bus, but it suits me better.

I need to embrace my non-sportiness before I move back to Boulder, home of many enthusiastic hikers and bikers. I don't mind getting together with someone who wants to hike, mountain bike and ski, as long as he's not expecting me to partake. And as long as my absence doesn't give him the right to hook up with ski bunnies! I will be back at the lodge, curled up in front of the fire with my novel, preparing spiked hot chocolate for his return, maybe even lying naked on the (fake) bearskin rug. Hey, someone's got to do it!

As we continue our approach to Aguas Calientes, the

mountains get higher. Waterfalls dangle on a high craggy slope, so still at this distance they look like strands of lace hanging on the rock. The scenery is lush and green as the train slows and pulls into the station.

At the train station many people stand with signs. I spot my name, and two other travelers join us, then the man walks us a few blocks to the hostel. My room is neat, with two beds and a private bathroom. I deposit my things and set off to walk around the town.

Aguas Calientes is small with streets of bricks and cobblestone that wind up and down hills. There are many stands and stores selling all the same things I saw in Cuzco. I wander the streets, making my way up to the famous thermal baths, where I rent a towel, store my things, and enter. From the path above the entrance, you can look down and see people lounging in several pools. A tropical bar on the terrace overlooking the baths sells drinks, and you can wave up to the waiters, who will take your order and serve your drink in a plastic cup to enjoy while you bathe.

I enter the pool and end up talking to a lady from Lima who is there with her family. She invites me to visit her in Lima. I love how easy it is to make friends here, how people extend invitations and give their phone numbers freely. I'm not sure that I will have time, but it is nice to have the offer. On the way back I choose a small restaurant and eat a trout dinner, then make my way back to the hostel for an early bed time.

Early in the morning I eat a simple breakfast at my hostel and then find the line of busses heading up the hill to Machu Picchu. The bus chugs out of town and crosses a bridge, then bounces up the switchback winding up the mountain. As we ascend, a thick fog hangs in the air. Mist haloes trees and rocks, giving me just a peekaboo view of the lush green jungle. Droplets of water cling to the plants. I hold my breath, already feeling the beginning of something magical.

There are places in the world we are told are mystic. Others we just feel. Machu Picchu is a bit of both. If it feels even more special by virtue of our being told of its spiritual qualities, does that make it any less impressive? There can't be any harm in buying into the legend. Machu Picchu is a wonder, but I cannot explain exactly why. Is it the fact that the Incas brought all of these stones up from Cuzco to build the structures, in a time when transportation was by foot or hoof? Is it the lush green landscape, the stair step terraces, the majestic mountains surrounding the ruins? Perhaps it is the mist that floats in by the morning, shrouding the whole place in an eerie magical cloak of grey, then dispersing to let the radiant sun bathe the fallen buildings in dancing light, while llamas graze placidly, ignoring the hordes of people.

This morning the ruins are obscured by a low grey fog hanging over the stones and covering the site in a mysterious sense of wonder. Our guide leads us through, telling of the sacrifices that were most likely made on the stone tables, making us curious about the improbability of these ancient people building a city that housed hundreds of Incan people, way up on this mountain and far from other cities. We climb up to the top as a group. A computer engineer from Seattle starts chatting with me, telling me he doesn't even have a camera, so I take a few pictures of him and promise to email them. Imagine coming to Machu Picchu and having no way to record the experience!

The guide takes us all through the Temple of the Condor, and we go through the narrow opening, symbolically being born again through the guts of the bird. Somehow, as I crouch down and crawl through the cave-like space, I feel it. I am indeed subtly reborn in this place.

I depart from the group as the tour is done and take a path that passes an arrow pointing a different direction. It is still a path, I reason, so I'm okay to follow it. Other tourists are going up where I went down, and I pass the terraced hillside and find myself blissfully alone.

Miraculously, I find a quiet place facing several craggy green rock faces. A canopy of clouds hovers above, but the sky directly overhead is clear, letting the sun shine through to bathe me in its light. I work my body into triangle pose and side angle and do a few sun salutations. Here in this sacred ancient place, beneath the temple of the sun, and having been spiritually reborn through the entrails of the condor, I pay homage to nature. Deciding to meditate, I sit cross-legged on a rock and rest my upturned hands on my knees. Birds chirp as they flitter above and the voices of tourists: German, Spanish, Japanese, echo lightly down towards me. I deepen my breath. A large dry leaf falls, crackling, and lands beside me, brushing my knee as it flutters to the ground. I drift into otherworldliness, and I seem to be right at the edge of something quiet and profound. I slowly open my eyes. My palms feel like they hold tiny glowing balls of sunlight. My butt is numb from the rock. I know that no matter how many pictures I take, I will never quite capture the essence of this place. And I feel gently grateful to be here alone; for if I had a traveling partner, I would not be free to do yoga, to meditate, to sit down and write. More and more often, I have these moments of feeling at peace with myself and my place in the world. Cloud cover drifts again over the glare of the sun. The breeze carries birdsong and touches me as if the birds caress me with their wings. If only I did not have to pee, I could have sat here for hours.

I make my way back down to the entrance to retrieve the bag containing my lunch and a drink, planning to eat and go back into the ruins on my own afterwards. A young woman and her mother join me at the table. They look weary and happy, as they tell me that they walked the Inca Trail.

"How was it?" I ask.

The daughter glances at her mother with a half-smile. "Hard."

"But good," Mom assures her.

I smile inwardly, glad I am lazy. They go on to tell me that they were both sick from something the first two days, that sleeping in the tents on the ground was uncomfortable, that carrying their packs was almost unbearable, and that when they finally arrived it had all seemed worth it.

Many travelers are at the picnic benches, eating food they have brought in or purchased from the snack stand. Everyone seems to have the same glow that I feel. I dispose of my garbage, shoulder my mostly empty pack, and head back up on the winding path that leads to the first part of the ruins.

I explore some more, doubling back on the same places I visited with our guide. It's a magical place, alright. I happen upon wandering llamas in one of the ruins, and I pet one as it strolls by. I spend a few more hours exploring, but I am tired. The guy from Washington had given me his return bus ticket, and although I would love to be the girl who hiked all the way back to town – actually, that is a lie, I don't care – I take the bus back.

That evening I am back in the hostel in Cusco, retrieving my bag and getting some sleep. In the morning I take off for the longest bus ride of my journey – forty hours total – to arrive at a beach town at the north end of Peru. From there I will take the flight to Costa Rica (which cost me nine hundred dollars!) I am at the beginning of "my time of the month," which totally sucks on a bus, but I shall spare the gory details and fast forward almost two full days.

Las Chisperas

A friendly llama

In the mist of Machu Picchu

Lobitos, Peru: Surfin Safari

After more than forty hours on buses I finally arrive in Talara. There are cabs and motos waiting at the bus station. Motos? Yes, the motorcycle with a carrier attached, like the tuk tuks of Asia. I don't want to take one of those with all of my luggage. The cab to Lobitos is forty soles, about thirteen dollars. It seems like a lot but I don't care; I'm tired and want to get to my destination.

The cab driver keeps up a steady patter as we drive. I have asked him about taxi safety, and he relates a story of a tuk tuk driver who killed a gringa tourist for the six hundred soles, about two hundred dollars, in her pocket. He assures me that there are guards who record the license numbers of the cabs and motos, and that the boy was caught. Yes, I say, but that does not help the tourist lady, does it?

He cordially helps me with my bags when we get in and makes sure I am in the right place. Vanessa, the manager, greets me warmly and introduces me to a scattering of people sitting on the wide porch of the house. The house itself, Casona, used to belong to a general. Now it is being used as a hostel and restaurant. It sits up on a bluff about one hundred and fifty yards from the beach. Waves tumble consistently, and surfers play in the tunnels of glassy blue water. Casona is painted a salmon color with a porch that wraps around the perimeter of the wood building. The windows are leaded glass, the floors wide wooden planks. Hammocks are strung on the porch and in nearby trees. Vanessa leads me upstairs to the dorm, where they have a few guests.

"We have six helpers here right now," she tells me. Six? Wow! I didn't think there would be so many. I take a bottom bunk in the spacious dorm room. Other helpers are in other rooms of the great house.

Downstairs the walls are painted sky blue. Robin, a California surf girl, is painting a huge octopus on the dining room wall. Beside her, Juan from Argentina works painting water bubbles, smearing them with his fingers as he goes. There is a large kitchen where we will take turns working, helping the young chefs, who go to cooking school three days a week and live at Casona. Around the other side of the reception area is a game room with a pool table and foosball table, and beyond that is the library, where books are spread out on the table, mostly Spanish books and magazines.

Robin and her friend Caroline are going to town and ask if I would like to come. It's about half an hour ride, and there are little combi buses that run back and forth, charging three soles, about a dollar, per person. We go to the store and through a fruit and veggie market, then back home. I put up my supplies and fall into bed for a siesta. When I get up there is plenty of time to do a yoga session. I roll out my mat in the empty library and practice for an hour, and my body thanks me.

That night is the birthday of the owner, Oscar. He invites us all to have dinner and drinks. His family and friends are all around. Dinner is fried rice and potato salad, which has ham that I pick out. There are big slabs of pork which of course I pass on. Thinking sadly that I won't have much to eat, I am delighted when two big plates of ceviche are served.

People come and go, buying beer and soft drinks from the cooler. I start ringing sales as Vanessa is busy and probably a little drunk. I am too, and I am very careful with the bills and change, trying to make sure I don't make mistakes. I get into bed as soon as the party dies out, because Oscar has informed us that there is a group coming tomorrow to use the library for a presentation, after which they will have lunch, so we will all be busy.

The work here is not bad; a little time in the morning either cooking breakfast or cleaning, and then we work in shifts so that someone is always on staff to help with the restaurant and the reception area.

All around Casona are signs of the desert, which I find curious for an ocean setting. Big black buzzards lurk around the house, sitting on the roof and watching balefully. *I'm forty-nine, but I'm not dead yet,* I think, as I stare back at them. Little black birds with gracefully painted wings and bright white bellies cruise around, their angular bodies decorating the breeze. And in the ocean, bizarre bi-plane looking structures, the oil decks, sit on top of the water, immobile in their shadowy bulky shapes as the waves roll in.

One sunny morning I go for a walk with some of the others. We walk down a dirt road and onto the pier, which is full of brown weather-beaten fisherman, some old, some young. A man is fishing with hand reels. One of the men has caught some plump grey fish. The fish lay gasping their last breaths, mouths puckered like cherries, little shimmery sides heaving slightly. I glance at them nervously then look away. I don't want to start feeling sorry for the only creature that I still sometimes eat! We make our way to the end of the dock, where there is a straight drop of about twenty feet into the water below. Robin and Caroline jump, encouraging me. "You can do it!"

I look skeptically at the water as I stand teetering on the edge. I am slightly afraid of heights. But I can't back down now, so I jump before I can think any more about it. Down, down, I plunge, sinking into the damp cold caress of salty ocean then popping up, gasping. I blink against the salty sting in my eyes.

As I climb to the top of the ladder that leads back to the dock, Robin is grinning at me. She is the age of my daughter. "Would your mother jump off?" I ask.

"Probably not," she admits.

Later that day I face down another challenge. Oscar has come to surf and he wants to take someone with him. He wants to show one of the helpers how to surf. Many of them are already surfers, so I am elected. An Argentinian helper, Shanti, svelte and athletic, joins us. As we hit the beach a friend of Oscar's, a surfer nicknamed Bokita, is there. It is he who will patiently give this gringa her first surf lesson.

On the sand, Oscar shows me how to slip the Velcro cuff onto my ankle. "This is your lifeline. You may go under, but the board will float." Then he shows me how to paddle with my hands close to the board, lift my chest by grabbing the sides, then stand. On the sand it doesn't look so hard, but I know in the water it will be different.

Bokita takes me out, hanging on the back of the board and shouting encouragements and instructions in Spanish. I paddle out, gasping when the water hits me in the face. He tells me to duck my head when I go through these waves, the small ones we must traverse to get to the ones I want. I look at the vast expanse of dark water, white foam cresting in waves as they roll in. I gulp down a slice of terror and paddle.

"Rema, rema!" Paddle, paddle! Bokita coaches from behind me. Then he turns the board as a bigger wave comes rolling towards us. I grab the sides of the board like I was shown, and suddenly the wave scoops me up, a force from behind. It is strong yet gentle, and the board glides along. Wobbly, I lift my foot forward like a lunge in yoga. My other leg refuses to budge on the tumbling force of the board, so I raise up half kneeling and let the wave carry me almost to the shore before I spill off the side.

Oscar and Shanti wave and shout bravo from the beach. It feels like a minor success. Not standing, but almost. Reveling in the feeling of the benevolent water carrying me along from underneath, gliding along and balancing my body on the board as smoothly as a seasoned waitress carries a tray of cocktails. It is as close as I will come to the feeling the real surfers must get when they catch the wave and ride it, for I try another dozen times and never get up on the board. Still, I am happy that I did it, and I think I might try surfing again another day.

I return to the hostel coated in sand like a piece of Shake and Bake chicken. Tired as I am, I can't help but grin triumphantly. I'm facing fears, one at a time, and conquering them. It may not be anything grand or impressive, but I am doing it all by myself: finding the bus, climbing the hill, riding the wave. Making small leaps of faith every day.

Casona is more of a restaurant and social gathering place than a hostel, with more helpers than guests. People swirl about in the evening like dust devils: here are some of the blond dreadlocked surfers I saw on the beach, here is a woman staying with a friend nearby who comes for a coffee in the afternoon. Some people are regulars, some are more transient. The nearby hostels vary from a huge hangar-like building where tents are pitched for shelter to a more modern hostel where they charge, Vanessa informs me, fifty dollars a night for a room, an insane price for Peru.

The house being in a desert location, water is scarce. There is a delivery three days a week, but, like many things here, it is not reliable. We find ourselves without water for showers for almost a week. The lot of us helpers troop down to the ocean with empty containers to fill them with enough sea water to at least flush our toilets. The house, although Oscar has fixed it up in many ways, still needs some major repairs. The deck in back is riddled with rotting or missing boards. One night in the dark I walk back to deposit a bottle and step right through one of the holes, badly scraping and bruising my entire right leg. The internet, too, is unreliable. When I can get online, I can't always open my messages. I long for news from my children, and just like in Spain at about the three-month mark, I am getting painfully homesick. But it won't be long now, and the in-between time holds the promise of my long-awaited yoga training, bringing with it a new group of friends and a challenge for my body and mind.

In the mornings I awaken at seven when the sun initiates its insistent call for me to begin my day. I use the bathroom and try not to be disgusted by the state of the toilet, which has no seat and often no water, so that it is rarely flushed and might harbor an unpleasant surprise in the bowl. I use bottled water to make my coffee in the French press. Then I sit and gaze out at the ocean. So, while I feel I am living in squalor, it is a little slice of heaven in other ways. The constant roar of the ocean is a soothing primal song. Fishing boats come and go from the pier. My favorite thing to do is to watch the surfers waiting in the water with anticipation of the next wave, like a Labrador waits for someone to throw the tennis ball. They bob gently in the sea until suddenly a white-crested wave comes rolling in, and some are borne up on it, riding like royalty on its power, swooping in toward the beach with amazing agility. On the shore, people are walking, swimming, surfing, in the rhythm of an ocean-based life.

I know that this week has some important lessons for me. My hair, dirty and salty, stands up on my head in persistent, wiry curls, matted together, almost like dreadlocks but not as cool. I am sure I have never gone this long without showering or washing my hair. And it's not an experience I would like to repeat! But I guess what I am learning is to define what is necessary and what things are bonuses. Really, we need so little to just live and survive, and the rest is a blessing. Why should I, by virtue of being born in a certain place to a certain kind of family, automatically have so much more than my spiritual brothers and sisters in poorer places? It's a mystery to me and I am profoundly grateful for my good fortune. Here we have food, electricity, music and friends, and a spectacular view of the ocean. With a three-minute walk I can be swimming in it. We are short of water and the internet is unreliable, but for the rest of it, I am lucky.

Blog Post: Simplicity

Lately I have been thinking about the difference between wanting and needing. From the basics in life: food, water, clothing and shelter, to the more luxurious things like fine food and wine, really cute shoes, and fast internet, what is really important?

In the last few years there has been a rash of "end of the world" movies, cashing in on the Incan prediction that the world will end in 2012. Twice on South American buses I have seen the one with John Cusack saving his family from such threats as fiery explosions, the earth cracking wide open to swallow up cities, and ocean waves engulfing and destroying everything in their paths. If the world is ending, I guess I am ready, but I really don't want to fight off explosions and ocean waves, thank you very much. Just take me quickly and I will go peacefully!

But if there were really an end of the world scenario, could I handle it? I mean, aside from worrying about loved ones and lost pets and possessions, when it comes down to the bare bones of life and survival, how tough am I, really?

For the last week or so, I have been staying in Peru in a gorgeous old run-down grand dame of a house, with a name befitting a grand dame: La Casona. She sits on a little hill looking out over the ocean, and from the broad, wraparound deck, you can watch surfers bob upon the water as they vie for the next big wave. Casona is a beautiful spot. However, with this little bit of heaven comes sacrifice. We have been without proper water for a week. There is currently a shortage of water, usually brought in from the municipality to the tank that supplies the showers and toilets. No water means no showers, and no showers means my hair starts to look a bit like Bob Marley's, but it was way cuter on him. To top it off, the typical Peruvian toilet has no seat, and you can't put toilet paper in the bowl; it goes in a trash can next to the potty. No me gusta!

Now if this sounds like no big deal to you, I applaud you. And although I'm trying not to whine, it has made me think about appreciating the luxuries that we in America (as well as other places that are blessed with modern conveniences) have at our fingertips every day. I am the last person to go around waving an American flag, and there are many things I don't like about my country (such as lack of health care or affordable education) but I must say that three months in South America has made me feel a little spoiled. I also know that poverty exists right in our own backyard; that I don't have to travel far to see it. It makes me want to do something to help my struggling neighbors (before I save Peru!) Oh, but first I have to get a job. And possibly take a shower.

So if it comes down to the end of the world, how am I going to survive running through the streets in tattered clothes, ducking into burned-out buildings, scrounging for food, when I can't even deal with going without a shower for a week?

I guess I'll have to ask John Cusack how it's done....

Lobitos is not much of a town, really, just a few buildings scattered about and some hostels and guesthouses by the beach for the surfers. But Talara, the closest town, is bigger, and it's a real dump. I go in for groceries, taking a colectivo for three soles that bounces over the ragged dirt road between the two, strewn with rocks and crossing the occasional rivulet of water. A few scrubby horses attempt to graze in the desert land at the side of the road. Oil rigs - I used to call them "dinosaurs" when I was a kid – chug steadily away, making their signature little "pop pop pop" as they pump up and down. Fishing and oil are the big industries here.

Slowly we roll into the edge of town, almost like a shanty town with brightly colored box-shaped houses with corrugated tin roofs. Laundry is strung along lines, stubbornly drying in the fish-scented breeze. Little kids play barefoot in the dirt streets. Garbage is everywhere: plastic bottles and ripped-open bags that the street dogs rummage through. It is ironic that a place that survives on bottled water like this does not have a way to recycle the plastic bottles. I think again about the differences in the quality of life between cultures; that the things that I take for granted in the USA are not readily available in poorer places.

When I return from town, laden with my groceries, Vanessa announces that although the regular water delivery still has not come, she has found someone to deliver water in jugs for cleaning and doing dishes, and she has ordered enough water for each of us to be allowed a two-gallon container that we can bathe with. I am ecstatic. I have longed for showers before but never have I been quite so desperate. I grab my supplies and run upstairs to sit on the edge of the tub and do what I can. I am so conservative with my little allotment that I get to wash my hair twice. I lather and scrub and rinse and come out smiling and feeling one hundred percent better.

Soon I will go to Mancora, the last stop on my trip. I find out through Facebook (which I accessed at the internet café in town) that one of my friends, Mary from Iguazu, was robbed there. I don't know details, but it makes me anxious about the safety of my last week of freestyle travel.

After talking with Caroline over coffee on my next to last day, she convinces me that traveling to Cuenca, Ecuador, would be a better last stop than Mancora. She tells me about the cute small city, its winding streets that are fun to explore, expansive and cheap markets, the arty vibe, the hostel she stayed in with hot running water and toilet seats. It sounds divine. And the best part of all, it is nine or ten hours away, not twenty or thirty, as I'm used to. I'm ready to change plans, and I'm excited. In my last week here, I can go to one final country!

After scrubbing out the fridge, which was desperately in need of cleaning and re-organizing, and trooping down to the ocean a few more times for toilet flushing water, I take some free time to spend one last day working on my tan. I spread my sarong out, but first I do a twenty-minute yoga session in my small bikini. The funny thing about this week is that I have shed even more of my self-image issues, spending time with my roommates Robin and Caroline, who run around in small bikinis, letting it all hang out. Their bodies are cute and tan, but not lean and model-perfect. Still, they wear their confidence and comfort in those beautiful young bodies like I have never done. I admire them for it. It makes me not care anymore how fat my butt is in my teeny suit. It makes me not worry so much if people notice my stretch marked belly that isn't exactly flat. Instead of covering up as usual, I do the session in the bikini. Nothing falls out, no one walks by and tells me to put clothes on. It's just me. Little me, or big me, out there in the sand and sun with the waves roaring, doing my thing.

On my last shift at the desk, Marian, the French girl, steps out to have a cigarette. It is close to sunset. A few surfers, as always, dot the ocean landscape.

"Quick," Marian says to me, beckoning. "You want to see this!"

Curious, I step out from my post. Dolphins! There they are, majestically bowing through the water, a pod of ten or so, crossing our horizon. I can't see their silky grey bodies, but I know the sheen as if they were right in front of me. I dash back in and grab binoculars, and I am rewarded when they get by the pier; one jumps out and arcs above the water, then splashes seamlessly back in, waving goodbye to me with his tail flukes. I am moved to tears. Dolphins are a good omen!

That evening I am treated to one of the finest sunsets I have ever seen: the sun slowly sinking, glowing brighter and more fiery with its descent, into the sea, like a sparkling slice of candied orange. A quote comes to me from a movie I saw about someone facing their death: "Most people are asleep inside. They walk around every day, asleep. It's only very few that are awake."

I want to be awake. I want to dream and feel and experience. Not just the big stuff, not just the stuff that everyone else deems important, but everything, everything, everything! I have touched on moments of this, little times of perfection while practicing yoga, or having a conversation. It occurs to me that life could be like that, always. I wonder if it's the same thing as enlightenment? I could be drastically awake. And, maybe for the first time ever, I want to be.

After my last shift at La Casona, I say goodbye to all my new friends and begin the descent down the dirt hill to the bus stop that will take me to Talara, then Mancora, then Cuenca. Caroline, barefoot, takes my big bag, strapping it on her back. We hug goodbye as the colectivo driver fastens my bags onto the top of the car along with a few surfboards. And off I go again on my own!

Finding the bus station is easy, and the bus to Mancora leaves every hour. But at Mancora, my confusion begins. Caroline told me there should be a direct bus. When I get to the makeshift CIFA bus station (really just a slipshod hostel with a desk out front manned by a fat lazy young man) I am happy to see the sign advertising "Cuenca" along with other destinations. Inside are wall posters of Ecuador, two featuring Cuenca. But when I ask my uncooperative friend at the desk, he says no, there are no direct busses to Cuenca. I will have to go to Machala. I have not researched Ecuador at all; where the hell is that? His cell phone rings as I am about to ask him for more information; he spends at least ten minutes talking to a friend about ordering Chinese food while I grow more and more impatient. Finally I interrupt:

"Please, can you help me?"

"To go to Cuenca, no. You have to get another bus."

"Can you sell me the ticket to Machala?"

"No, the system is closed. You can ask the bus driver. The bus comes at nine."

"What time does it get in?"

"Two in the morning."

"And I'll be able to get a ticket to Cuenca there?"

"I don't know. Probably the station is closed then."

I sigh with frustration. "Can I please use the bathroom?"

"No. The lady for the bathrooms is not here right now." He goes back to his phone call, dismissing me.

I go outside, where a kindly looking woman is sitting. I say, "Excuse me? Do you know about getting a bus to Cuenca? Where are you going?"

"I'm waiting for the bus to Guayaquil."

"This … person…" I roll my eyes toward the desk, fuming, and she nods in sympathy.

"It's terrible, his job is service." We glance at the portly boy, yakking away on his phone.

"Apparently his real job is talking to his friends on the phone. In my country, he would no longer have a job! He tells me I have to go to Machala, but he cannot sell me a ticket, I can't even use the bathroom…"

"Machala is small; you should not go there. Go to Guayaquil, it is a big city. From there you can get the bus to Cuenca. We'll see about the bathroom."

She stands up, nods at me to watch her things, and goes in

to exchange words with the boy. Soon, a woman comes out and escorts her to the bathrooms in back.

When my new friend returns, she says, "Go use the bathroom," with a smile. She promises to watch my things.

I use the facilities and check the Ecuador map on the way back. Cuenca is inland, Machala is south of it, and Guayaquil is north; quite a bit north. Will it be worth going that far only to double back? It is the middle of the night, I reason, and I won't have much else to do. I return to my bags and express my concerns to my friend.

"Machala is much smaller and the station will be closed."

"I can sleep until it opens?"

She shakes her head. "You need to be careful, even in the small cities. If the whole station is closed up, will you sleep on the street? In Guayaquil, the station is open and you will find your bus. It's better for you."

I agree and thank her. The bus pulls up. I buy a ticket, get on, and realize I have forgotten once again to pull out a sweatshirt to cover up with. As the whole world knows by now, it is difficult for me to sleep on a bus without being covered in butter! But I resign myself to being cold, pull out my inflatable pillow, grab an apple from my bag for my dinner, then settle in to try to sleep.

La Casona

Surfing beach at Lobitos

Cuenca, Ecuador: Breaking My Fast

There are two border crossings, the exit of Peru and the entrance of Ecuador. At the first, I wake up and grab my passport and paperwork and stumble from the bus. I realize I am slightly nauseous. Great. We go through the line, get passports stamped, and get back on the bus. At the other border, the tripulante, or bus attendant, asks me where I am going; I tell her Cuenca, eventually. She asks if I would rather get off now. What? I don't get it; is this a language thing? My friend who helped me in Mancora looks around from her seat, fiercely shaking her head. No, I say, I want to go to Guayaquil, where I will find my bus to Cuenca, thank you very much. Well then, she says, I will have to pay the difference of seven dollars. Fine. My stomach roiling, my head dizzy, I give her the money.

The entrance to Ecuador frontera has a long line; it is just our bus, but they seem to be taking forever. I hit the bathroom three times, hoping something will relieve me from my upset stomach, but no such luck. I ask the tripulante if it is possible to retrieve my sweatshirt from my bag, as I am cold and sick. She promises to bring me a blanket when we re-board, and later makes good on that promise. I sleep fitfully, my neck stiffening in the awkward bus-sleep position I am coming to know and hate. At about four in the morning, we disembark at the bus station in Guayaquil.

As promised, it is a big station: the biggest I have seen! It gives Penn station a run for its money; three floors with shops and children's play areas, like a mall. I buy a ticket to Cuenca for five o'clock, get a front seat and sleep the whole way into town, waking occasionally to note the green, lush landscape as we move farther in from the coast.

I'm still feeling ill when we arrive, but I find the bathroom and then an internet stand to book my hostel. I choose the Monastario, which makes me smile- here I am on my nun trip, staying at a monastery. I get a cab, check in early and go straight to bed to sleep another four hours. When I awaken, I walk around a few blocks, still dizzy and shaky. I get a cup of tea and a bowl of soup, then return to the hostel, am asleep by five and don't wake up until almost seven the next morning!

After a good breakfast, I go for a wander. Cuenca is a cool city – large and colonial. It has big glorious churches and cathedrals, green parks, and colorful plazas with vendors. Adjacent to my hotel is the flower plaza, a small square with stands selling fresh blooms and bouquets. It is across from the old cathedral, a magnificent structure that spans the entire block. Its façade is ginger colored brick and it is topped by shimmering blue and white domes. I walk through the plaza, inhaling the heady air, marveling at the immense cathedral, and then I wander on through the streets of Cuenca. I window shop a bit, go into a tour office to look at various tours, and decide, since I am still a little weak, that I will go on the double-decker bus ride that will take me through the city with a guided narrative. And all for just five dollars!

It begins to rain as we take off, which makes the whole top level of people scamper down to the bottom. After about ten minutes the rain subsides and we return to the top. The narrative is in Spanish, but I am the only gringa on the bus so I content myself with either concentrating hard on the words or zoning out. There are many more small squares and ornate churches on our route. We pass the Panama hat museum, with its giant hat glued to the front of the building. We cruise alongside the River Tomebamba, watching the water tumble along between the lush green banks. The bus makes its way out to the edge of town and ascends a hill to Turi, a viewpoint from which the entire city can be seen. I spot the familiar blue domes of the cathedral.

I stop to pet a street dog on the way back; a small grey terrier. His eyes are glued shut from weepy matted scum, as if he has a cold and is very sick. He leans against me and his ribs feel like sticks beneath my hand. I ask the woman selling the brochettes of meat how much they are, one twenty-five is the answer. I debate which kind to buy. "Do you think dogs like chorizo?"

A chorus of laughter breaks out as the group of locals enjoying their meat sticks poke fun at the crazy gringa. The dog does not complain, wolfing down both chorizo and chicken with equal zeal.

Back at the hostel, I chat with Enrique, a Hare Krishna man I met earlier who is staying there. His friend Cesar is with him. For some reason, the conversation turns to romance. I say jokingly that I am a nun, not looking for any romantic involvement while traveling. I tell him how it has made my life easier.

"But you have to be open," he insists. "Have an open heart. No one belongs to anyone else. If you meet someone and enjoy each other, for a moment, for a day, for a month, what does it matter?" I give up on explaining that it does matter to me, I don't want to have someone just for a moment. And I don't want to share myself for a moment with someone who does not care to know me longer. I have the feeling Enrique wants to be my man of the moment. No dice, chum. But still, his words swirl in my head. Be open.

"Necesito tu ingles," says the man at reception, popping his head around the corner and addressing Enrique; he needs his English. Soon Enrique returns with a young brunette girl wearing a backpack. Her name is Ashley and she is from Alberta, Canada. We chat for a while; she is sweet and friendly. We all sit around the table, talking about how nice Cuenca is. Night darkens the sky and we can see the lights of the many churches and the big cathedral.

"It's so beautiful by night!" I comment. "But I don't walk around by myself at night."

"I don't like to either," Ashley says.

"Would you two like to go for a walk tonight, all four of us? We can take you down by the river, show you the broken bridge, and you will be safe with us," offers Enrique.

We agree. Soon we are all strolling through the evening streets. A parade of Catholic devotees passes by, singing and carrying candles. A litter bearing the virgin, lit by candles, is born aloft by four men. We walk past, and on to a street overlooking the river.

An art café has intriguing sculpted figures on its façade and even on the roof: two curly-haired dogs with human faces are a bas relief in the wall. A cherub leers out from above the door. Ashley and I, proper tourists, whip out our cameras and begin to take photos. We move on to a square with a large pole with statues of traditionally dressed Ecuadorians surrounding it, looking up in excitement. At the top of the pole dangle utensils and pots and pans of shiny copper. The sculptor cast two boys attempting to climb the pole, which Cesar explains is greased; if they can climb up, they can keep the gifts. Each thing he says in Spanish he then asks me to translate for Ashley.

We make our way down, passing the river, which is lit in colors by the lights overhead: blue, green, purple. It is a haunting effect. I walk with Enrique, who is trying to get romantic. He plucks a flower and hands it to me. Cesar and Ashley walk together. She has a boyfriend back home, so I know they are not sprouting a romance. We walk past a club called Zoocieadad. Cesar comments that it gets wild there later at night.

We climb a few stairs and are at the broken bridge, Puente Roto, a stone bridge that is indeed broken off, leading to nowhere. As we ascend the stairs, Enrique pinches my side, grabbing the part that no woman wants grabbed, ever – the bulge of flesh that stubbornly persists, poking over my jeans waistband. I am horrified.

"Don't do that. Do not ever do that to a woman! "

"What? I am being affectionate!"

"No, no, no. That is not friendly, that's mean. You don't grab someone's fat places. Ever."

He sulks and I walk on. As Ashley and I admire the night sky, we notice that Enrique has disappeared. Maybe he is waiting at the top of the stairs? But he is nowhere to be found.

Cesar and Ashley and I decide to go to a bar; Ashley and I get mojitos. Next, we go back to the Zoosciedad and dance a little. Ashley says she does not know how to dance salsa, so Cesar attempts to teach her.

A drunken bearded guy with a backpack on his shoulders asks me to dance. I do so for one song, and then hide away on the other side of my friends. Ashley is getting into it, looking like she is having fun. I am suddenly, just for a moment, painfully lonely. Here I am in a club full of people, nursing a warm beer and watching the world go by. I miss the days of having someone to dance with, someone whose body moves with mine easily because we know each other as lovers. Cesar sends a friend, a short sweet young boy, over to dance with me. Then someone else is dancing with Ashley, but a tall white guy is watching them intently. Is it a gay couple and the tall one is jealous? Whatever it is, it's creeping me out and bringing out my protective mama instincts.

I exchange a look with Ashley. "Wanna go?" I ask. She nods quickly.

We walk out into the night air. It is midnight. Cesar asks if we want to go to one more place, a calmer one. It's late, but we say okay. He leads us to a place where we can get tea. We are the only people in the establishment, which is a welcome change after the crowded zoo.

Soon an old man with a guitar enters. He grins widely at us, his eyes popping comically. He begins to play a song very animatedly, thumping the guitar body, spinning it around. He must be at least sixty, with stringy hair and a clownish manner. I ask him to play "Besame Mucho." Sometimes it still makes me cry, but I know I am pretty safe with this crazy guy singing it. He has me laughing. I give him a dollar.

As we settle in with our tea, the guitar clown hangs around a bit, saying I am his true love and he wants to come back to the US with me. I laugh as he hugs me. This is not quite what I was looking for!

A group of men enter the café and draw his attention, and he goes to play for them instead. We breathe a sigh of relief and as I notice a small statue of Ganesh in the window, Cesar treats us to the story of why Ganesh has an elephant head, as I translate for Ashley.

Meanwhile the old man guitarist has handed his guitar over to one of the men at the other table. I look up, distracted from my group by the change in guitarists. He is playing Spanish songs, but also some Elton John, Jim Croche, Billy Joel. He picks the strings of the guitar in a flamenco style as he sings along. He is very talented.

I drift over to listen. The group gives me a seat, and they look at me sympathetically when the old man once again pulls me close and proclaims his love. I watch the real guitarist, whose name is Carlos, his fingers nimbly moving over the strings. I can tell that he enjoys playing; he goes into his own little world, unlike our more flamboyant friend. He has a quiet intense passion about him as he plays. I sit there for a few songs, transfixed.

I go back to our table and lean over towards Ashley, my eye still on Carlos. He has close-cropped hair and glasses. He is wearing a plaid shirt with an ill-fitting sports jacket. Not my usual type, but yet….

"The more he plays, the sexier he seems to me," I say.

She nods and giggles. "You should go for it," she teases.

I adamantly shake my head. She seems happy to talk to Cesar and the men call me back over, so I join them again.

Carlos goes from Jim Croche's "Operator" into a song in Spanish. I listen intently to the words, trying to understand. He bends over the guitar, passion furrowing his brow as he plays. He does not look up, so I am free to openly watch him.

"Casi todos sabemos querer, Pero pocos sabemos amar"

Almost all of us know how to want, but few know how to love….

I find tears in my eyes, streaming down my cheeks. As he finishes, he looks up, coming out of his trance.

"It's a beautiful song," I say, almost in a whisper.

He smiles a thank you, and then does a double take. "Wow. I made you cry?" I nod. "I never made anyone cry before." His tone is astonished. He looks at me closely, concern on his face.

"It's a song about love. It's beautiful. I don't mind showing it when I am moved. To me, the ability to be moved by music is a gift. I don't have to hide it. But I'm not sad," I assure him.

He goes on to play a few more, and the clownish old man plays too. Soon they are trying to close the café and we all leave. Carlos offers a ride back to the hostel, as it is late, almost three, and some areas are not safe at night. We pile into his car. Cesar tells us about the water festival that he is speaking at tomorrow, in Santa Domingo square. Carlos says he will come by and say hello. We thank him and get out, and I stumble sleepily to bed, so tired.

I awaken to voices in the kitchen next door; it is right next to my bed through a thin glass wall, so close I can eavesdrop on the conversations at the breakfast table. I don't feel like eavesdropping, though, I want to be sleeping! I groan and pull the pillow over my head.

When I get up, Ashley is having coffee. We get ready and hit the street, walking and talking as we make our way to Santa Domingo square. I don't really expect to see Carlos, but we want to support Cesar and there are supposed to be lots of vendors selling their crafts.

We find the square and walk around. Cesar is speaking about water conservation, then leads the group in chanting. We chat with an Argentine couple who are making their way through South America in a small Volkswagen, selling handcrafted jewelry to raise gas money. I pick up a necklace, fingering the crocheted loops of thread.

"Do you like it?" says a voice at my shoulder. I look up, and there is Carlos.

"Hey! You made it." I kiss his cheek, as does Ashley. We stroll around and then it begins to rain, so we decide to go back to the hotel so I can change out of my suede boots.

I invite Carlos into my room while I change shoes, and we end up sitting on the bed, door open wide, as hostel guests are not supposed to have outside company in the rooms. He tells me about a relationship he has just gotten out of; a three-year long distance one with a Swiss girl. He packed up his life to move there and marry her, until she told him about a fling she had while in Mexico. It broke his heart; he ended the engagement and moved back to Cuenca.

"How long ago was this?" I ask

"Just two months."

Ah, a recently broken heart. I look at him with sympathy, knowing how long it really takes to get past these things.

Ashley pops her head in and we go out to explore Cuenca some more. We walk around the streets, visit a reptile museum and are treated to feeding day for the boa constrictors. The attendant tosses yellow fuzzy chicks into the cages. Carlos and Ashley watch, fascinated. I can't look. Then we visit the Panama Hat Museum, which is really just a big store selling the hats. Carlos mentions that he has to go to a conversation group. His English is really quite good.

"I lived in the states for several years," he tells me. "I tried to get a visa to stay, but it didn't go through. They recommended that I go back to Ecuador and try to meet some gringa girl who will marry me. Ha!" he laughs at his joke. He also takes salsa dance lessons, he tells us, and invites us to go dancing that evening with him. He will stop by the hostel at seven.

"What do you think?" Ashley asks me.

"Well, I wouldn't mind a little date," I say. "But you're invited too."

"I had enough dancing last night," she laughs. "I'll probably stay in."

We spend the rest of the day exploring and walking the streets of Cuenca. We find a huge market where they are selling fruit, vegetables, and meat. I avoid the meat aisles. These places never seem very sanitary to me, and the slabs of meat sitting on tables, flies buzzing around, are even more repulsive to me now that I am a veggie girl. We try morocho, a drink made with rice and milk and cinnamon.

I get ready for my non-date, check to confirm that Ashley does not want to go, and head downstairs to wait for Carlos. He pulls up, I hop in, and he suggests an Italian restaurant for dinner.

When we get to the place, which is just around the corner from the place we will go dancing, he tells me he got too hungry and he ate already. I laugh. I'm still ordering ravioli, I tell him, and he settles for a coffee and a brownie.

We talk candidly while we eat, about life and relationships. He tells me more about his time in the US, and about his family of six brothers and sisters. I tell him about my travels and the life I hope to build in Colorado. We are both starting over and relocating after wrecked relationships. I am surprised at how open Carlos is. I have been finding this often on my travels; men who will talk about life without censoring their thoughts. It is so different to me after how guarded and closed off Brad was, so reluctant to talk about anything but work. It gives me hope that there are men out there who aren't scared of life!

Carlos and I go to the dance club, a small and intimate bar with two floors. We find a table upstairs to wait for the band to start. I tell him that I can be a bit clumsy when dancing, and he assures me that he is still learning too. When the band starts up, we remain upstairs, where we can see and hear the band playing but have the whole place to ourselves. I am relaxed, not worrying about being watched by other more experienced dance couples. Carlos spins me and holds me and laughs when I make a misstep, then pulls me back in. He is easy going and confident, and I am beginning to reconsider my convent vows. I wrap my arms around his neck, letting my body fall into his. After a few songs, they play one I recognize: "Sweat" by Inner circle. Of course, the lyrics are now in Spanish, but this is a very sexy song. When it finishes, I bring my lips to Carlos, kissing him softly.

"Nice song," he says, pleasant surprise in his voice.

After the band stops (he tells me they only play for one hour) we decide it is time to go home. Ashley wants to go to Cajas Park tomorrow and we want an early start. Carlos drives me back to the hostel and we sit in the car, kissing, for a while. "I don't want to push you," he tells me. At dinner I told him that I am not interested in vacation romances, but a girl can change her mind, right?

I don't sleep well that night, thinking about kissing Carlos. I toss and turn.

In the morning, Ashley and I decide to get a cab; Cajas is just out of the city. For twelve dollars the cab driver takes us. I know nothing about where we are going, except that it is a park with lots of lakes. Carlos warned me that it might be cold. He said he would take us himself, but he does a radio show on Sundays and would be busy. He will come by when it's done, though. Thoughts of another date with him keep me warm as we trudge down the road where the cabbie dropped us.

Here is the park of the Virgin, with a small chapel. It's beautiful, but where, we wonder, is the rest of the park? It is indeed cold, and opportunistic vendors at the entrance are selling hats and gloves. I buy a hat with warm ear flaps. Ashley and I enter the park and walk around.

It is lush and green, with misty fog all about. A few cows graze nearby. Other people are walking around; locals from the looks of them. We ask several people where the rest of the darned park is. Where are the lakes? We are told that we can walk up the hill and find a big lake at the top. I look skeptically at the climb, in high altitude and with no real path to guide us. But it seems this is our only option from here; the rest of the park must be farther up the road. I put on my game face, tell Ashley I might have to rest occasionally, and we begin.

The climb is hard, picking through rocks and mud, and needing to stop to catch our breath with alarming frequency. My heart is pounding. I force myself on, grumbling to myself that I did not do the Inca Trail for this very reason. At the top, we are finally rewarded by a spectacular view of an expansive lake nestled among the hills. We stand and stare, shivering, then nod at each other in agreement to turn around to go back down, at one point both stepping a foot in black mud up to our ankles.

Back down at the garden, we hike up the road to the actual park entrance, and talk to the man at the entrance point. Farther along are several hikes, but you have to drive into the park, and of course we don't have a car, and we are also cold and wet. A little restaurant is next to the entrance, and we sit down and order horchata, a hot pink drink that tastes of flowers, like hibiscus tea. I hold the warm mug against my face to warm it.

The bus takes us back into town and we get a cab from the bus station to the hostel. Ashley will be moving on, and I have another date with Carlos! I hug her goodbye, another friend for a few days come and gone and befriended on Facebook. I burrow under my covers for a much-needed nap.

At the agreed-upon time, Carlos pulls in and we agree to go for pizza. As we wait for our food I tell him that I am debating moving my things to another room of the hostel that is less noisy. I have paid for four nights and need to decide how much longer I am staying.

"You can come and stay with me," he offers. "I am in my brother's house, and it's big. You can have your own room. We can talk in the living room and go to our separate rooms at night." His sincerity touches me.

After our pizza we go to his place, which is a little way out of town. He assures me that he can play tour guide for me, since he is not yet working after his move back to Cuenca from Switzerland. The house is in a wealthy neighborhood, and it is indeed large. He tells me that his brother, an architect, designed and built it. It is a rustic country style with brick tile floors, exposed ceiling beams and brightly painted walls. He shows me the rooms, introduces me to his guitar, and we go upstairs to see the room where I can stay. His brother is working out of town and so Carlos has the place to himself. The master bedroom upstairs is large, with an adjoining walk-in closet and bathroom.

We sit on the bed. He leans over to kiss me. I want this to happen, after all my convincing myself that I am destined for celibacy. I could not ask for a sweeter man to break my sex strike. And I know if I tell him to stop he will.

But I don't.

Afterwards we lay together. "Do you believe in fate?" he asks me.

I smile. Like, destiny? I don't know. I think we have a hand in our fate, that our choices shape our destiny."

We talk about our meeting; that night he had dropped into a place where he sometimes plays and found it empty. Another place he likes to go was closed. He was about to go home when his friends called him and asked him to get together with them, and they had ended up at the café where we met. In my case, we might not have gone to that place if Enrique had been with us, for he doesn't like bars. And even if we had, I would not have drifted over to their table, leaving three behind, it would have seemed rude. All the little events of the evening conspired to throw us together.

We go downstairs and Carlos gets out his guitar and plays and sings for me. I could really get used to this!

The next day I move in. We have just a few days together and we both know it. We spend time in the house, making love, telling our stories. I ask him to learn a Springsteen song for the next time we see each other. I play him "Thunder Road" on You Tube, he shows me some videos he has made of some original songs. We wander around Cuenca together. One afternoon he takes me on a day trip to San Bartolome, where they have guitar workshops, and then we go to Chordeleg where they are famous for silver jewelry. I buy a pair of bird-shaped earrings and name them my "Carlos pajaritos."

When we make love, he wears his glasses. He looks at me

during the act, and we meet eyes and smile fondly. I think of Brad, always with his eyes closed tight against the intimacy. It occurs to me that trying to connect with someone who avoids getting close is like plugging a live device into a dead socket. I know my next lover will not be dead inside; I want the vitality of a true union. I don't have the soul connection with Carlos, but he is teaching me some things about love, whether he knows it or not!

"It takes a new good relationship to get over the last one," he assures me. "Un clave saca otro." One nail gets out another. I think he's right; when I do meet someone to have something real with, I will finally forget about the disappointment of the relationship with Brad.

It is my final day in Cuenca. Carlos notices that I am getting antsy. We stop at the bus station to get my ticket and a girl in a very short black dress passes in front of the car while we are waiting to park. He cranes his head to watch her all the way down the sidewalk, which annoys the hell out of me. Later, at lunch, I ask him what he really thinks about couples being faithful to each other. He broke off his engagement because of infidelity, but in further talks, I find that he had also cheated on his fiancée while they were apart! The difference is that she told him about it, while he never told her of his transgressions. The double standard is really bothering me.

"She never should have told me," he protests. "Why did I need to know that? It ruined everything!"

"Girls want to know, and they want to confess if they do something. Guys feel like it's all fine if they got away with it."

"But those times didn't mean anything to me."

"They would have meant something to her."

"That's why I didn't say anything to her, why hurt her?"

I shake my head at my frustrating inability to understand this point of view.

He tries to explain again. "We were apart for eight months. That is difficult for a man. In Spanish we have a saying: Amor de lejos, amor de pendejos." I laugh in spite of myself. *Long distance love is love for assholes.* I think about the three years that Brad and I spent doing long distance, and the times he was vague about his time away at conferences and work-related meetings. I think about how much cheating he did in his marriage, and can't imagine why I would think that suddenly would stop because he was with me. I try to express these doubts to Carlos.

"I was married eleven years, and I never cheated on my wife. If you're happy in your relationship, why make trouble for yourself? Why start a double life? It is possible for a man to be faithful if he's happy. Now," he says with frustration, but tenderly, "stop picking on me!"

Our last night together has come. We have been inseparable for days, and it will take some time to get used to being on my own again. I know that Carlos and I are not a love affair that will last, but it is one I will remember fondly, and I hope he will too.

Back at the house he plays songs for me, love songs, sad songs. I watch him bent over the guitar, remembering the first time I saw him just days before. Tears once again run down my cheeks; why does goodbye have to be so sad? He sees me, smiles mischievously, and begins to play "La Cucaracha," spinning and slapping the guitar like the old man did, just to make me laugh. I know I will miss him: his talent, his passion, and his sweet and easy humor.

"We'll be in touch," he says. "I've always wanted to visit Colorado." But we both know that we may never see each other again. "We will remember each other in a special place in our hearts." He touches his chest. "There is a place only for you, for no one else."

All too soon it is time for me to take my bus to Piura, where I will fly out the next day and catch my flight to Costa Rica for yoga training. I'm not in love with Carlos nor he with me, but we have shared something special these few days. I hope that I have helped him heal from his broken engagement, and I know that meeting him has helped me to move past some of the hurt I have been holding onto.

I cry when I catch my bus, hugging him tight to me one last time.

Blog Post: He Plays Me Like a Guitar

It's funny, having a whirlwind relationship that was never meant to last. It's like you go through mini phases of a real relationship at warp speed. When I met Carlos, I was enthralled. You might say that my old groupie days resurfaced upon meeting a guy who could really play guitar, and I'm sure that was part of it. But that wasn't everything. There were other things about him that I was drawn to: his sincerity, his humor, his ease of being. And in short order, I learned about his impatience, his superior air, and his sexist attitude. Four days through infatuation, frustration, and I'm outta here!

I knew, of course, that Carlos and I were not going to last. That's rare, and it wasn't what I was looking for. In truth, I wasn't looking for anything. Perhaps that is the best reminder: it's not "seek and ye shall find", but "good things happen when you least expect it."

When I sat in the kitchen and watched his fingers fly across the strings in a style he told me is called "tremolo", I was content for the moment. I could appreciate his artistry. He told me he would love to travel like I am doing, and I encouraged him to make his CD, grab a few clothes and the guitar, and hit the road with them. I'm sure I will never know if he took my advice.

Some people are brought into your life for a brief moment, and you drink in the nectar that they provide. Perhaps you also provide something sweet to enhance their life. Carlos was licking his wounds, and I was searching for myself. We were two shooting stars that crossed in a dark night sky, and we each illuminated something for the other.

He told me he would never forget me. But he deleted me from his Facebook friends before I had gotten on my plane to Costa Rica. Pocos sabemos amar. So few of us know how to love.

I am sad to say goodbye to South America. I was in the groove of buses and visiting new places, and now I have another new landscape to visit as I slowly creep my way north towards the United States.

I feel like I have grown in many ways during these months, but I hesitate to put it into words. Best to let it percolate a while, let the new attitudes seep into the old places. And I still have a month, the month of yoga teacher training, to get through. I am ashamed to say that I have not been able to keep up the yoga routine as much as I would have liked. The online videos have helped, but it is difficult to do while traveling. I have tried my best. The training, I am sure, will kick my fat butt.

A little glitch crops up in my plans: at the airport in Lima they inform me that I need the yellow fever shot to enter Costa Rica. This is because I have been in Peru, where yellow fever is a danger in the jungle regions. Even though that is not where I was! The attendant tells me that I cannot get on this flight; I must get proof of the shot and then I can board the next flight, a few hours later. Okay, fine. Oh, and by the way? The shot needs to be dated ten days before my travel. Oh, crap! I tell her, my voice trembling, that I have spent almost four thousand dollars on a yoga training that begins tomorrow; that I can't possibly miss ten days of it! Is there a way to get the shot record back dated? She shrugs. I can ask.

I will do whatever it takes to get this solved. I sit calmly, applying some makeup. My feminine wiles are getting old, but they are all I've got. Will it take tears, money, flirtation, or more? I don't know, but I will be ready. A young man who works for the airline takes me back through customs and points me in the direction of the clinic. Here goes nothing.

I ask the nurse at reception about getting the shot, and she reminds me that it needs to be ten days before traveling. I ask if I can please talk to somebody, imagining a fat perverted doctor lurking in the back waiting to take advantage of his power, but when I enter, a dark pretty woman sits in the doctor's office. I begin to explain but I can't help starting to cry.

"No llores," she says gently. *Don't cry.* I gulp and try to tell her about my predicament calmly. "Go pay for the shot," she says, and the receptionist nurse takes my money and leads me to the other room, where she unsheathes a needle, pokes me, and returns to the desk. The doctor gives me the card, backdated. Tragedy averted! I thank them both heartily and leave with my virtue intact.

Costa Rica, Yoga For Dummies

When I originally devised this trip, I decided to end my journey with a two-hundred-hour yoga teacher training in Costa Rica. I am excited for the possibility that yoga might be a new career for me, at least part time. This will be my biggest expenditure, but isn't that why God made credit cards? The training was billed as "coast to coast," encompassing three training locations. I met Troy, the teacher, in Colorado, and liked both his teaching style and his yoga philosophy.

Yoga training programs are approved by an organization called Yoga Alliance. The program must incorporate elements such as lecture on the eight limbs of yoga, meditation, anatomy lessons, and teaching practice. The poses in yoga are called asana, but this is just one part of the practice. Each teacher or studio offering training has a choice of what to emphasize, but all the essential elements must be included.

Troy's month-long training will begin at a retreat center called Samasati, located near the coastal town of Puerto Viejo de

Talamanca on the Caribbean Sea, and not far from the Panamanian border. We will spend two weeks there, move to a resort in the Heredia district in central Costa Rica, then end with our final week on the Osa Peninsula at a third retreat center, Luna Lodge.

Most of the trainees have already left the San Jose airport for the shuttle bus to the retreat center, but Alesa, also from Colorado, kindly volunteered to wait for me so we could travel together. We quickly bond; not only are we both yogis and single moms, but both of our husbands had affairs with barely-of-age girls!

I ask, "Is he an Aries?"

Alesa looks surprised. "Yes, he is! His birthday is March twenty fourth." It is my turn to be surprised. Our ex-husbands share a birthday! We commiserate over wine until bed time. I have a feeling we will build a strong friendship.

We wake up early to share breakfast and take a four-hour bus ride to Puerto Viejo, then a cab. We finally get to Samasati Lodge, where Troy greets us enthusiastically.

We are shown to our rooms. Mine is the least expensive accommodation; I have been through bedbugs, bunk beds, and a week without a shower; why would I need top of the line now? The Monkey Lodge guest house is a long wooden building with five rooms and a shared bathroom at each end. My room has two single beds and a little wardrobe. A mosquito net is hanging above each bed. The mattress is soft and slightly lumpy, but the room is clean and I don't have to share. I settle in for a nap before the orientation meeting. And, miraculously, even with the noises of the jungle and the chatting of fellow yogis echoing around me, I sleep.

At the evening meeting we all greet each other: yogis and yoginis from all over: New York, Colorado, Hawaii, Canada, and several traveling like me, without a fixed home. There are fourteen of us: twelve women and two men. We will get to know each other very well, I am sure, over this month of living, eating, traveling, and doing yoga together.

Meals are served buffet style, which scares me, and it will be vegetarian, which pleases me. Our first dinner has soy "meat" balls in marinara, rice and beans, broccoli in pesto, green salad, hearty bread, roasted potatoes and carrots, green salad, and a buttery squash soup. We are at this lodge for twelve days and I know there will be plenty of eating opportunities. I remind myself that slimming, not gluttony, is the goal. Even so, it is the first night so I try a little of everything.

Early to bed, early to rise will be the theme here, as yoga classes start at six every morning. The soft sound of rainfall permeates my sleep, lulling me into slumber as I feel the fishnet embrace of the mosquito net around my shoulders.

An eerie sound awakens me at four-thirty.

"ooo, oooo, aaaa,eeh…"

What the hell is that? I remember that Troy forewarned us about the howler monkeys that often sing a pre-dawn song. I listen, imagining them in the trees, although it sounds like this one is just outside my window. Nervous, I get up to use the bathroom. Two other yoga ladies are on our porch, sleepily peering out into the dark morning.

An hour later it is legitimately time to get up. The meditation lodge is just up the hill; I have given myself ten minutes to get dressed and get into class. Yawning, I unroll my mat in the last available spot. Troy begins class with gentle breathing and stretching, and moves us through sun salutations, triangles, warriors, and more, until an hour and a half has passed. The class reclines collectively in Savasana, or corpse pose, lying on our backs. The rain is tapping on our roof like drum beats, all but drowning out Troy's soothing instructions.

It is Sunday, a day in which we have a big chunk of free time. We can go to town, check out the beaches, or take hikes, but all these things are rendered unlikely by the continuous rainfall. Instead, I think, as I chat with new friends at breakfast, it might be a good day to do some writing.

I retire to my room and get my laptop, then sit on the deck with a cup of tea. I take in the humid feel of moist rain-soaked air, watching droplets form on broad green leaves. Tiny red and orange frogs frolic just outside my perch, one climbing the tall above-ground roots of a rainforest tree, another clinging to the stem of a plant, his little round toes hugging its width. We were told that these frogs are only poisonous if you play with them and have an open wound, or if you kiss them and put them in your mouth. Perversely, I think about doing that, just to see. The thought makes me smile, and the frog, perhaps sensing my evil intent, climbs down from the plant and hides under a brown leaf on the ground. Don't worry, froggy boy, I wasn't serious.

A bushy plant across the road sports bright fuchsia blossoms, and hummingbirds dart among the jade-colored leaves despite the drizzling rain. Occasionally, a bright Morpho butterfly, neon blue as if plugged into an invisible extension cord, flits by, showing off its radiant color. The flowers here are breathtaking: bright and showy and tropical. A damp pink blossom, pleated like the skirt of a young ballerina, clings to a plant just outside my door. For today I don't mind the constant barrage of rain, but I hope it doesn't continue like this all week. I already lost a lot of my tan, and I am hoping to refresh it while I'm here.

After dinner, there is a bright golden glow through the canopy of trees, like a misplaced street light. It casts a slight halo through the spread of dark leaves. I point it out to Alesa and we go over to the rail, peering through to see if the moon is full.

She straightens suddenly. "Do you hear that growling?"

I lean over, peering into the darkness. An other-worldly sound rumbles up to my ears. It doesn't sound quite like an animal, but what the hell is it? I look up again at the moon, my mind leaping to werewolves. I don't believe in werewolves, of course. But what is that strange growling sound? Heart pounding, I walk to the corner of the railing, the dark jungle spreading out below.

"Is it one of those howler monkeys?" Alesa whispers. She is hiding behind me, peering over my shoulder.

"No, I don't think so," I whisper back. "They sound totally different." Part of me wants to identify the animal, but the other part wants to go back up to the warm safety of the restaurant, where unsuspecting guests and yogis are lingering over the last of dinner, blissfully unaware of the wild beasts that we now know are out there.

"I'm going to go get Troy!" Alesa says, going back up the stairs.

Alone, I wait, trembling. The sound gets closer, changing in pitch. I shrink back from the railing. Oh dear God, what could it be? It comes closer and closer, but now… wait a minute? Is it sounding different? It's less like a beast now, and more like… a frog? I walk close to the square patch in the floor that leads down to the water pipes below. Echoing through the pipes is a definite frog-like croak.

Alesa returns. "He says maybe it's a frog?" she tells me, doubt in her voice. I point to the pipe, and she moves closer. She begins to giggle.

"No werewolves tonight!" We laugh at ourselves and say goodnight.

The first few days of training go smoothly: six AM yoga classes, lectures in the afternoons, and more yoga in the evening session. I am enjoying learning everyone's stories; why they are here and what they hope to do after. People seem eager to share their narrative with others. We are discovering a lot about each other. Alesa and I are becoming good friends and support partners. I meet a girl Veronica's age who is struggling with heart arrhythmia and fears that she won't wake up each morning. Others here have health issues, or life-changing events like the death of a parent or divorce. Most are here for more than yoga; this is a step in personal development for them. As for me, I feel centered and grounded. After all the travel I've just done, I don't think this training will be an emotional journey for me.

Then my hormones hit. I didn't get my normal debilitating PMS symptoms this time: crying, suicidal thought, despair, and the urge to isolate myself. But my period starts, and the symptoms which forgot to plague me before decide to come along with it. So now, with the body issues, I also have the emotional issues.

A group is going to town and one of the girls generously offers to pick up anything the rest of us need. One girl, Stephanie, a young dark beauty from Brooklyn, jokes that she would like a six-foot-two boy. The rest of us order chocolate. But the talk turns to dating, and suddenly I am crying and completely sure of the fact that no one will ever love me. To cover up the sudden swell of despair, I make a joke about becoming a "Yoga Nun" or a "Yoga Hooker," as we have been talking about trademarking unique brand ideas in class. With the joke, I recover, but the sadness lingers. I go to my room, try to play some music, but my music player is going crazy from the humidity, changing songs when I try to adjust volume, adjusting softer instead of louder. When I am in this frame of mind, every little thing like that feels insurmountable.

I know it's stupid. I know it makes no sense. I can intellectually justify everything, noting it's hormonal, but here is the thing: it does not make it any less horrible. The feelings are there and they feel real. Knowing I can't hide, knowing there is class in a few minutes, I take a Xanax to calm me, and cry all through meditation until it kicks in and blissfully just zones me out.

Drinking peppermint tea on the deck of the restaurant later, I take in this location: Costa Rica, in the middle of the rain forest. I taught a unit on the rainforest in kindergarten, and am now getting first-hand experience of the forest layers, the birds, and the beautiful Morpho butterflies that coast around like messengers from a brighter world. The ocean today is almost the same color as the pale sky, blending the two elements together as if they were painted on the inside of a globe, curving up towards a bluer ceiling with white puffs of cloud that I view through tall palms and vine-covered tree trunks. Flowers of scarlet and gold and lavender surround the deck railing. The house cat, a sweet pregnant calico, young as a teenager, curls up purring on my lap. I should be content. I need to be. I will work through this surprising funk; I know I will.

And I do. There is much to digest. We learn about mantras and mudras in class. I work my body hard when I can, raising a leg in plank pose when I come down, working on strengthening my core and my spirit. In class, we begin practice teaching with each other. I feel slow, cumbersome with the instructions, unsure of the inhales and exhales, certain that everyone here is more adept at this. I plug along, apologizing to my yoga partners, stopping to read the manual. I need something to make me feel sure of myself.

One morning, I get a much-needed boost; something that literally gets me high. It is Friday, and Troy has promised to work on some new things with us. He talks about headstand, having us roll our skulls around on our yoga mats. I am apprehensive. I have never tried headstand because it looks impossible. If I never try it, I don't have to say I can't do it, right? From the rolling motions, Troy has us do some ab work, core building. Oh, thank God. No headstand today, I think.

"If you're working on headstand, give your students something to become aware of their core muscles first," Troy tells us. *Uh-oh.* And then he guides us into a tripod. I remember tripod from a gym class, probably thirty-five years ago. Two hands flat on the ground, knees supported on bent elbows, and head on the ground as the third point of the triangle. I used to like this.

Well, looky there. I can still do tripod. Upside down, I chuckle to myself.

Troy says we can raise our legs up from here. Yeah, I think not! Still, it would be interesting to try. Slowly I ask the muscles to lift, expecting nothing. And yet, something seems to be happening. Something like, could it be? Are my legs lifting, are they off my elbows? Are they now even further up, am I straight up with my toes in the air? *Really?*

Yes, yes, yes! And shakily I lower down, amazed. I look around the room, as surprised as if I had suddenly grown antlers. Did anyone SEE that? But all the others are busy with their own versions, or laying down after their attempts. No one seems to have noticed this marvelous feat! I stare around, gaping like a fish. I feel extraordinary. I did it! Just for a second, but I did it. And that, I think to myself, is quite enough.

But I wonder if I could do it again.

So I try, and there go those wobbly legs again, trembling but up. Indeed they are up. This time, Troy comes over to help me hold it.

"Squeeze your quadriceps!" he encourages, holding my ankles. But I'm not sure that I even have quadriceps, and I wobble back down. He gives me an earnest grin and a thumbs up.

I grin back. "Holy fuck!" I whisper.

I feel my body getting more fit even after a week. This is great, but the problem with feeling good is that it makes me, for lack of a better word, horny. I want to share that physical energy with someone. Some days I am like a randy fourteen-year-old boy. Poor Alesa, my good friend by now, is bearing the brunt of my spinning energy: the lame jokes and the offhand sexual references. On Saturday, our partial day off, we go to the beach. There are a bunch of us frolicking in the warm ocean, bouncing in the buoyant water. A pair of men with shiny black shirtless bodies are throwing a Frisbee. I am practically purring watching them. I send up a prayer for another lover; it seems like my week with Carlos has reawakened my sexual spirit and it is ready to spring forward. The aura surrounds me like a buzzing cloud.

Alesa and I have margaritas and nachos, and watch an amazing sunset from the deck of a restaurant on the beach. The sky becomes peach, then baby pink, then a fiery molten lava splashed with orange. The drooping palm trees and a solo man standing in a boat become black silhouettes against the flaming sky. In darkness, we stroll through open-air stands selling woven bracelets, coconut shell earrings, clay pipes with lizards clinging to them. Alesa and I both buy a hammock at a colorful store, and I buy carved wooden boxes for my daughters. Then we grab a taxi to take us back, although a few girls have elected to stay in town to drink and skip six o'clock yoga tomorrow morning. I envy them, but it already feels late to me.

I'm a little tired the following day, but I make it through our morning class, taking it easy. It's Sunday once again, so there is free time. I decide to try to catch some sun before I walk down the hill to use the internet. I am feeling blue, fidgety, and out of sorts. I get into my swim suit and lay out by the Jacuzzi, but it is an overcast day. Why do I always seem to miss the clear bright sun? I take out my book to read but cannot focus; it's a book Alesa loaned me about listening to your instincts when making decisions. I'd rather lose myself in fiction.

After a while there is a rustling noise, and a welcome sight: two dogs approach, tails wagging. They are hounds with large spots and long dangling ears. I call them over. They are heartbreakingly skinny. There is a granola bar in my bag, which I break into pieces for them. They eat it and sniff around for more. Sorry, guys. Suddenly it seems all the poverty, famine, and scarcity in the world is represented by these kind souls: long eared, bony friends who come around and appreciate the affection they get, even though they need so much more. They are still able to give love. How, I wonder, can I ever help the need in the world? I have so much and cannot truly appreciate how lucky I am. Others will always suffer, always struggle. I begin to cry, then to sob in earnest.

The larger dog stays close to me, looking into my face, snuffling the scent of my falling tears. I stroke his long silky ears, scratch his neck. He understands. I am crying and he comforts me, even though he is the hungry one. I hug him close. He puts his paws up on the lounge chair like he wants to climb up. I help him up, trying to make room for him to lay by my feet. But he has other ideas, pushing his chest against my legs and thrusting his hips. He has decided that all this love is a prelude to humping me. Isn't that just like a man?

"Hey I don't feel that way about you," I say, pushing him down. "I'm really not into the inter-species thing." He is persistent, though. I give up and jump into the Jacuzzi to avoid his advances.

Really, God? I pray for a little bit of love, and you send a dog over to hump me? I laugh at the absurdity of the situation. Someone up there has a bizarre sense of humor.

In class, we are learning about anatomy, yoga philosophy, and how to do physical assists in all the poses. We practice these daily, and it is beginning to feel more natural, less awkward. I still don't know how I'm going to make this all happen in my life: writing, teaching yoga, whatever else is coming down the line, and I realize that this might be the cause of some of my anxiety. The uncertainty of life is approaching me as I come to the end of my sabbatical. I have got to get back into the real world and I don't really remember how!

Twelve days at Samasati go quickly. I am getting to know most of my fellow yogis. Alesa and I are the only ones who have children, which deepens our bond. Ashton has the room next to me. She's twenty-six, a strongly independent girl who loves to travel. In class we partner for teaching practice, based on drawing a ticket at the door. It's funny; I have worked with some people a lot, others not at all. I find myself paired with Zeno, a very odd but hilarious guy from London, a spoiled trust fund baby, who wears homemade clothing and rarely showers. Still, he is fun to play with, like a giant good-natured kid.

On the evening we study the bandhas, I am paired with

Stephanie, which is a good thing, as we can snicker about clenching the vagina and anal sphincter to engage Mula Bandha and not offend anyone. The next day, as I'm practicing poses with Zeno, he says, "If you're losing your balance, tighten your vagina!" I just about fall over laughing.

On our final day at the lodge, to celebrate summer solstice, we are all getting up and meeting at five AM to do one hundred and eight sun salutations on the deck while we watch the sun rise. This would sound wonderful to me if only I were a morning person. My limbs feel heavy and cumbersome. But as I keep going, it's becoming more fluid. Watching the others helps. It takes over an hour to get through, but I feel strong, capable, and spiritual. Toucans zip through the trees, blue butterflies float above me. It is indeed a magical time and place. My skin glows with sweat and the light of the golden sun. *Remember this,* echoes in my ears. When I reach the last sun salutation, I collapse on my mat with a smile on my face.

This afternoon it is time to make our way up into the mountains to our next location, Montana Azul. The van ride is almost twelve hours, with heavy rain, traffic, and stopping a few times for people to throw up. We stop for lunch and I gorge myself on food that is so different from what we have had: a fried empanada, guacamole, and tomato soup. None of it is very good except the guac, and I feel like I have a little Buddha belly as I squeeze back into the van for the rest of the trip. The backrest is straight and the leg room is nonexistent, and it's all I can do not to ask, "Are we there yet?" When a girl named Season begins to sing along to her music player I grind my teeth, but fortunately someone else speaks up to silence her.

Finally, we arrive, the van grinding gears to make it up the huge bumpy hill. The road to this place is a mess. We pass the dining hall, an open, cone shaped white building with a thatched roof. It is lit up with candles on the tables, and the staff stands waiting inside, hands folded in front of them, smiles on their faces. We get our bags unloaded and troop back to the dining hall, settling down on pillows and colorful woven blankets around a small blazing fire pit. We are exhausted, but the weariness of the group seems to be fading as we take in the beauty of our new home. We are served a light dinner and shown to our rooms.

It is darker than dark, and we will have wait until tomorrow to see the place by day light. Our group of six who are staying in the more rustic lodging (which means we all got the cheaper package) trudge up the hill. There are only two flashlights lighting the path. The altitude is making me huff and puff. My legs are sore from yesterday's sun salutations and the eleven-hour squished van ride. How long is this God-forsaken path that leads straight up the hill? If I fell down and died would anyone notice? Finally, we are shown to our Nature Lover's Tent, which is enclosed with a roof, and a floor, and has electricity. I think they call this Glamping. I say goodnight to my roomie, Ashton, and close my eyes for the night. Yoga is at seven tomorrow, a gift of an extra hour!

We are only at Montana Azul for two full days, but I intend to enjoy them. This place is beautiful: winding paths lead to hidden gardens that seamlessly incorporate the natural habitat with intimate landscaping. One garden, Jardin de Estrellas, has a firepit in the center, a stone bench that overlooks the main paths, and a serene Buddha statue with blue curls sitting beneath a tree. The flowers are a riot of color throughout the property, and iridescent hummingbirds dance among them, their feathers of green and dark blue a striped blur of shining hues, as if a handful of sapphires and emeralds had taken wing. My favorite flowers are a pale lavender shade and shaped like a daffodil with the frill and the cup, and set upon a tall stalk, so that they wave in the breeze at a height that flirts with my eyes as I walk the path down to breakfast. Usually the rain comes by afternoon, heralded by rumbling thunder until the sky breaks open and soaks unsuspecting yogis who forgot their umbrellas.

The yoga space is like a temple: a square room with open sides that looks out at a view of mountains bordered by green fields. A large Buddha statue, carved of wood and painted with fading colors, sits towering at the back of the floor, one hand raised in a peaceful greeting as his hooded eyes stare out and a half-smile adorns his lips. It is colder here, lacking the humid jungle air of Samasati, and we sit with vanilla colored fleece blankets around our shoulders at our dawn yoga class.

Too soon it is time to leave this magical mountain retreat and move across to Luna Lodge, our last location for the training. The van ride will be shorter this time. I take a half a Xanax so I will sleep, and the hours melt peacefully away until we arrive at Puerto Jimenez. A two-hour bumpy ride through the jungle takes us deep into the natural wonder that is the Osa Peninsula, where the Lodge rests at the top of a verdant green rolling expanse of hills peppered with tall trees, overlooking the ocean.

I am tired when we arrive, and we are shown into the open-air dining hall: a tile floor in an open-sided room that is covered by a palm frond roof. At the edge, a curved platform looks out over the trees, and hammocks are strung between support beams of carved and gleaming blond wood. At night, the bats occasionally flit through the restaurant. Dinner is served buffet style, and my fellow yogis are all thrilled that there is chicken. I load my plate with salad.

I am sharing another tent with Ashton. The strong and agile guide leads the way in the dark, illuminating the path with a flashlight while he slings my fifty-pound suitcase up onto his head, takes Ashton's pack on his back, and we hustle up so many stone stairs that I am sure I will expire before we reach the top.

The next day I ask Leah to count the stairs when she goes up, as her tent is next to ours. I almost don't want to know. There are one hundred and sixty. I remember the stairs to the beach in Maitencillo, Chile, just a few months ago. There, the number was three hundred and fifty, but I will have to do these three times per day! At least, I console myself, the yoga platform is close to our tent and I will only have to walk down about fifteen in the mornings. That is the payoff for having only a tent again; those in the nice bungalows will have to do one hundred and fifty or so stairs going up before six o'clock in the morning!

The meals here are exquisite. It is not vegetarian, but there are always many choices. Here we hear, but do not see, the howler monkeys, roaring their strange cries in the distant trees. It sounds like someone's stomach growling with ravenous hunger, heard through a stethoscope. Every night at dinner, a frog takes his place under one section of decking where his voice echoes, and he sings to us all through the evening. "Whoop, whoop," is his call. He is soon known as "Party Frog," and I imagine him raising the roof with his little froggy hands, wearing a lampshade on his head and a lei around his neck, a tropical drink by his side. "Whoop, whoop," we yogis sometimes say to each other to elicit a smile. Party time!

Despite the strenuous climb to reach it, the space for yoga is beautiful. The yoga platform looks out over the treetops. Down the stone path, thatched roof cones of the bungalows pop up here and there, embraced by green fan palms and orange and red birds of paradise growing wild. The stained wood plank floor stretches out, inviting you to unroll a mat and practice while gazing out over the trees to the shimmering ocean far below. The walls are maize yellow and tribal masks flank the open space at the back of the room, where plants wind up a stone gully. When it rains there is a trickle of water that dances down the stones. A bronze Ganesh sits in the corner, looking out benevolently over the space.

Ganesh holds a special interest for me. Just after my divorce, my mom brought me and my sister to a Buddhist meditation center in the mountains above Boulder. During a long chanting and moving meditation, I was drawn to the altar at the front of the room, which was filled with flowers and statues. A giant Ganesh sat upon a platform. Like a child, I swayed in front of him, eyes closed and tears streaming down my cheeks.

Now I know that Ganesh, among other things, represents the removal of obstacles in our lives. I think about where I was then, before I had a steady yoga practice, but was just beginning. So much of my present path was just opening to me. I had yet to meet, love, and let go of Brad. My kids were still young, sweet, and dependent. My job had yet to transform to the stressful finale it became. So much of what I have been through since then has made me stronger, although it was excruciating to endure. Sometimes I can look at all that has happened and be excited about the possibilities in my future. Other times, the future terrifies me.

I have only a week to pull this all together. Have I accomplished what I set out to? It seems too subtle to put into words. I've certainly learned more about traveling! I've learned how to teach a yoga class and help my students. I've learned patience; I've become open to change. But how I will take these lessons and use them in my life, I still don't know.

Soon the rain comes, heavy and steady. Thunder rolls,

grumbling softly. A thick mist hangs in the treetops, enveloping the jungle in a cloak of white vapor.

In this final week of training, we will be preparing to teach an actual class. This terrifies me, although it's what I've been training for. One day Troy says we are doing our last practice teaching session. He is giving us time and space to plan our own ninety-minute classes, which will start next week. We have "tribes" of four yogis, and an ambassador from another tribe will attend the class, giving us each five students.

My class is Tuesday afternoon. I work on it all morning on Saturday, digging into the notebook pages I worked up with some sample flows in Con Con at my beach condo. It seems so long ago! I figure out approximate times for my sections of asanas, and decide I have worked hard enough to go to the beach with a bunch of yogis.

The ocean here in the Osa peninsula is wild: a pebbly dark beach leads up to the edge of the water, and waves crash in, threatening to knock you off your feet if you're in the water past your ankles. Even then, the undertow pulls so much sand out with each rolling wave that you are in danger of falling over. Alesa and I work through some of our sequences on the beach and time them. Stephanie and Bhojak walk across the road to another lodge to have a drink.

When we join them, they are excited; they found a path called the Stairway to Heaven, hundreds of stairs leading through the jungle and past several wooden platforms where you can rest and sometimes see animals. They show a video on Stephanie's phone of howler monkeys swinging in the tree.

"We're sorry you missed it," Stephanie says.

"We should come back tomorrow," Alesa says, since our ride has come to take us back up the hill.

"Maybe. If I get my class done."

But when Sunday comes, I don't feel like going back. I stay by the pool all day, work on my class section by section in my bikini until I have the timing down and have renewed my tan. When Alesa returns, she shows me a video.

"Did you see monkeys?" I ask as she hits play.

"Nope!" she says, but she is grinning like she has a secret. I soon find out, as the camera zooms in on the wooden platform and a fat puma lying on it, twitching its tail. Its eyes narrow as it watches the interlopers, and Alesa pans back over the terrified faces of the group. The cat didn't move, but they all backed down the stairs after admiring it for a few minutes.

Tuesday is the day I get to teach. I take Amber's class earlier in the day, and I think she does a great job. She seems so together! When we talked at the pool the day before, she had said she was nervous, sure she was going to suck. I reassured her. And here she was, poised, laughing, encouraging us all like an old pro.

I wonder if I can do that too?

For in all of my travels, in all of my growing and learning and becoming more grounded in myself, I still have mad insecurities. They are not present all the time, but I know they are still there.

And unfortunately, they decide to take this opportunity to surface.

Three thirty comes, and I begin my class in child's pose, talking about starting with the body you walk into class with. I'm breathing too fast, talking too fast. Am I leaving them in child's pose too long? The doubts continue, ebbing and flowing throughout my class. I don't lose my pace, but I feel like I must keep my audience - five yogis whom I know and love - entertained somehow. Here are five pairs of eyes, earnestly looking my way for guidance, and all I can think is, "what the hell do I know?" I guide through three posture flows, trying to focus on alignment and breathing, but my own breathing is out of whack.

And later, when it is all done, I get some positive feedback, but I'm still frustrated with myself. Is this the same girl who used to take off her clothes nightly in front of a bar full of strangers? Maybe I should just teach my yoga classes while drunk and naked!

Speaking of which, I decide to go down to the bar. Even though drinks are seven dollars, I deserve one now if ever! Troy reassures me about my class, even tries to cheer me with an off-color joke, a rarity for him. I tell him I'm working on many of my poses and I will be sure to put mirrors in my practice space at home.

"Just take some of the ones off your ceiling!" he suggests.

I laugh.

The remaining week flies by while I spend my time attending other people's classes and lying in the sun, exhausted, when not doing yoga. I am amazed at the growth in my fellow yogis. The girl with heart problems has turned into a relaxed, confident young woman. Season, relatively new to yoga, has learned so much that she teaches like an old pro. Alesa seems happier and ready to change her life. We have all gone through amazing metamorphosis.

Soon it is time for our graduation night. In the morning, Troy has concocted a class where each of us teaches for five minutes, building on what the previous person has done. It is hilarious and invigorating, a veritable round robin of yoga incorporating everyone's unique style. I use my Warrior Flow that I created for my own class, and later when I realize I called Reverse Warrior "Warrior three" (it's a different posture altogether!) and confused everyone for a moment, I don't even stress. I laugh about it.

Troy puts us into pairs to talk about our yoga training

experience to a partner. My partner, Leah, is thirty and confident, an army major taking a hiatus from military life. I confess to her that it is weird to be the oldest person there, but I hope that I serve as an example to others: that it is never too late to try something new. That maybe someone will say, "When I'm your age, I hope I am just like you!"

That afternoon Alesa and I put on form-fitting black yoga clothes and take some photos by the pool and on the deck, showing off our form and the location in the most photogenic poses. I am pleased with the progress I have made, and ready to make more. I look hot! My body has gotten leaner and more muscular, not to mention a bit more tan! I can add a yoga pose pic to my next dating profile and be proud of it.

In the evening we all dress up. The mood is light. Fourteen yogis have been through a lot this trip and we are ready for it to be over, but sad to leave each other. There is laughter and there are tears. Troy has set up a circle of certificates face down on a centerpiece of blankets with a huge vase of tropical flowers. Chocolates are scattered about. The method will be to pick a chocolate and a certificate, and award them to each other. Troy begins and then we all take turns. It is a beautiful process.

Leah picks up a certificate to present. She smiles at me. "Cathy," she begins. "Congratulations on completing your training. When I am your age, I want to be just like you!"

I hug her tight, tears stinging my eyes. As the ceremony continues, the skies crack open with a giant thunderclap and rain pours down outside. It is as if God himself – or herself – is crying along with all the yogis.

Blog Post: The Yoga of Life

I am in Costa Rica, practicing yoga daily and learning about chakras, bandhas, yamas, and niyamas. My brain is filling with new information. My body is learning to do things it could never do before simply because I attempt them. Who knew I could do a headstand or an arm balance? I will emerge from this training with new abilities and an expanded mind.

What I didn't bargain for was an expanded soul.

The yoga training came upon the heels of almost a full year of travel: meeting wonderful new people, confronting my discomfort in new situations, and facing challenges. Sometimes failing. But always moving forward.

Isn't that just the thing called life?

I have had the good fortune to be a moving human laboratory; experimenting through travel. I have come face-to-face with my own biases and pettiness, and given myself time to work that out. Nothing was at stake, yet everything was. Because life is a series of the chances we take and the lessons we learn. If we don't grow, what are we doing here?

There has been time to figure out what matters most to me. I have shed some concepts that I thought might be the answer: that I must have a loving partner, that I have to look a certain way, and that I need to have so much "stuff" that it becomes a burden.

Everything shifts and changes in life. This year has been no exception. Friends come and go, fall turns into winter (or sometimes into summer!) and time marches on. The answers to the big questions in life are not one size fits all. We each must figure it out for ourselves.

What I have determined so far is that love comes in many flavors: the encouragement of your parents, the way your kids need you, a warm horsie flank or a cold doggy nose. A friendship that blooms from a brief connection.

As I come to the end of my adventure, I have discovered a fleeting peacefulness that I hope I can hold onto. I know I'll still stumble and fall, I will be a bitch sometimes, I'll play the victim, I'll sink into dark places and sleep too much. But maybe I'll catch myself sooner. Maybe I'll learn to be my own best friend. Maybe I'll recognize that while I can and will do a lot of things myself, it's okay to need other people.

And perhaps I can allow my life to unfold and contain surprises, both good and bad, and stand back and marvel at the simplicity and complexity of it all.

That night we have dinner and drinks, and some stay up all night. Although I am not one of the all-nighters, they move the party to the yoga platform around one in the morning, cranking the music and laughing and hooting into the wee hours. Determined not to be the old lady who spoils everyone's fun, even though I am supposed to leave at five o'clock, just a few hours away, I eventually shove earplugs in my ears and pull the extra pillow on top of my head. I catch just a few hours of sleep before my 4:30 wake-up call, which consists of the guard quietly calling my name through the screen of the tent flaps and then, thankfully, hauling my bag down the one hundred and sixty stairs.

Troy and the yoga crew

With Alesa on graduation night

Return To The U.S.A.

I am at the airport in San Jose, Costa Rica. The final stop before my return to the states. I don't know how to feel. My year of travel is finally over. It's bittersweet. I am ready to go home, to see my family, to drive my car, to shop at a Target. But I take this last moment to gaze at the fertile hills of Costa Rica, where I chose to end my journey. Tears well up in my eyes. Confusion. Aren't I happy to be going home?

"Como dormir a un elefante," the tune scampers through my head, illogically. Where did I sing that? Was it Spain? No, Argentina, I think. The edges of the landscapes blur in my memory, the faces of people I met like a giant mental collage. Some, when I see them on Facebook, are momentarily mistaken for someone else. In this one year, I have lived such a full and strange life.

And now, finally, it is time to put it all together. I must take the crazy quilt of this year and transform it into a memory that will sustain me as I settle back into reality – or rather, as I create a new reality. For now I am a changed person, in some ways subtle, others more obvious. I can teach yoga now. My Spanish has improved, but it is far from perfect. My patience with the little bumps on the road of life has increased. I am more at peace. I am more tolerant of myself and others. I have traversed the maze of a celibate-on-purpose existence, at least for a bit, and I have discovered the joys of abandoning that existence with no expectations. I have ripped my heart and soul open to the Universe and learned to live with a sense of humor.

I don't know where my life will lead me next, and I have come to terms with this. I have hopes and ambitions, but very little attachment. I am alternately giddy with anticipation and terrified, but in between these two emotions lies a widening gulf of peaceful acceptance. I am learning to just be.

At Denver International Airport my mother will greet me at baggage claim. To make her smile, I'm changing into the cool boots I bought in Peru, to remind her of the unique and sometimes daring things I would step off the airplane wearing in the eighties: strapless leopard skin jumpsuits or silver go-go boots. Mom has teased me that she will wear a red carnation so that I recognize her after all this time.

There she is, smiling knowingly. The familiarity of her warm embrace is like a long exhale. In a few weeks I will also be reunited with my children. I am home as if nothing has happened in the meantime. Things are the same. Yet I am different.

In the car going home, I tell my mom about the South America trip and yoga training, reliving it as I relate the stories. She listens and nods, happy to share in the adventure. And what an adventure it was, I realize! In ten months of travel through Spain, Morocco, most of South America, and Costa Rica, I have become a different person. And now, grateful for the gifts that this past year of travel has brought, I am eager for my next phase of life to begin.

And I am already planning my next trip.

www.ingramcontent.com/pod-product-compliance
Lightning Source LLC
Chambersburg PA
CBHW071134130626
46553CB00004B/1374